PRELUDE TO GREATNESS

Prelude to Greatness

LINCOLN IN THE 1850's

Don E. Fehrenbacher

STANFORD UNIVERSITY PRESS
Stanford, California

Stanford University Press
Stanford, California
© 1962 by the Board of Trustees of the
Leland Stanford Junior University
Printed in the United States of America
Cloth SBN 8047–0119–9
Paper SBN 8047–0120–2
First published 1962
Last figure below indicates year of this printing :
79 78

To My Mother and Father

Preface

THE CENTER of my attention in each of these seven essays is the relation between a man's rise to power and the historical process in which he was involved. It is an emphasis that has often led me not only beyond the range of Abraham Lincoln's personal experience but to a critical review of various conclusions reached by other writers. The essays are consequently a mixture of biography, history, and historiographical commentary. They are by no means a complete exposition of Lincoln's political career in the 1850's, for instead of telling the familiar story once again in all of its detail, I have sought the answers to certain important questions, selecting data and arranging my presentation accordingly. What part, for example, did Lincoln play in the founding of the Republican party? How did he manage to become the unchallenged leader of Illinois Republicanism? What conditions produced the anomalous senatorial contest of 1858? What were the consequences of that campaign for the two participants and for their respective parties? How did Lincoln, with his undistinguished political record, establish himself as a major contender for the presidential nomination by the spring of 1860? Such questions have been asked before, of course, and many of my answers are far from original. I have tried, however, to make a more pointed investigation than one will find in standard biographies and histories, hoping that the results might at least palliate the sin of adding still another volume to the enormous mass of Lincoln literature.

Approximately one-third of this book has already appeared in print. From "The Origins and Purpose of Lincoln's 'House-Divided' Speech," *Mississippi Valley Historical Review,* March 1960, I have taken the opening paragraphs of Chapter Three and most of Chapter Four. Chapter Six is a revision of "Lincoln, Douglas, and the 'Freeport Question,' " published in the *American Historical Review,* April 1961. I thank Editors William C. Binkley, Boyd C. Shafer, and their staffs for permission to reprint these two articles and for editorial improvement of the submitted manuscripts. In addition, certain passages in Chapters Three and Five are drawn from "The Historical Significance of the Lincoln-Douglas Debates," *Wisconsin Magazine of History,* Spring 1959; and that portion of Chapter Seven which deals with the Republican National Convention of 1860 is borrowed in considerable part from my essay, "The Republican Decision at Chicago," in Norman A. Graebner, ed., *Politics and the Crisis of 1860,* published by the University of Illinois Press in 1961. I am grateful to Editors William C. Haygood and Donald D. Jackson for allowing me to repeat myself.

I greatly appreciate the courteous services of various libraries, especially the following: the Newspaper Room and the Manuscript Division of the Library of Congress, the Illinois State Historical Library, the Illinois State Archives, the Chicago Historical Society, the University of Chicago Library, and the Stanford University Library. I have received help in finding materials from Marion D. Pratt, and in arranging interlibrary loans from Florence Chu. The Institute of American History at Stanford University contributed financial aid. To my profit, Thomas A. Bailey, George H. Knoles, and Otis Pease read parts of the book while it was in progress, and the final draft underwent the expert scrutiny of Paul M. Angle. Helen Kmetovic skillfully typed the manuscript. Theressa Gay patiently checked quotations and citations. Ruth, Susan, and David Fehrenbacher lent their youthful voices to the task of proofreading, and my wife, Virginia Fehrenbacher, has been nothing less than a silent partner in the project from beginning to end. To every person and institution that has given me assistance, I return both my gratitude and complete absolution from responsibility for all errors and misjudgments in the pages that follow.

One final debt remains to be acknowledged. I have depended heavily upon the work of numerous scholars who preceded me in the study of Lincoln's rise to the presidency, including some with whom I have at times found myself in disagreement. This book is little more than a footnote—and a respectful one, I hope— to the sum of their extensive labor.

DON E. FEHRENBACHER

STANFORD, CALIFORNIA
December 1961

Contents

1. Illinois and Lincoln in the 1850's   1

2. Lincoln and the Formation of the Republican Party   19

3. The Senatorial Nomination   48

4. The Origins and Purpose of the House Divided Speech   70

5. A New Look at the Great Debates   96

6. The Famous "Freeport Question"   121

7. The Path to the Presidency   143

Bibliographical Note   165

Notes   173

Index   199

PRELUDE TO GREATNESS

One

Illinois and Lincoln in the 1850's

O N HIS FORTIETH BIRTHDAY, February 12, 1849, the Honorable Abraham Lincoln sat in Congress as the only Whig representative from Illinois, but this was a dignity that he must soon lay aside. His term would end in less than three weeks, and he had not been re-elected—not even renominated. Worse still, his successor was a Democrat, whose victory at the polls in a traditional stronghold of Whiggery could only be interpreted as a repudiation of "Spotty" Lincoln's views on the Mexican War.[1] Driven by circumstances and his own partisan zeal into a political blind alley, the lame-duck Congressman now had little choice but to settle back into private life, resume the practice of law, and watch for another opportunity.

His wait was a long one, streaked with further disappointment. The Whig administration of Zachary Taylor offered him a position that he did not want and awarded the one that he actively sought (Commissioner of the Land Office) to a less deserving rival. Twice, in the years that followed, he tried and failed to win a seat in the United States Senate. This was the prize that he coveted most, and his defeats were all the more agonizing because they came so close to being victories. For twelve years after the termination of his brief and undistinguished congressional career, Lincoln held no public office of any kind.* Then, in the nation's most tragic hour, he took the oath as its chief executive.

[1] Numbered notes will be found at the back of the book, pp. 173–95.
* Elected to the state legislature in 1854, he resigned without serving in order to become a candidate for the Senate.

Of all the paths that have led to the presidency, Lincoln's was probably the most inconspicuous. None of the familiar "dark horses" of American history had such a meager record of prior achievements. Yet Lincoln himself cannot be classed as a dark-horse nominee; his was no name pulled from obscurity to break the deadlock of an exhausted convention. Neither was he a mere "favorite son" who unexpectedly caught the fancy of Republican delegates. Even before the proceedings began in the Chicago Wigwam on May 16, 1860, it had become more or less apparent that the Lincoln men offered the main challenge to the numerous supporters of William H. Seward. The devastating swiftness with which the New Yorker was overhauled and beaten on the third ballot can be explained only in small part by the noisily partisan galleries and the bargaining talents of Lincoln's managers. Somehow this former Congressman and twice-defeated senatorial aspirant had come to be regarded by a majority of Republican leaders as the candidate who best combined devotion to party principles with the ability to win. The results of the ensuing election, in which he received practically the entire electoral vote of the free states, fully vindicated their judgment.

The sudden rise of Lincoln to national leadership will never be stripped of all its mystery, but when studied against the background of the preceding decade, it ceases to appear miraculous. During those years, his way to greatness was being cleared by certain important changes in the world around him, while he, without knowing it, was preparing himself admirably for the role that awaited him. In the end, when opportunity sought out the man, it found him neither reluctant nor unready.

*

The upheaval of the 1850's in American politics, which produced the modern alignment of parties, was one aspect of a more comprehensive revolution already begun, but subsequently accelerated by the Civil War. Most plainly visible in the growth of factories and cities, the advance of railways and telegraph lines, the agglomeration of capital, and the multiplication of societies for the improvement of mankind, the revolution manifested itself also in a social viewpoint which welcomed change as indisputable evidence of progress and nursed a mounting impatience with those men and institutions that were out of step with destiny. If political discussion had been distributed along the range of problems posed by the emerging new order, the old Whig-Democrat alignment might have served as well as any to articulate the conflict of opinions. But in the 1850's, an abnormal condition— the submergence of other public business in the all-absorbing controversy over Negro slavery—compelled a reconstruction of parties on sectional lines. For a variety of reasons, it was the Whig organization that disappeared from the scene to make room for the Republicans, while the center of balance in the Democratic party shifted southward, and the brief flaming of the Know-Nothing movement confirmed the impossibility of subordinating slavery to other issues.

Constitutional restraints and political necessity confined the sectional controversy to narrow limits. The Republicans proposed to circumscribe the slaveholding system, not destroy it. Yet this was bound to be regarded in many quarters as an intermediate rather than an ultimate objective, and it did undoubtedly reflect a growing conviction that slavery was not only an odious wrong but an insufferable barrier to social progress. Southerners were not entirely unreasonable in their belief that the status of the institution in the territories was an index to its security at home, and thus to the vitality of the whole cultural pattern associated with it.

The restricted ground of the slavery controversy is one of the curiosities of American history. From the Missouri Compromise, through the Wilmot Proviso, the Compromise of 1850, the Kansas-Nebraska Act, the Dred Scott decision, and the Lecompton affair, to the final crisis of 1860, the vexed question was invariably linked with the process of constructing new states out of Western territories. The long debate was narrowly constitutional, became tediously repetitive, and, strangest of all, grew more and more rancorous even though the issue itself steadily lost most of its concrete significance. The slave population of the territories in 1860 was ridiculously small and unlikely to grow much larger. Yet, almost as a matter of uncontrollable habit, the South continued to demand the confirmation, and its adversaries the extinguishment, of a right that could not have been exercised. This irrational behavior provides a basis for the view that the Civil War was a needless descent into violence, induced by the emotional inflation of an artificial problem. But in order to reach such a conclusion, one must virtually ignore the symbolic function of the territorial issue and minimize the more fundamental conflict underlying it. By the late 1850's, in any case, it was apparent that Republican pressure and Southern inflexibility must lead to some kind of emphatic decision, although not necessarily to civil war. Lincoln, for one, saw a crisis approaching, but predicted that it would have a peaceful ending.

In the period of fluid politics which preceded the crisis, party loyalties were shuffled, power was redistributed, and a new set of leaders entered into prominence. For Lincoln, the death of the Whig party, although he watched it with no little sadness, meant release from an allegiance that had become suffocating. The Whigs were an irredeemable minority in Illinois, while the Republicans from the start proved to be more than a match for the Democrats, and in that simple fact lies much of the reason for the contrast between his earlier and later careers. Achieving eminence in both parties, he found that one was a dead end and the other, a broad highway leading to many opportunities. During each of four elections from 1854 to 1860, he was nominated or strongly supported for high office: the Senate in 1854, the vice-presidency in 1856, the Senate again in 1858, and the presidency in 1860. And only his lack of interest kept him out of the running for governor. Such things would have been impossible if the Whig party had somehow survived.

But many another career besides Lincoln's was immensely benefited by the political revolution that created the Republican party. What special advantages did he possess, what distinctive qualifications, that he should have been singled out for the presidential nomination? The full answer to this question is bound up in the complex historical developments of the time; yet one can begin simply enough with Lincoln's good fortune in his place of residence. The same man living in Wisconsin or Iowa, for example, would have been unlikely to rise so high, but Illinois was a pivotal state in the national politics of the 1850's, and its leaders were objects of unusual interest as a consequence. The support that Lincoln received for the vice-presidential nomination in 1856 was probably not so much a tribute to an obscure Western lawyer as a recognition of the importance of his state. Four years later, after the Republican National Convention had made its memorable choice, Joshua Giddings, one of the delegates, explained to a friend that "Lincoln was selected on account of his *location.*"[2] The Illinois environment thus deserves careful attention not only as a backdrop but as one of the basic reasons for Lincoln's emergence.

*

It is a significant fact that the rise of Lincoln in politics coincided with the rise of Illinois to pre-eminence among the commonwealths of the Mississippi valley. Growth at a dazzling rate was the striking characteristic of the 1850's. The population of the state doubled in those ten years (going from 851,470 to 1,711,951), and this was proportionately three times greater than the increase recorded in the country as a whole. At the end of the decade, Illinois had moved past seven other states to become the fourth largest in the nation.[3] Much the greater part of this growth occurred in the northern half of the state, where communities were newer and more progressive, and where the antislavery strength was concentrated.

With a few exceptions, the composition of the swelling population remained stable throughout the period. For example, a representative group of twenty-five Illinoisans, assembled at any time between 1850 and 1860, would have included ten persons born within the state, three from the rest of the Old Northwest, three from the Middle Atlantic region, and one from New England. The other eight would have been natives of the slaveholding states or foreign countries, but here an important change was taking place. Reflecting a national trend, the percentage of Southerners in the Illinois population fell from 17 per cent to 10.5 per cent during the decade, while that of the foreign-born, who nearly trebled their numbers, rose from 13 per cent to 19 per cent. Only down in "Egypt," at the lower end of the state, did the Southern influence continue to be predominant. The foreigners, on the other hand, were more numerous in the northern counties, except for a heavy concentration of Germans along the Mississippi opposite St. Louis.[4]

Place of birth did not necessarily determine a man's outlook in politics (Douglas came from Vermont, Lincoln from Kentucky), and the people of southern Illinois, by their very choice of residence, had more or less turned their backs upon slave society. In general, however, they represented the extreme of Northern conservatism on the slavery issue, and their steady decline in numerical strength had visible political effects. Illinois, with an aggressive, reform-minded north and a backward, defensive south, came to resemble in some degree the divided nation itself. "Talk of 'sectionalism' in the Republic!" wrote a Chicago newspaper correspondent in 1857. "There is not between South Carolina and Massachusetts . . . a more deadly hostility than between the ninth and first Congressional districts in this State."[5]

As for the foreign elements, they certainly added to the complications of Illinois politics. Courted and exploited, amenable to mass influence, and posing the most serious threat to the purity of elections, they were a force to be reckoned with at every turn, and the Germans in particular virtually held the balance of power in the state. The Democratic party had long been the favorite of European immigrants, but many of them were alienated by the Kansas-Nebraska Act, with its apparent capitulation to the slavery interest. In Illinois, as elsewhere, the sons of Ireland generally remained loyal Democrats, while the Germans, together with the Scandinavians and certain other lesser groups, went over in large numbers to the anti-Nebraska coalition, which soon adopted the name "Republican."

Meanwhile, resentment of the foreigner's expanding power and dismay at the rapid growth of the Catholic church had inspired the Know-Nothing movement, which might have built a major party on a foundation of political nativism if it had not been broken apart by the weightier slavery issue. By and large, the Illinois Know-Nothings were of Whig background, traditionally hostile to the Democracy, and committed in a moderate way to the antislavery cause. When their own organization began to disintegrate in 1856, many of them likewise leaned toward Republicanism, but not without serious misgivings. Thus the Republican party, needing support from foreigners and nativists alike, faced the task of submerging their mutual antagonism in the battle against the extension of slavery.

*

Just as remarkable as the population growth was the expansion of the Illinois economy in the 1850's. In agriculture, as corn production doubled and wheat production increased nearly threefold, the state became by a wide margin the grain-raising leader of the nation. Yet at the same time, industrialization proceeded at a rapid pace, merchants and professionals multiplied, and by 1860 almost half of those gainfully employed were engaged in pursuits other than farming. The frontier stage had been left behind, and Illinois, with diverse ways of living and making a living, with mills and factories to lay beside its magnificent farms, with its own flourishing metropolis and a revolutionized transportation system, had achieved a considerable degree of economic maturity on the eve of the Civil War.

Above all, it was the coming of the railroads that transformed Illinois life in the 1850's. The ten-year span saw the inception and completion of the mighty Illinois Central, and, beginning with

the Chicago and Rock Island, the establishment of links between
the Great Lakes and the Mississippi. A puny 110 miles of track
in 1850 grew to a network of 2,868 miles crisscrossing the state
by 1860.[6] The railroads opened up wider markets for all types of
producers, created new towns overnight and raised some of the
older centers to the rank of cities, attracted hordes of unskilled
laborers into the state for construction and maintenance work,
dominated the interest of the financial community, and reduced
the isolation, while quickening the tempo, of everyday living. The
famous Lincoln-Douglas campaign of 1858, during which the two
men traveled a combined total of nearly ten thousand miles in
less than four months, principally by railroad, would have been
impossible only a few years earlier.

Upon political behavior the railroads exercised a potent and
manifold influence. Excursion rates swelled the attendance at
major conventions and rallies. The mobile army of gang-work-
ers, mainly Irish, served as a pool of illegal voters, who descended
in clusters upon strategic districts at election time. But most
important of all was the interlocking leadership. There were few
prominent figures in Illinois politics who did not have close ties
with the railroad interest. Some, like Joel A. Matteson and Norman B. Judd, were active promoters and officers or directors;
others, like William H. Bissell, John Wentworth, and Abraham
Lincoln, rendered professional service as attorneys, lobbyists, and
publicists. The railroads needed the friendship of public men and
openly courted it with judicious distribution of their legal business, printing contracts, and other patronage, not to mention free
annual passes. Speculation in lands along railway routes also
gave many politicians a private stake in the prosperity of the
roads.

Lincoln, although not a railroad promoter or investor, acted
as counsel for a number of companies in the 1850's and was on
a regular retainer basis with the Illinois Central during much of
the decade. After helping to win an arduous and extremely important tax case for the Central against McLean County in 1856,
he submitted a bill for $5,000. This, measured against his usual

charges, was nothing short of exorbitant, and he had to bring suit in order to collect. The company offered only token resistance, however, and continued him in its employ after paying what he asked. That such liberality was not without an ulterior purpose is evident from a letter written by the resident director of the railroad to its president. Lincoln, he explained, might turn against the company and could be a formidable enemy because of his intimacy with state officials. Settlement of his claim would mean retaining the good will and services of a man who was "not only the most prominent of his political party, but the acknowledged special adviser of the Bissell administration."[7] By no means does it follow that Lincoln deliberately engaged in a form of extortion. He undoubtedly thought that the high fee was warranted by the extent of his labors and by the great financial benefit accruing to the Illinois Central from the favorable decision. At the same time, it would be difficult to believe that he saw no connection between his position in politics and his success in collecting the full amount.

The practice of law is the main corridor to public office in America, and the Western lawyer of the mid-nineteenth century was especially well fitted for the role of political leader. Ordinarily a general practitioner rather than a specialist, he moved facilely from one kind of case to another and came to know government, business, and society in a wide variety of aspects. Schooled by his profession in the art of oral persuasion, he was more likely than not to be a master of the sonorous eloquence that his age admired. He set his own work routine and could adapt it to the demands of politics, while his regular travels on the court circuit kept him in close touch with popular opinion. Thus Lincoln, even in periods when the law occupied most of his attention, was never more than a short step from the center of the political scene. Indeed, the fact that Illinois, unlike many states, concentrated its major elections in the even-numbered years imposed upon his life a definite rhythm of annual alternation between his two careers.

If politics was the second profession of many lawyers, it was often the marrow of the day's work for the newspaper editor, whose public influence and fierce partisanship usually made him a member of the political elite in his community. Practically all of the Illinois men prominently associated with Lincoln's rise to the presidency were either leaders of the bar or lords of the press. As a business enterprise, newspaper publication in the 1850's was characterized by feverish expansion, instability, and desperate competition. During the decade the number of dailies in the state rose from 8 to 23, and of weeklies, from 84 to 228, but most of these establishments changed hands one or more times, and there were several hundred others that started and failed.[8] Many a small-town Greeley found that operating a newspaper was a short road to bankruptcy. And the financial hazards of journalism, all too considerable in themselves, were multiplied by the demands of political strategy, which often caused two or three papers to be set up where only one was really needed. As a result, the rival editors in a typical locality were not only political enemies but competitors in a savage struggle for survival, and their venomous running debates covered all subjects and seasons. In some places, moreover, journals of the same partisan faith fought each other with no less bitterness. This was especially true of the Republican press in Chicago, whose incessant quarrels became a prime source of party discord.

The average newspaper of the 1850's was a modest enterprise, owned by a single proprietor or close group of partners, operating with limited capital, simple equipment, small staff, and reaching only a local audience. In the cities, however, journalism was fast becoming a big business. Technological innovations like the rotary press had revolutionized the printing process. The increasing use of paid correspondents and stenographic skills meant fuller coverage of the news, while the advent of the telegraph speeded its transmission. Urban growth provided an expanding source of patronage at home, but the major newspapers also took advantage of railway progress to enroll large numbers of subscribers in distant parts of the country. For example, the circulation of the New York *Tribune* in Illinois reached 20,000 by 1860, and in Iowa it was probably double that of any other publication. On a smaller scale, the Chicago *Tribune* was gradually emerging as a journal of state-wide and even regional importance.

The operation of a big city newspaper in the new industrial age therefore required substantial capital resources and the pooling of many talents. It could not be a one-man affair. Yet bigness did not immediately eliminate all the characteristics of the old personal journalism. The idiosyncrasy of its chief editor was still the distinguishing feature of more than one great newspaper, and as his audience grew, so did the political power of a Bennett, Raymond, or Greeley. Such men might with good reason aspire to the role of president-maker. Every ambitious politician needed some equivalent of Seward's Thurlow Weed to speak for him through the one medium of mass communication. In Illinois, the Chicago *Times* and the *State Register* at Springfield were the principal organs of Stephen A. Douglas. Lincoln, whose political reputation was built largely in the newspapers, took great pains to cultivate the Republican editors of his state. He was especially close to the *State Journal* in Springfield, and the Chicago *Tribune* contributed so much to his eventual success that one of its editors has been extravagantly labeled "The Man Who Elected Lincoln."[9]

*

So firmly were journalism and politics bound to each other that the nonpartisan editor was a rare and unappreciated creature. But then, any person of consequence in a community found it difficult to stand clear of political controversy. The professional competence of local officials, teachers, and even clergymen often counted for little if they were "wrong" on the great issues agitating the nation. Of particular significance was the interpenetration of religion and politics throughout the decade. It is well known that much of the original impetus and moral fervor of the antislavery movement came from evangelistic Protestantism, and that the slavery question divided several of the major church organizations before it disrupted the national parties and government. Less attention has been given to the disturbing effect of the controversy upon local religious affairs.

In Illinois, as in other Northern states, the primary issue before ecclesiastical bodies was not the merits of slavery but the extent to which churches and their leaders should become directly involved in the sectional conflict. For instance, the Rock River conference of Methodism, covering the northern part of the state, went on record in 1855 as favoring the exclusion of slaveholders from church membership. The Illinois conference (in the middle of the state), while affirming its repugnance to the system of slavery, opposed a step that would inevitably compel Methodists of the border slave states to join those of the deep South in withdrawal from the national church.[10] Similar divisions between antislavery activists and organizational conservatives developed not only in other denominations but within many individual congregations, and the close correspondence of such factions to the two major political parties was usually obvious. Sunday did not necessarily mean a day of rest from politics. A large number of Protestant clergymen were, of course, openly committed to the war against slavery and willing to prosecute it week after week from their pulpits. But whether a minister spoke his mind or held his tongue on the subject, he was likely to have trouble maintaining harmony among his church members during periods of general excitement. Here is one man's summary of the problem, written when the presidential campaign of 1856 was at its height:

> A minister's political sentiments are at once, in coming here, inquired into, and soon ascertained, then a portion of those who differ from him in this, withdraw from his preaching and his support, then he is expected to look to his political friends for support—the others discard him. This, though undesirable appears to be unavoidable.[11]

The slavery question was the most important link between religion and politics, but there were others. Church leadership dominated the crusade against strong drink, which reached a climax in 1854–55 when a Maine-type prohibition law was enacted by the state legislature and then rejected by the electorate in a special referendum.[12] The alignment of voters on this issue made it clear that the temperance and antislavery movements drew their strength from similar segments of the population, but there was also a strong scent of nativism to the prohibition measure, and it could not have been incorporated into the Republican program without alienating the great mass of Germans. Party editors with temperance leanings found it convenient to denounce Irish whiskey and omit mention of Teutonic beer.

Religious feeling was also an essential element of nativism, and the one that Republicans could most safely exploit in their efforts to please both Know-Nothings and Germans. Republicanism, said the Chicago *Tribune* in 1856, offered full scope to the exertions of the man "who would repress the political tendencies of a false but arrogant church, without ostracizing the foreigner whose political and religious sympathies are as true and ardent as his own."[13] The loyalty of Irish Catholics to the Democratic party, the conservatism of their church on the slavery question, the fact that the author of the Dred Scott decision professed Catholicism and that Douglas had become allied to it through marriage—all furnished material for repeated charges that popery and slavery were united in a plot against American liberty. The Lincoln-Douglas campaign of 1858 was pictured in some of the leading Republican newspapers as a contest, in part, between Protestant morality and the degrading influence of Rome. "It is the Pope . . . who says that Abraham Lincoln shall not be United States Senator," declared the Chicago *Democrat* in June, and when the results of the election were known it added: "The triumph of Douglas is as much a triumph over Protestantism as it is over free labor."[14] Again in 1860, an anti-Catholic clamor was raised against Douglas, and it was even rumored that he had been secretly converted to his wife's faith. "Is Douglas a Catholic?" demanded a Bureau County editor. "If he is a Catholic, he owes allegiance to a foreign despotic power, and if elected President will not be the President of the people, but an instrument of evil in the hands of the Pope of Rome."[15]

Lincoln, to be sure, did not echo such appeals to religious prejudice and undoubtedly disapproved of them—but silently, for political prudence induced him to repress much of his aversion to the principles of nativism. He was likewise repelled by the self-righteous fanaticism with which some religious leaders burdened the antislavery movement. In this case, however, he objected to methods rather than basic premises, sharing with every abolitionist preacher the conviction that slavery was a great moral wrong. His thinking on the subject, although primarily secular, reflected also the distinctive ethical influence of American Protestantism. Not himself a member of any church, he revealed an increasing awareness of the fact that he had enlisted in a cause with deep religious roots. It was perhaps not entirely a coincidence that the famous House Divided speech, with its biblical phrases and prophetic tone, followed closely upon the great revival which swept across the country in the early months of 1858.

*

The pervasive and unremitting popular interest in politics was the most striking feature of Illinois life in the 1850's. Political discussion filled the newspapers, extended from pulpit to saloon, and fell like monsoon rains from the lips of countless stump orators. Eastern and European visitors to the state were amazed by the size, frequency, and enthusiasm of rallies and parades, by the uniformed bands and marching clubs, lines of floats, banners, torches, fireworks, turpentine balls, cannon fire, illuminations, pole-raisings,* picnics, river excursions, fistfights, and riots. At-

* In the typical town, come election time, banners bearing the names of parties and candidates were fastened to poles and erected in public places, often with elaborate ceremonies. The object was to raise a higher pole than the opposing party, and some standards fluttered more than a hundred feet above the ground. At times, it was also necessary to guard them against enemy forays. The *State Journal* of August 8, 1860, announced that "on

tendance at political meetings was often immense, considering transportation facilities and the limited range of the unamplified human voice, and speeches were customarily so long that one wonders whether to marvel most at the stamina of the orators or the endurance of their audiences. The latter expected plenty of jokes, partisan insults, and extravagant accusations, but they also listened attentively to fine-spun technical arguments and lengthy rehashes of past utterances and events. The wave of popular excitement rolled to its crest on each election day, then subsided in a brief period of emotional exhaustion. Soon, however, another contest was sighted not far in the distance, and a new campaign had begun. This sustained passion for politics testified to the vitality of the democratic system, but it also proved to be dangerous. One of the major factors contributing to the disruption of the Union, in the opinion of Roy F. Nichols, was "the baneful influence of elections almost continuously in progress, of campaigns never over, and of political uproar endlessly arousing emotions."[16]

There is more than one way of explaining the excessive political enthusiasm of the 1850's. Most important, of course, was the explosiveness of the slavery issue and the sense of mounting crisis, which swept away apathy, patience, and dispassion. But in addition, the people of that simpler age found keen enjoyment in political activities and bestowed upon them all the devoted attention that many later Americans would reserve for athletic contests. Politics was a favorite form of mass entertainment, and the larger meetings were holiday affairs, attended by whole families looking for diversion from their daily routines. No one wanted to miss the fun and excitement. Lincoln and "Long John" Wentworth, while waiting to address a crowd at the little town of Oregon during the Frémont campaign, amused themselves by

---

Monday night some miserable, infamous, low-flung, narrow-minded, ungodly, dirt-eating, cutthroat, hemp-deserving, deeply-dyed, double-distilled, concentrated miscreant of miscreants, sinned against all honor and decency by cutting and sawing down two or three Republican poles in this city."

counting the babies nursing in their mothers' arms. They agreed that there were more than seventy, all present, as Wentworth remarked, "to receive their political christening."[17]

Another reason for the intense and widespread interest in politics can be discovered in the very structure of the American political system. The national party itself was really little more than a loose federation of state and local units, functioning as an entity only during presidential campaigns. This pronounced decentralization, while it undermined party discipline and made doctrinal consistency virtually impossible, did foster a vigorous grass-roots participation in the democratic process. The workings of the political convention, which by now had become the accepted method of nominating candidates for nearly every public office from coroner to president, drew great numbers of ordinary citizens into active political service at the community level. Everything, in fact, began with the local convention. Here campaigns were launched, party credos were rough-drafted, and the first set of delegates was started up the ladder of representation. Here, where the pulse of popular opinion beat sturdily, and the voice of the individual could be plainly heard, the Republican party was born.

In Illinois, especially, there was an added stimulus from the approximate equality of Democratic and Republican strength, which meant that every state-wide election would be excitingly close. Within the state, however, this even balance of opposing forces prevailed only in the middle counties. The region that had previously been the heartland of Illinois Whiggery now became the battleground where each contest was decided. It was here, for instance, that Lincoln and Douglas concentrated most of their efforts in 1858, making only token expeditions into the north and south. To live in Springfield was thus to be near the center of conflict, and a prime political advantage; for the Republican party, secure in the northern districts, lavished special attention upon the middle section and awarded its major nominations to men like Trumbull, Bissell, Lincoln, and Yates, whose names carried weight there.

The striking thing about the political pattern in Illinois was its resemblance to the situation on the national scene, where a belt of border free states held the balance of power in the electoral college and in Congress. Of particular importance were New Jersey, Pennsylvania, Indiana, and Illinois, which gave their votes to Buchanan in 1856. Without substantial gains in these states, the Republicans could not hope to capture the presidency in 1860. Here, then, was a zone of decision like the middle counties of Illinois, whose Republican leaders were certain to exercise an enormous influence upon their party's choice of candidates and declaration of principles. Lincoln's place of residence was therefore doubly strategic, and it not only endowed him with geographical "availability," but made his ear keenly sensitive to the crosscurrents of public opinion and conditioned his fortunate assumption of a position somewhere near the emotional and doctrinal center of Republicanism.

The fact that Lincoln was situated in the pivotal section of a pivotal state did not give him a unique advantage, however, and it only begins to explain the amplitude of his success in politics. One must still ask how it happened that he, instead of some other man like Trumbull, became the pre-eminent Republican of Illinois, and then why it was Illinois (rather than Pennsylvania, for example, with thrice the electoral votes) that furnished the presidential nominee in 1860. The various factors contributing to this result will be examined more extensively in later chapters, but there is one that should be mentioned here because it heads the list of political benefits accruing to Lincoln from his residence in Illinois—namely, the dominant influence of Stephen A. Douglas in the politics of the 1850's.

Unquestionably the most vibrant and controversial public figure of his time, Douglas drew the attention of the nation to Illinois and to the lawyer-politician who pre-empted the role of his chief local adversary. Lincoln achieved prominence without election to office by making a career of opposing the famous Little Giant. His speeches throughout the decade constituted one long running rebuttal to what Douglas said and what Douglas did.

And when the latter was compelled in 1858 to acknowledge him formally as a rival, Lincoln at last began to acquire a national reputation. Indeed, it would be no great exaggeration to say that Douglas for a number of years was unwittingly engaged in clearing Lincoln's path to the White House.

In a considerable degree, then, the sudden emergence of Lincoln during the 1850's can be attributed to a set of exceedingly favorable conditions, which resulted in part from certain fundamental changes in the political environment. Yet even the most complete tabulation of extrinsic factors would not tell the whole story; for in the man himself there was also a perceptible change—a strengthening of mind and will in response to the challenge of circumstances. Much has been written about the extraordinary capacity for growth revealed in Lincoln the president, but anyone who follows him through the preceding decade will find ample evidence of this same quality and may even conclude that the moral stamina, the humane judgment, and the profound sense of history had long been there within him, waiting only to be called forth. The task of organizing discordant elements into the Republican party of Illinois tested and developed Lincoln's genius for leadership, while the great question at issue sharply stimulated his powers of thought and expression. The party statesman who delivered the Cooper Union address in 1860 bears more resemblance to the author of the Second Inaugural than to the petty politician whose inelegant harangue entertained the Scott Club of Springfield in 1852. On the smaller stage of state politics he had already demonstrated his mastery of words and of men.

Two

Lincoln and the Formation of the
Republican Party

DURING THE SPECTACULAR political upheaval that occurred between 1852 and 1856, the Whig party all but disappeared from the national scene and in Illinois ceased to function entirely. In its place there arose the Republican party, which promptly demonstrated great sectional strength by carrying eleven of the sixteen nonslaveholding states for Frémont and, in Illinois, by capturing all of the major state offices. It would be a mistake, of course, to think of the Republicans as just Northern Whigs with a new name; for what happened was much more complex. Some Illinois Whigs, for example, went over to the Democratic party, and a larger number found temporary refuge in the Native-American movement. At the same time, many antislavery Democrats and most of the old Free-Soilers were entering the Republican ranks. Nevertheless, it is probably safe to say that a majority of the Whigs in the state turned Republican along with Lincoln, and that they constituted the largest element in the new party.[1]

Lincoln's role in this mass transfer of political allegiance and in the founding of the Republican party has naturally received much attention from historians and biographers. With a few exceptions, they have generally agreed that while figuring prominently in the opposition to the Kansas-Nebraska Act, he was a latecomer to the organization that grew out of it. They picture him as standing aloof and irresolute for all of two years, then, with a "hearty shove" from Herndon, joining the Republicans "after it was apparent they were going places."[2] Like so many misjudgments of historical events, this interpretation has some basis in fact and needs substantial revision rather than outright refutation.

*

The period from 1850 to 1854 was not unusually placid. Yet it appears so in retrospect because of the violent political storms that preceded and followed it. For Lincoln, too, these were relatively quiet years of concentration upon the practice of law, and we have his own testimony that he had begun to lose interest in political affairs when the repeal of the Missouri Compromise "aroused" him again.[3] Such a tendency is hardly surprising in view of the character of the times and his own unfavorable situation, but the assertion of numerous writers that he "retired" from politics considerably overstates the case.[4]

Although Lincoln's congressional term ended in March 1849, he was busy during the months that followed with the patronage claims of his state upon the new Taylor administration. The biggest plum was the commissionership of the General Land Office, which had been allocated to Illinois. Lincoln first tried in vain to get the position for another man, then became a candidate himself, with no better success. The Administration was not ungrateful, however, for his services in the election of Taylor and offered to make him Governor of Oregon Territory, but this appointment he declined.[5] While concern for his family probably determined his decision, political considerations no doubt reinforced it. Oregon, with its strongly Democratic population, would have been a poor field of action for an ambitious Whig.

Lincoln waited five years before seeking public office again, but this was a sensible adjustment to circumstances, not actual retirement. A Whig had few opportunities to choose from anyway, and he preferred to bide his time rather than take a backward step into the legislature or attempt some hopeless task like running for governor. Of course there was always his old seat in Congress, lost to a Democrat in 1848. But he knew that his opposition to the Mexican War still counted against him and prudently stepped aside for Richard Yates, a more available candidate, who won back the district in 1850. Meanwhile, Lincoln remained active in local party proceedings and continued to be regarded elsewhere as one of the state's leading Whigs. In 1852, his name appeared on the Scott electoral ticket, and he was appointed national committeeman from Illinois. It is true that he made only a half-dozen speeches during the campaign, but this was consistent with the general apathy of Illinois Whigs in a cause they considered hopeless. Furthermore, since the odd-numbered years were ordinarily fallow in Illinois politics, Lincoln's inactivity during 1851 and 1853 was entirely normal and to a great extent duplicated in 1855 and 1857. Thus the tradition that he abruptly withdrew from political life for five years and then made a dramatic "return" in 1854 is a mixture of fact and fiction.

However much his interest had waned, it was completely revived in the furor over the Kansas-Nebraska Act. Suddenly he had a new purpose and a new chance. For the next six years he poured his energies without stint into the battle against the extension of slavery and in the process raised himself to the presidency. But whether devotion to principle or rekindled ambition was his primary spur has been a matter of some dispute. The appraisal of Lincoln's motives swings back and forth between two extremes and as a rule is decisively influenced by a given writer's general views on the slavery controversy. Panegyrists like Josiah G. Holland and Isaac N. Arnold, never doubting the justice of the Republican cause, stress his lifelong hatred of human bondage and his moral indignation at the repeal of the Missouri Compromise.[6] On the other hand, those "revisionist" scholars who sympathize more with Douglas than with his anti-Nebraska critics are likely to lay emphasis upon Lincoln's self-interest and opportunism. Donald W. Riddle, for example, sees only hunger for office in his famous Peoria speech of 1854, with its "specious arguments" against popular sovereignty. "Lincoln," writes Professor Riddle, "was not fighting for a cause. He was using the slavery issue, conveniently presented by the Kansas-Nebraska Act, to advance his own political standing."[7]

Between hero worship and cynicism there is a middle view which recognizes in Lincoln both the man of deep moral conviction and the practical, aspiring politician. His ambition, as Herndon tells us, "was a little engine that knew no rest."[8] But at the same time, there is no reason to believe that he was any less sincere in his protests against the Kansas-Nebraska Act than the thousands of other Americans who rose up to denounce it. The intensity of that mass response is hard to recapture now, partly because subsequent events seem to indicate that Northern apprehensions in 1854 were not entirely justified. Historians like James G. Randall have repeatedly pointed out that Kansas had only two slaves in 1860, and that it entered the Union as a free state under the very organic act which the antislavery forces so violently condemned.[9] There is a double fallacy, however, in the inference commonly drawn from these facts. First, without the great outburst of indignation in 1854 and the unremitting agitation of the following years, no one can be sure that slaveholders would not have entered Kansas in larger numbers or that the effort to make it a slave state would have failed. The argument that the Kansas climate alone was a sufficient barrier to slavery amounts to nothing more than an unverifiable assertion. Second, it is unreasonable to use the ultimate disposition of the Kansas problem as the primary basis for judging the motivation and wisdom of the anti-Nebraska uprising in 1854. Historical perspective in this case drains much of the emotional content, and therefore most of the meaning, from the crisis that followed the repeal of the Missouri Compromise.

Back in 1846, the issue of slavery in the territories had precipitated a similar crisis, but the controversy that began with the introduction of the Wilmot Proviso ended in compromise four years later, and the Free-Soil movement did not develop into a major sectional party. The far different course of events after 1854 must be attributed at least in part to the thunderous impact of the Kansas-Nebraska Act, for it stirred previously moderate Northerners to unwonted alarm and anger. In their fight for the Proviso, the opponents of slavery had been on the offensive, demanding that all newly acquired territory be made forever free, and the settlement of 1850, though a disappointment, was not an utter defeat. In the repeal of the Missouri Compromise, however, they were resisting an assault upon ground long since guaranteed to freedom, and they did so in greater numbers than ever, with all the fierceness of an army defending its homeland against invasion. The widespread belief that the "slave power" had entered upon a program of aggression, fortified by such later developments as the turmoil in Kansas and the Dred Scott decision, accounts in no small measure for the broader base of the antislavery movement after 1854.

Lincoln's reaction typifies the awakening of many soberminded men in the North. Always opposed in principle to the institution of slavery, he had not hitherto enlisted actively in the crusade against it. As a congressman, he had been neither outspoken nor entirely consistent in his support of the antislavery cause. This can be explained in some degree as a concession to party unity and to the conservative mood of his constituents, but it also reflects the essential mildness of his own views, down to the moment when he was "aroused." The Kansas-Nebraska Act transformed his thinking on the whole subject down to its very roots. Thereafter, he became increasingly convinced that slavery and free society were absolutely incompatible.[10]

Lincoln saw much more evil in the obliteration of the old compromise line than just the revival of sectional conflict and the opening of two territories to slavery. Not that he regarded either of these effects as unimportant, but his primary concern—and this cannot be stated too emphatically—was with the moral status of slavery in a nation originally dedicated to the inalienable rights of man. Believing that the Missouri Compromise, like the North-west Ordinance before it, had recognized the priority of freedom, and that Negro servitude had been tolerated by the founding fathers only as a local necessity, he discovered in popular sovereignty an odious new principle which placed slavery and freedom on the same ethical level. The difference between the two was now reduced, he thought, to a matter of mere economic interest. The moral distinction had been erased along with the compromise line. Repeal of the Missouri Compromise was therefore doubly wrong: "wrong in its direct effect, letting slavery into Kansas and Nebraska—and wrong in its prospective principle, allowing it to spread to every other part of the wide world, where men can be found inclined to take it." Beyond the immediate, practical problem of Kansas, then, was the question of whether national policy should continue to embody some kind of commitment to freedom, or whether it should yield slavery a place of absolute equality. "I particularly object," said Lincoln in his Peoria speech, "to the *new* position which the avowed principle of this Nebraska law gives to slavery in the body politic. I object to it because it assumes that there *can be moral right* in the enslaving of one man to another."[11] After 1854, he never failed to take this bifocal view of the territorial issue, or to lay his heaviest stress upon its symbolic importance in the "eternal struggle between . . . right and wrong."[12]

The Kansas-Nebraska bill was the center of bitter controversy for the first five months of 1854, but the extent of its disruptive influence upon politics did not become visible until after preparations for the autumn elections were launched throughout the country. When Lincoln began to speak out publicly against the measure late in the summer, he had already given the subject many months of study and reflection. In all probability, his thoughts were well crystallized before there was anything more than the vaguest prospect of political advantage for himself. Nevertheless, since a man often has more than one reason for what he does, the depth and sincerity of Lincoln's conviction can be affirmed without the slightest discounting of his intense, unsleeping ambition. He simply had the good fortune to find that a cause which moved him deeply also offered glittering rewards.

*

It must be remembered, however, that Lincoln's opposition to the Kansas-Nebraska Act in 1854 did not imply any change in his allegiance to the Whig party. The egregious measure bore a bold Democratic stamp. Endorsed by President Pierce, driven through Congress by Douglas, it was a partisan as well as a sectional issue. Northern Whigs were overwhelmingly against it, and Southern Whigs, at least divided on the subject. Lincoln was therefore not unreasonable in the expectation that the party of Henry Clay would become the rallying point for a grand move to restore the Missouri Compromise. But two basic conditions prevented the Whigs from exploiting their opportunity: the internal weakness of the party itself, and the heterogeneous composition of the anti-Nebraska forces, which could achieve solidarity only in a new organization.

The passing of the Whig party and the rise of the Republicans was like a motion picture "dissolve," in which one scene slowly fades from view while another gradually takes its place. These two complex events were not merely connected but inseparably part of one another, and for many men like Lincoln there was no exact moment of ceasing to be a Whig and becoming a Republican. Furthermore, the timing of an overt commitment usually depended more upon external, local circumstances than upon the inner progress of a man's thought or the strength of his conviction. Not all the founders of Republicanism were among those persons who first adopted its name.

There is no simple explanation for the sudden demise of the Whig party within three years after its last president, Millard Fillmore, departed from office. Citing the divisive influence of the slavery question rather deepens than dispels the mystery. Sectional antagonism was, after all, an equally heavy strain upon Democratic unity. A Democrat had introduced the Wilmot Proviso; Democratic votes had helped send both Charles Sumner and

Salmon P. Chase to the United States Senate; and no less a Democrat than Martin Van Buren had run for president on the Free-Soil ticket in 1848. Yet adhering to this same party, with varying degrees of fidelity, were Southern extremists like James M. Mason, Andrew P. Butler, and Jefferson Davis. For many Democrats, as well as Whigs, sectional loyalties had become paramount, and the survival of their party a relatively minor concern. Both organizations were, in fact, badly divided, and one historian has insisted that it was very much a "toss-up" between 1848 and 1852 as to which "would be able to remain a nation-wide party."[13]

In the end, of course, neither party stood up under the besetting pressures of sectionalism. But the Democrats, with a more vigorous tradition and somewhat wiser leadership, managed to postpone disaster for a few years by choosing an ideally nondescript candidate in 1852, by sloughing off their radical antislavery element in 1854 (thus reducing internal discord), and by achieving an evasive, ambiguous, and precarious accommodation on the territorial question. The Whigs, on the other hand, could not make the necessary adjustment. Always deficient in tensile strength, their party had become tainted with nativism and opposition to the popular Mexican War. Their old battles for a national bank, protective tariffs, internal improvements, and the distribution of proceeds from the sale of public lands had been given up entirely or reduced to spiritless gestures. By 1852, Whiggery in many parts of the country seemed aimless and anemic—a receptacle for the deposit of anti-Democratic feeling, and little more. Then, during that year, it suffered an irreparable loss of leadership in the deaths of Clay and Webster, followed by the worst defeat in a presidential election since the last agonies of Federalism. From these heavy blows the party did not recover, and, tending to disintegrate rather than break neatly in two, it rapidly lost identity and became raw material for other political movements.

To men living in the early 1850's, however, the trend of events was far from clear. The historian, knowing what happens next, is excluded by the very certainty of his knowledge from the contingent world of those who make history. And in spite of all his precautions, he may tend to forget that signs of the times are easily read only when the times are past. Professor Riddle says that after the election of 1852, "it should have been evident to Lincoln that the Whig party was dying."[14] Yet the evidence was actually too inconclusive to justify such a positive judgment so soon. Some Whigs looked ahead with gloomy resignation, others, with stubborn hope; but all were spared the illusion of inevitability.

The election results, although discouraging enough, were in themselves hardly grounds for complete despair. Winfield Scott, to be sure, carried only four states and was overwhelmed by Franklin Pierce in the electoral college, 254 to 42. But the popular vote was less decisive: Pierce, 1,601,274; Scott, 1,386,580; Hale (Free-Soil), 155,825. Scott's total surpassed that of any previous presidential candidate, and his percentage was not far below Taylor's for 1848. In Illinois, where the Whigs were accustomed to defeat, Pierce won easily, as expected, and yet Scott's percentage of the total vote was almost equal to what Taylor and Clay had received in the two preceding elections. Also, while the Whigs were beaten as usual in the contest for state offices and control of the General Assembly, they profited from a redrafting of congressional districts to capture four of the nine seats in the House of Representatives, where they had held only one before. On the whole, then, and especially in Illinois, the Whig setback in 1852 was not an unmitigated rout, and under less abnormal conditions the party might have been able to renew its vitality.*

---

* The following table shows the percentages of popular vote for the three parties in the elections of 1848 and 1852:

	United States		Illinois	
	1848	1852	1848	1852
Democrat	43	51	45	52
Whig	47	44	43	42
Free-Soil	10	5	12	6

In terms of popular votes, the defeats of Democratic candidates in the 1920's and of Republican candidates in the 1930's were more overwhelming than

At least a responsible Whig like Lincoln had to proceed for a time on the assumption that such a renewal was possible.

Unfortunately, the bitter post-election analyses indulged in by the Whigs had the effect of aggravating the very weaknesses which had led to their defeat. For instance, the widespread belief that Pierce's margin of victory had been supplied by foreign-born voters strengthened many Whigs in the determination that "Americans should rule America" and inspired a mass movement into Know-Nothing lodges. This, in turn, intensified the foreigner's distrust of the Whigs and bound him all the more securely to the Democratic party. Political nativism, flourishing first on the local level, did not in its early stages necessarily imply the dissolution of orthodox party ties, but after 1852 it moved swiftly toward national organization and became increasingly an alternative, rather than a supplement, to Whiggery.

Another reason for Scott's poor showing was the defection of many Southern Whigs who considered him lukewarm toward the recent Compromise and a potential tool of Seward and company. This conservative revolt was not confined to the South, for the hostility of disgruntled Fillmore men in New York probably cost Scott that state, and in Massachusetts, where Webster told his friends to vote for Pierce, the party's erstwhile majority was greatly reduced. Antislavery Whigs, already unhappy with a platform that acquiesced in the Compromise, were infuriated by these acts of "treachery" and more disposed than ever to shake loose from all political association with slaveholders.* Thus the

---

the one suffered by Scott, but by that time the two major parties were more firmly institutionalized. The Whig party had only twenty years of history behind it in 1852 and was perhaps too callow (rather than decrepit, as usually pictured) to withstand the extraordinary pressures placed upon it.

* The disaffection of certain radical Whigs because of their party's acceptance of the hated Fugitive Slave Law was not a decisive factor in the election. Although the Free-Soil organization probably did draw off more Whigs than Democrats (in sharp contrast with 1848), its strength was cut in half, and it had only a negligible effect upon the final result. The idea that the Whig party underwent martyrdom because of its contribution to the great Compromise does not square well with the evidence. On

Whig party emerged from the election weakened and discordant, showing definite signs of disintegration.

There was consolation and some hope for Whigs, however, in the fact that their victorious rivals were likewise plagued with dissension. The semblance of Democratic unity which had assured the election of Pierce began to disappear even before he took office. Personal animosities, patronage quarrels, and the President's bumbling efforts to conciliate all factions of his party caused trouble everywhere, but especially in New York. There the old fight between Barnburners and Hunkers was resumed with such fury that the resurgent Whigs carried the state in the 1853 election. Furthermore, it was obvious that the Democratic ascendancy in national politics depended heavily upon maintenance of the shaky sectional truce. Both logic and history supported the expectation that a revival of the slavery controversy would, in the free states, at least, redound to the advantage of the opposition.

We know now, of course, that the Kansas-Nebraska excitement spelled the virtual end of organized Whiggery, while the Democratic party escaped with the amputation of its free-soil wing. But the point is that for a time, while matters hung in the balance, other outcomes were possible, or seemed so to contemporaries. Douglas's explosive measure, by dividing Northern Democrats, actually raised the stock of Northern Whigs. Only gradually did it become apparent that the latter, in order to profit fully from the situation, must submerge their identity in a new coalition. For the observer and participant like Lincoln, the signs pointing to the imminent demise of the Whig party were mingled with a variety of other signs, some of which pointed in the opposite direction.

The delay between Lincoln's denunciation of the Kansas-

---

the contrary, it was the suspicion of Whig unreliability on the Compromise that apparently swelled the vote for Pierce in a year when there was a deep desire for sectional peace.

Nebraska Act and his relinquishment of the name "Whig" accurately reflected the general state of politics. For the lines that were so quickly and sharply drawn on the Nebraska issue cut through organizational allegiances and brought confusion to the party system. Even after the elections of 1854, in which the North registered an emphatic protest against the abrogation of the Missouri Compromise, the shape of the future was only dimly revealed. The results unquestionably added up to a severe defeat for the Democratic party, but just who had won the victory was still far from clear.

*

The birth of Republicanism was no more a simple, instantaneous event than the death of Whiggery. The elements of a Northern sectional party had existed for a number of years and needed only time and certain favorable conditions to assume a definite form. Although it was inevitable that opposition to slavery should be the head and front of such a movement, other motives prodded its growth. The Southern oligarchy was resented not only for its ownership of slaves but as a concentration of political power which bent the federal government to its will and barred the road to economic progress. Men who wanted protective tariffs, cheaper public lands, and liberal internal improvements came more and more to identify their enemy as the slaveholding South.

The Free-Soil party of 1848 made the first organized effort to exploit this generic sectional feeling. Broader in appeal and more moderate in temper than the earlier Liberty party, the movement nevertheless proved to be premature. The strain placed upon the major parties by the fierce conflict over the Wilmot Proviso was not enough to overcome their cohesive strength, and they held together until the Compromise of 1850 gave them a temporary respite. Yet the ordeal had weakened their resistance to divisive influences; the Compromise quieted the territorial controversy only to stir up another over the Fugitive Slave Law; and the forces that had achieved but partial expression in the Free-Soil movement continued to gather momentum. The results of the 1852 presidential election are misleading because on the surface they indicate a return to the two-party system and a subsidence of antislavery politics. But at the state level, a rearrangement of political structures was under way before 1854, and the beginnings of the Republican party can be seen in coalitions such as those that sent Charles Sumner of Massachusetts and Ben Wade of Ohio to the Senate and organized the abortive People's party of 1853 in Wisconsin. There were vaguer signs of a similar trend in northern Illinois, and the Chicago *Democrat* in the summer of 1853 predicted an effort by the Whigs to join with Free-Soilers and other reform groups in the formation of a new opposition party.[15] At about the same time, the passage of a severe law prohibiting the entrance of free Negroes into the state set off a violent public debate which helped prepare the ground for what was to come.

Thus the formation of the Republican party had some fragmentary beginnings prior to 1854. Then the great anti-Nebraska uprising of that year swiftly converted a raw tendency into a recognizable and formidable movement. But structural coherence came more slowly, and the process of organization was not completed until 1856. In the meantime, Republicanism evolved plurally, in many places, in various ways, and from diverse origins. Any designation of a specific birthplace and birthdate for the party is therefore highly arbitrary, and the claims entered in behalf of communities like Ripon, Wisconsin, and Jackson, Michigan, are based to a considerable extent upon something quite superficial— that is, early adoption of the right *name*.

The transition from protest meetings to improvised coalitions to well-ordered party organizations did not proceed everywhere at the same rate. The most rapid progress was made in areas where the antislavery spirit met little resistance from Whiggery and little competition from nativism. Conditions in Michigan and Wisconsin, for example, were particularly favorable, and the anti-Nebraska forces had united, organized, and labeled themselves

"Republicans" by the summer of 1854. In other states, like Maine, Vermont, Ohio, Indiana, and Iowa, the results were similar but not identical. Fusion organizations appeared in each case and swept to election victories over the Democrats. There were variations, however, in the degree of solidarity achieved, in the extent to which Whig machinery was dismantled, and in the use of the name "Republican."

The most complicated situations developed in lower New England and the Middle Atlantic states, where Whiggery remained potent either in its familiar form or as the backbone of Know-Nothingism. In New York, Greeley urged the establishment of a Republican party, but at the insistence of Seward and Weed, the anti-Nebraska campaign of 1854 was fought and won under the Whig banner. In Massachusetts, the Know-Nothings got the upper hand and elected their candidate for governor on a platform that combined nativism with anti-Nebraskaism. A separate Republican party was also organized, but it made a poor showing at the polls. As for Pennsylvania, it presented the most confused picture of all. An amorphous Whig-nativist-prohibitionist-antislavery coalition carried the election and issued one more stern rebuke to the Pierce administration. Just what political structure would emerge from this jumble was uncertain, but the future looked bright for the Know-Nothings, and there were as yet few signs of an independent Republican movement.[16]

Illinois was likewise a scene of confusion. Efforts to draw the diverse anti-Nebraska elements into a single organization met with only fragmentary success. The fusion movement made considerable headway in the northern counties, and some conventions adopted the Republican name. Yet even in that favorable climate it was not always easy to detach men from their old allegiances. The lack of unity among the anti-Nebraska forces was well exemplified in the Chicago congressional district where they put three candidates (a Whig, a fusionist, and an independent Democrat) into the field against the regular Democratic nominee. Farther south, the Nebraska issue divided public opinion more evenly and had a less disruptive effect upon existing political structures. The Whig machine remained intact, hoping to make capital from the intense excitement, and the influential *State Journal* rejected the idea of forming a new antislavery party.[17] Democrats who condemned the repeal of the Missouri Compromise did so in most cases without renouncing their party, although many of them were eventually driven out of it by Douglas's vindictive tactics. Know-Nothingism, which promised to become a complicating factor in the central and southern parts of the state, was not organized as a separate political movement in 1854.

Thus Lincoln, in continuing to act as a Whig, displayed neither timidity nor stubbornness, but merely followed the only course possible in his section of Illinois. Any attempt there to translate anti-Nebraska feeling into a fusion or Republican movement would have weakened it seriously. The diversity of the forces opposing the Kansas-Nebraska policy meant that the battle could be fought in each locality under a popular banner: Republicanism in some places, Whiggery and independent Democracy in others. Consolidation was utterly impracticable in 1854 and expensive when subsequently achieved. Ten counties, most of them Whig strongholds, which returned anti-Nebraska majorities in the election of 1854 would be in the Democratic column six years later.

It was as a Whig, therefore, that Lincoln plunged into the unusual political campaign of 1854, and as a Whig that he became a candidate for the state House of Representatives. This sudden willingness to return to the legislature after an absence of a dozen years is rather curious in a man of Lincoln's political stature and ambition. Perhaps it was simply zeal for the anti-Nebraska cause —a determination to play some part, however small, in the impending struggle. He himself later asserted that he had entered the race only in order to help Yates win re-election to Congress.[18] But another consideration must have been at least in the back of his mind. The new legislature was due to elect a United States senator, and if the anti-Nebraska forces could capture this prize it would be a humiliating defeat for Douglas on his home grounds. That Lincoln was looking ahead to the senatorial contest and even giving some thought to his own chances seems more than likely.

*

Lincoln had already made several political speeches when his candidacy for the legislature was announced on September 4. Thereafter, he averaged about one a week until election day. Three times he spoke in direct reply to addresses by Douglas, and at Springfield on October 4 their encounter assumed the appearance of a true debate when Douglas responded with a long rebuttal. In each of his appearances Lincoln went over approximately the same general arguments. His presentation was well polished by the time he spoke at Peoria on October 16, and here for once his words were fully recorded. Thus it was the "Peoria Speech" that became famous.

Lincoln's assault upon the repeal of the Missouri Compromise was powerful enough to delight even the more extreme antislavery men among his listeners. But at the same time one must note certain sharp contrasts between his views and the radical resolutions passed by various "fusion" or "Republican" conventions in the northern part of the state. He dealt gently with the Southern people, saying, "They are just what we would be in their situation." He admitted having no ultimate solution for the slavery problem and rejected any suggestion of raising Negroes to a position of social and political equality with the white race. He acknowledged the Southerners' constitutional right to have an effective fugitive slave law. He did not demand the abolition of slavery in the District of Columbia. Neither did he insist that there should be "no more slave states." His indictment of the Kansas-Nebraska policy and the consequent opening of federal territories to slavery was eloquent and unqualified, but not abusive. Even the unfriendly *State Register* remarked after one of his speeches, "Mr. L. spoke of Judge Douglas in a less denunciatory manner than is the custom on such occasions."[19] When

Lincoln eventually joined with men of more advanced beliefs in forming the Republican party, he adopted their name, but they accepted a platform that was closer to his way of thinking.

In the audience that heard Lincoln's speech of October 4, 1854, there was a group of antislavery radicals who had come to Springfield for the purpose of organizing a state-wide Republican party. Deeply impressed by the Whig leader, they sought to enlist him in their enterprise and even placed his name, without permission, upon the central committee of their organization. Lincoln declined to become involved in the movement, however, and it soon fell apart. That is about the substance of this well-known incident, but some colorful embellishments were added by William H. Herndon, whose retentive memory yielded at times to his lively imagination.

According to Herndon, he decided that his partner could not afford to associate with the radicals, or to offend them either, and so should get out of town until their meeting was over. Lincoln took his advice, made a hasty departure "under pretence of having business in Tazewell County," and thus was "saved" from a "great danger."[20] It is an amusing picture—the future Emancipator scurrying away in his buggy to escape contamination from a little group of abolitionists—but scarcely a credible one. The fact is that Lincoln went to Pekin because he had a number of cases to try in the fall term of the Tazewell Circuit Court. The trip was part of his regular professional routine, and he made it in other years at approximately the same date, without traveling on the "wheels of political prudence."[21] Herndon's biographer, David Donald, finds other flaws in the story; it is, he declares, inconsistent with the characters of both men, unsupported by contemporary evidence, and consequently "open to grave suspicion."[22]

In any case, this abortive "Republican" movement of 1854 had no connection with the party organized two years later. The Springfield meeting, called by an abolitionist weekly published in Chicago, and attended by a few dozen extremists who represented no one but themselves, cannot be considered an authentic state convention. Lincoln's understandable reluctance to become formally identified with such a group was less significant than his willingness to cooperate with its members and all other radicals in opposing the Kansas-Nebraska policy. "Stand with anybody that stands *right*," he urged his fellow Whigs in the Peoria speech. "Stand with him while he is right and *part* with him when he goes wrong. Stand *with* the abolitionist in restoring the Missouri Compromise; and stand *against* him when he attempts to repeal the fugitive slave law."[23]   Illinois Republicanism in 1854 was a trend rather than an organization, and Lincoln's relationship to it can best be described as one of limited collaboration. In a letter to Ichabod Codding, one of the leaders of the Springfield meeting, he attempted to define his position: "I suppose my opposition to the principle of slavery is as strong as that of any member of the Republican party; but I had also supposed that the *extent* to which I feel authorized to carry that opposition, practically; was not at all satisfactory to that party."[24]   Nevertheless, many fusionists were sufficiently satisfied with Lincoln to support him for the Senate, and in the end they came to accept his more moderate views as a doctrinal basis for the new party.*   In other words, when he did embrace Republicanism, it had been modified to suit his specifications.

Illinois voters went to the polls on November 7, 1854. The results, although somewhat less one-sided than those in many other Northern states, amounted to a clear-cut defeat for the

* Codding, Owen Lovejoy, and other radical leaders of the early Republican movement in Illinois were well aware that a moderate program would attract wider support. The platform which they drew up at Springfield was therefore surprisingly mild, but the *State Register* in reporting the proceedings slyly substituted the more provocative resolutions passed by a local convention at Aurora. In the debate at Ottawa four years later, Douglas unwittingly made use of the *Register*'s "forgery" and suffered much embarrassment as a result. (Basler *et al.*, eds., *The Collected Works of Abraham Lincoln*, III, 4, 43–44, 56–58.) What purports to be a true copy of the Springfield resolutions is published in Paul Selby, "Genesis of the Republican Party in Illinois," Illinois State Historical Society *Transactions*, 1906, pp. 282–83. Beveridge, *Abraham Lincoln*, falls into Douglas's error on II, 266, and then corrects it on pp. 646–47.

Democratic party and a repudiation of the Kansas-Nebraska Act on the home grounds of its chief author. Anti-Nebraska candidates captured five of the nine congressional seats (even though Yates lost by a narrow margin), and an anti-Nebraska majority also swept into control of the General Assembly. Lincoln, elected easily to the legislature, now decided that the Senate seat was within his reach and began to write letters soliciting support. Strangely enough, however, he paid only belated attention to a clause in the state constitution which made legislators ineligible for election to the Senate. Either his senatorial candidacy was a late-hour inspiration, or he had committed a surprising oversight for an eminent attorney at law.

Scholars are in considerable disagreement as to just when Lincoln was bitten by the senatorial bug. For instance, Donald Riddle insists that the Senate was uppermost in his mind from the very beginning of the campaign, whereas David Mearns declares that he "had no thought of becoming a candidate" until after the November election.[25] What little evidence there is tends to indicate that the idea of seeking the senatorship started as a vague hope in Lincoln's mind, but developed rapidly with the progress of the campaign and the conspicuous success of his speeches. All of his speaking engagements in the closing weeks of the contest were outside his own district and therefore of more benefit to himself than to Yates. His Chicago speech of October 27 in particular was almost certainly a bid for northern support in the senatorial election.[26] And the promptness with which he launched his letter-writing campaign on about November 10,[27] together with the fact that he seldom took a major step without first giving it serious thought, likewise suggests that Lincoln had decided sometime before the election to enter the senatorial contest if the legislative returns were favorable. Yet it was not until November 25 that he formally declined "to accept the office of Representative in the General Assembly," and by then the question of his eligibility had been raised more than once.[28] One can only conclude that he had indeed overlooked the constitutional restriction. In addition, he and the other Whigs of Sangamon County failed to exert themselves in the special election called to choose his replacement. As a result, the Democrats won a surprise victory and one precious vote was lost in the legislature.

Examining the composition of the new Assembly, Lincoln estimated that it would contain 57 anti-Nebraska and 43 pro-Nebraska members. Of the former, about two-thirds were Whigs and one-third were Democrats, although many in both of these groups, as he noted, had "gone into the Republican organization."[29] Even with most of the Whigs and Whig-fusionists supporting him, he would still need votes from at least a dozen anti-Nebraska Democrats to be elected. Whether that many were willing to carry their revolt against Douglas to the point of placing an old-line Whig in the Senate was clearly doubtful. Furthermore, some of his fusionist support from the north was unenthusiastic and likely to desert him if the contest extended beyond a few ballots. At the same time, the regular Democrats had little expectation of re-electing the incumbent, James Shields, and party leaders quietly pinned their hopes to the popular Governor Joel A. Matteson, who would presumably be acceptable to some of the milder anti-Nebraska Democrats. The switch to Matteson could not be made without great loss of face, however, until there had first been an earnest demonstration of loyalty to Shields.* Thus Lincoln, who was stronger than Shields but probably weaker than Matteson, would have his best chance in the early balloting.

Obstructionist tactics by the Democrats and a tremendous snowstorm in the Springfield area delayed the senatorial election until February 8, 1855. On the first ballot, Lincoln led with 45 votes, five short of a majority; Shields received 41; five anti-Nebraska Democrats voted for Lyman Trumbull, who had just been elected to Congress from the eighth district east of St. Louis;

* The election of Matteson would have been only a partial victory for the Democrats, first because it would not have constituted a direct endorsement of the Kansas-Nebraska Act, and second, because it would have elevated Lieutenant-Governor Gustave Koerner, an anti-Nebraska man, to the governorship.

and eight votes were scattered among other candidates. The little Trumbull bloc stubbornly refused to transfer its support to Lincoln, and on succeeding ballots his strength gradually declined, while the Shields vote remained stable. Then, in the seventh round of balloting, the Democrats suddenly executed their plan of abandoning Shields in favor of Matteson. The latter promptly attracted 44 votes, whereas a last desperate Lincoln rally could net only 38. The anti-Nebraska forces now began a wholesale shift to Trumbull in the hope of heading off the Matteson raid, and by the ninth ballot Lincoln's total was reduced to 15, Trumbull's had risen to 35, and Matteson's had reached 47. At this critical point, Lincoln finally faced up to defeat and dispatched his remaining adherents to the aid of Trumbull, who was elected on the next ballot with 51 votes.[30]

*

The outcome caused rejoicing in antislavery circles everywhere and gloom among the regular Democrats, who were especially chagrined to see such a prize carried off by a party "renegade." As for Lincoln, although his pleasure at the anti-Nebraska victory was obviously mixed with great personal disappointment, he exhibited less bitterness than some of his partisans. He did not bear a grudge against the five original Trumbull men whose steadfast opposition had contributed so much to his undoing,* but placed the primary blame upon the "secret Matteson men" within the fusionist ranks. "I could have headed off every combination and been elected," he wrote the day after the election, "had it not been for Matteson's double game."[31] Yet it must have been apparent also that one major source of his weakness as a candidate had been his continued attachment to the Whig name. The senatorial contest had demonstrated that Whig-

---

* Curiously enough, two of the five Trumbull stalwarts were State Senators John M. Palmer and Norman B. Judd. Palmer, as a delegate to the Republican National Convention of 1856, led the effort to secure the vice-presidential nomination for Lincoln, and it was Judd, of course, who nominated him for the presidency at Chicago in 1860.

gery in its old form could not profit from the political revolution in progress, and that party labels of all kinds were a serious hindrance to the maximum mobilization of anti-Nebraska strength.

Such a mobilization was thenceforth Lincoln's principal concern as a political leader, but he did not plunge immediately into action. For one thing, he had a family to support, and during the twelve months following his defeat for the Senate he quietly carried on the practice of law without much outward attention to politics. At the end of that period he would join decisively in the erection of a new political structure, but in the meantime he waited and watched and pondered the lines of procedure that might be followed. He did not join the Republican party. There really was none as yet in Illinois. He did not adopt the Republican name. There would have been no advantage in doing so. In fact, for the better part of two years Lincoln generally avoided calling himself anything but an opponent of the extension of slavery. The problem, he knew, was to achieve *inclusive* organization of the diverse elements that had risen up against the Kansas-Nebraska policy. And this would require prudence and tact as well as earnest conviction.

Lincoln's passiveness during 1855 is sometimes offered as evidence of his lingering devotion to the Whig party and hostility to the fusion movement.[32] But whatever substance there may be in such a view, it is not wholly accurate as an explanation of his attitude during this transitional period. In the first place, it must be stressed again that Illinois, unlike so many other states, had no significant elections in the odd-numbered years. Thus there was not the urgent need for immediate organizational activity that existed elsewhere in 1855. The few pertinent remarks to be found in Lincoln's writings leave the impression that he shrank from unnecessarily hasty and premature efforts at fusion, rather than from fusion itself. He seemed to think that Illinois anti-Nebraskans could act more intelligently after they had studied developments in other states and seen the results of the 1855 elections throughout the country.

The great destiny that awaited the emerging Republican party was still far from obvious in 1855. Indignation over the Kansas-Nebraska Act, for all its initial vehemence, would have been an insufficient basis for sustained political action, especially since there was little hope of repealing the obnoxious law. But the struggle in Congress proved to be only the first stage of the conflict. It was the subsequent disorder and violence in Kansas, verging at times on civil war, that kept the anti-Nebraska coalition alive and speeded its transformation into a permanent organization. Simultaneously, however, the Know-Nothing movement was taking formidable shape in both Northern and Southern politics. For a brief period it appeared to have the better chance of becoming a major party. But then many Know-Nothings in the North who had also supported the anti-Nebraska cause were driven to rebellion when their national council adopted a platform embracing the principle of nonintervention in the territories and renouncing all agitation of the slavery question. As a consequence, the new American party began to break apart almost as soon as it was formed. Lincoln, who disapproved of the Know-Nothings but considered their participation essential to the success of antislavery fusion in Illinois, believed that it would be easier to enlist their cooperation when this process of disintegration was further advanced. "Know-nothingism has not yet entirely tumbled to pieces," he wrote to Owen Lovejoy on August 11, 1855.

> Until we can get the elements of this organization, there is not sufficient materials to successfully combat the Nebraska democracy with. We can not get them so long as they cling to a hope of success under their own organization; and I fear an open push by us now, may offend them, and tend to prevent our ever getting them . . . . I have no objection to "fuse" with any body provided I can fuse on ground which I think is right; and I believe the opponents of slavery extension could now do this, if it were not for this K.N.ism.[33]

Two weeks later, in a letter to his old friend Joshua F. Speed of Louisville, Lincoln took stock of his own personal situation:

> You enquire where I now stand. That is a disputed point.
> I think I am a whig; but others say there are no whigs, and
> that I am an abolitionist. When I was at Washington I voted
> for the Wilmot Proviso as good as forty times, and I never
> heard of any one attempting to unwhig me for that. I now
> do no more than oppose the *extension* of slavery.[34]

It is scarcely surprising that he should explain himself somewhat
differently to a slaveholding Whig of Kentucky and the abolition
leader of Illinois, but there is no real inconsistency between the
two documents. The greater part of the letter to Speed is a vigorous defense of the anti-Nebraska position and a sad farewell to
political association with him. "If for this you and I must differ,
differ we must," Lincoln writes. He "thinks" he is as good a
Whig as ever, but this must be regarded as a justification rather
than a commitment. It is plainly Lovejoy, not Speed, with whom
he expects to act in the future. He looks forward to antislavery
fusion on a moderate platform at a suitable time and clings to
the spirit of Whiggery, not its structure.

The policy of watchful waiting which Lincoln pursued in 1855
can thus be interpreted as something other than mere reluctance
to make the change from Whig to Republican. It is true, of course,
that in central Illinois there was still much resistance to the fusion
movement, even among the most outspoken critics of the Kansas-
Nebraska policy. The *State Journal,* for example, continued
throughout 1855 to oppose the absorption of Whiggery by Republicanism.[35] Lincoln's views undoubtedly reflected the conservative sentiment of his region while at the same time he was
canvassing ways to overcome it. This was the ambivalence of a
mind in transition.

Contrary to the impression given by Beveridge and certain
other writers, Lincoln's rate of progress toward full membership
in the Republican party was not conspicuously slower than that
of many other men who eventually became state and national
leaders of the organization. Seward, for one, did not publicly

endorse the new party until October of 1855, on the eve of a significant state election. In the circumstances, he was a more laggard convert than Lincoln. Chase, to be sure, was already in the van of Ohio Republicans, but Simon Cameron remained a Know-Nothing and Edward Bates a Whig. These four men were Lincoln's major rivals for the presidential nomination in 1860, and all of them entered his cabinet. In Illinois, likewise, many outstanding anti-Nebraska leaders were slow to join in the fusion movement. Trumbull, Koerner, Palmer, and William H. Bissell still regarded themselves as Democrats at the beginning of 1856.* Whigs like Yates, Orville H. Browning, and David Davis proceeded no less cautiously than their friend Lincoln. In the northern counties, of course, the new party found earlier favor with the people and their representatives. Yet even John Wentworth of Chicago, the antislavery Democrat whom Beveridge labels "one of the founders of the Republican Party to which Lincoln finally attached himself," actually lagged behind Lincoln all the way—in denouncing the Kansas-Nebraska Act, in building the Republican organization, and in accepting the Republican name.[36] All things considered, the picture of Lincoln as an exceptionally reluctant latecomer to Republicanism is greatly overdrawn.

*

The various state elections of 1855 did not dispel much of the confusion in national politics. Democratic victories over the Americans in Virginia and over the heterogeneous opposition in Pennsylvania signalized a rapid recovery from the disaster of the previous year. Anti-Nebraskaism again carried New England, but in most cases under the Know-Nothing rather than the Republican banner. The American party also won in New York and California. For Republicans, the best news came from Ohio, where Chase was elected to the governorship. In addition, the

---

* Bissell, who was to be nominated for governor by the state Republican convention at Bloomington in May, remained more or less hostile almost to the last moment.

unhealed breach in the Know-Nothing organization bolstered Republican hopes of drawing the "North Americans" into their ranks. As for those persons who continued to call themselves Whigs, it was by now abundantly clear that they would soon have to choose between the three functioning parties and become Republicans, Americans, or Democrats.

The year 1856 opened on a note of rising excitement, with Kansas still in turmoil, the national House of Representatives locked in a seemingly endless struggle over the speakership, and a crucial presidential campaign drawing near. The time had obviously come for Republicans to complete the structure of their party, and in January a number of state chairmen set things in motion by calling a preliminary national convention to meet at Pittsburgh on Washington's Birthday. This move apparently stimulated action in Illinois, where there was still no state-wide Republican organization. A group of antislavery editors took the initiative and summoned their fellow journalists to a meeting on February 22 at Decatur. There plans were made for "a state convention of the Anti-Nebraska party of Illinois" at Bloomington on May 29.

In every way except formal use of the name, this Decatur "editorial convention" marks the launching of the state Republican party, and Lincoln, significantly, was the one prominent political leader who attended it. He conferred with the members of the resolutions committee and heartily endorsed the moderate document which they drafted. He discussed the problem of a gubernatorial nominee, withdrawing his own name from consideration and urging the selection of Bissell. And at a dinner in the evening he delivered a half-hour speech promising to "buckle on his armor for the approaching contest with the Pierce party."[37] If ever a man committed himself by deed and word, voluntarily and openly, Lincoln did so at Decatur, and there is nothing to indicate that he had any serious misgivings about it afterward. Yet in Reinhard H. Luthin's influential article, "Abraham Lincoln Becomes a Republican," we read that he "continued to remain aloof" through March and April, that up to the very eve of the Bloomington convention, his attendance was doubtful. Here again it is William Herndon who has led scholarship astray.

Professor Luthin points out that while Herndon busied himself with addressing county anti-Nebraska conventions, his partner "engaged in no such missionary endeavor." So Herndon "decided to force Lincoln's hand." Luthin then lets Herndon tell his own story, which may be summarized as follows: Believing that "the times were ripe for more advanced movements," the junior partner drew up a call for a county convention to select delegates for Bloomington. Since Lincoln was absent from the city, Herndon signed his name to the document. One of Lincoln's overcautious friends protested, and Herndon immediately wrote for approval of his action. Lincoln responded with a telegram, "all right; go ahead. Will meet you—radicals and all." Thereafter, Herndon concludes, "the conservative spirits who hovered around Springfield no longer held control of the political fortunes of Abraham Lincoln."[38]

Herndon's account, written many years after the event, was probably not an outright fabrication. The chances are that he did sign Lincoln's name to the convention call, but as a matter of mere convenience and with full confidence that his partner would want it so. There is no evidence whatever that the man who had committed himself decisively in February needed any prodding in May. At the Decatur meeting, Herndon had been appointed to the state central committee of the new party, no doubt with Lincoln's approval. Therefore, in calling a Sangamon convention he was not acting upon a sudden inspiration but simply performing one of his duties, and the same can be said of his "missionary" activities in other counties. As David Donald aptly puts it, "Lincoln had made the lead at Decatur; Herndon was now following suit."[39] Between February and May, Lincoln was hard at work on the court circuit, knowing that much of his time later in the year would be given over to campaigning. If he made no public speeches, there was less need for them at this stage of the fusion movement than for the private persuasion of certain key politicians. The plain truth is that Lincoln was well ahead of many anti-Nebraska leaders in promoting the organization of an Illinois Republican party, and his early support of the Bloomington convention had a powerful effect upon waverers among them.

The spectacular success of the Bloomington convention vindicated Lincoln's strategy of waiting for the most opportune moment to organize. Enthusiasm ran high, heightened by news of the assault on Charles Sumner in the Senate and the proslavery "sack" of Lawrence, Kansas. All the major varieties of anti-Nebraska sentiment were represented: Democrats and Whigs, Germans and Know-Nothings, radicals and conservatives. This diversity was reflected in the nomination of Bissell for governor, a German for lieutenant-governor, and Know-Nothing Whigs for the other state offices. The resolutions drafted by Browning were aggressive in tone but suitably moderate in substance. Oratory flowed freely and reached its climax in an address by Lincoln (unrecorded, and consequently known as his "lost speech"), which was from all accounts one of the most eloquent and effective performances of his life. From the day of this Bloomington convention, Illinois had a Republican party equal to any other in unity, discipline, and zeal.

A few weeks later, the Republican National Convention at Philadelphia nominated John C. Frémont for president. Second place on the ticket went to William C. Dayton of New Jersey, with Abraham Lincoln receiving 110 votes on an informal first ballot. Although he had favored Supreme Court Justice John McLean instead of Frémont, Lincoln plunged energetically into the campaign and by his own count delivered more than fifty speeches before it was over.[40] From the beginning, however, it was apparent that the Republicans would have a much better chance of electing their state ticket than of carrying Illinois for Frémont. In James Buchanan the Democrats had a strong presidential candidate who was free of close association with the

Kansas mess, and the Whig-American nomination of Millard Fillmore promised to cut Republican strength in conservative areas. As early as August 4, Lincoln predicted that Illinois would end up in the Democratic column unless the Americans withdrew from the field. He expended much effort in letters and speeches trying to persuade old-line Whigs that a vote for Fillmore was, in effect, a vote for Buchanan. But the election results verified his fears. Buchanan defeated Frémont in Illinois with a plurality of about nine thousand votes, while four times that number were "thrown away" on Fillmore. There was much consolation, however, in the victory of Bissell and his entire ticket. Illinois now had a Republican administration.

Even those scholars who picture Lincoln as a reluctant, last-minute Republican acknowledge that he was fully committed to the new party by the summer of 1856. It is therefore interesting to note that throughout the campaign he prudently avoided use of the name, speaking instead of the "Anti-Nebraska party" and the "Frémont men." The Republican label, with its radical connotation, was accepted only gradually and grudgingly in many circles. For several years, more innocuous names were used in southern Illinois and in states like New Jersey and Pennsylvania. Lincoln, it must be conceded, was somewhat slow to call himself a "Republican." But in the actual construction of an effective organization from the raw materials of anti-Nebraskaism, and in the determination of its essential character, no citizen of Illinois played a more important part than he.

Three

The Senatorial Nomination

THE CHRONOLOGY of Abraham Lincoln's rise from relative obscurity to a presidential nomination includes no more decisive date than June 16, 1858. At Springfield, late in that warm Wednesday afternoon, the Republican state convention unanimously designated him as its "first and only choice . . . for the United States Senate, as the successor of Stephen A. Douglas," and he responded in the evening with his famous "House Divided" speech. Either of these two events would have made the day significant; together they constituted a major turning point in his career.

The resolution endorsing Lincoln for the Senate was more important than anyone realized at the time, for without it there probably would have been no Lincoln-Douglas debates. Douglas saw little profit for himself in joint discussions and rejected Lincoln's suggestion that they canvass the state together. He proposed instead—and Lincoln accepted—an alternative plan for just seven debates.[1] Only the fact that his rival had been specifically named as the Republican candidate induced the reluctant "Little Giant" to go even that far. So the convention's resolution, amounting to an informal nomination, proved to be the door of opportunity for Lincoln. Through it he stepped to the memorable contest with Douglas, and thus, at the age of forty-nine, to the stage of national politics.

This was not an ordinary door, however, but something strange and new, carpentered especially for the occasion. The nomination of a senatorial candidate by a state convention had no precedent in American politics. Even in the casual form of a resolution from the floor, the action represented an intrusion upon the vested authority of the General Assembly, which was constitutionally free to elect any legally qualified person, regardless of convention pronouncements. The unique character of Lincoln's second bid for a Senate seat can be seen when it is contrasted with his first. In 1854, he had waited until *after* the general election in November to announce his candidacy, and then he had conducted a quiet letter-writing campaign among the *legislators,* with whom the choice rested. Four years later, he came forward as an avowed candidate in June, five months *before* the election, and carried his subsequent campaign directly to the *people.* This new way of running for the Senate had interesting implications because it tended to relegate the legislature to the passive role of an electoral college. When the time came to elect a senator on January 5, 1859, every Republican legislator compliantly cast his ballot for Lincoln, and the Democrats all voted for Douglas. According to George H. Haynes in his history of the Senate, the Lincoln-Douglas contest was the first important step toward the Seventeenth Amendment.[2]

The singularity of Lincoln's nomination received considerable attention from contemporaries, including Douglas, who remarked that it was probably the first time "such a thing was ever done."[3] Newspapers used words like "original" and "unprecedented" to describe the campaign, and one Philadelphia editor called it a "dangerous innovation," indeed, a "revolutionary effort to destroy the true intent and spirit of the constitution."[4] Yet the resolution of the Republican state convention did not spring from any passion for political experiment. Instead, it was a tactical maneuver, improvised to deal with a specific, vexatious problem. Upon this point Lincoln students are in general agreement, but there is a divergence of scholarly opinion as to what the problem was.

According to one view, the nomination of Lincoln was a rebuke to certain Eastern Republican leaders who had found a new hero in Stephen A. Douglas since his spectacular break with the Buchanan administration over the Lecompton constitution for Kansas. Horace Greeley, in particular, had appointed himself to

lecture his Illinois brethren on the advantages of returning Douglas to the Senate unopposed. The resolution endorsing Lincoln
was their way of rejecting this odious advice, their gesture of
defiance to the meddlesome editor and others like him who would
turn Illinois Republicanism over to its deadliest enemy. Herndon
expressed the common feeling of grim satisfaction when he wrote,
"I want to see 'old gentleman Greely's' notice of our Republican
Convention—I itch—I burn, to see what he says . . ."[5]

The other version is that Lincoln had a rival among Illinois
Republicans in the person of John Wentworth, who was scheming
to get control of the legislature and win the Senate seat for himself. A group of Wentworth's enemies determined to explode his
plot by persuading the state convention to give Lincoln an ex-
clusive endorsement. The "trick" worked perfectly, and Long
John was beaten. Writing to Trumbull a week later, Lincoln
observed: "The resolution in effect nominating me for Senator
I suppose was passed more for the object of closing down upon
this everlasting croaking about Wentworth, than anything else."[6]

Which of these two explanations is closer to the truth? Both
can be documented from the sources, and both have the support
of respected scholars. Generally speaking, the anti-Greeley explanation prevailed in earlier writings. But then Albert J. Beveridge, in his massive and influential study, described Lincoln's
nomination in dramatic detail as an anti-Wentworth stratagem
and nothing else. His judgment was widely although not uni-
versally accepted. More recently, it has been challenged, and
when Benjamin P. Thomas wrote his biography of Lincoln in
the early 1950's he treated the nomination solely as a rebuff to
Eastern Republicans.[7]

The fact that the resolution endorsing Lincoln had notable
consequences is enough to justify investigation of the motives
behind it. In addition, however, this little problem in historical
interpretation will serve conveniently as the framework for a
review of the events that led up to the great debates.

*

The emergence of Lincoln as a national figure was aided by the new sectional crisis that flared up in the closing months of 1857. The year began quietly enough. Threats of disunion subsided after Buchanan's victory over Frémont; some measure of peace had been restored in strife-torn Kansas; and the country was riding high on a wave of prosperity. The Democratic party had obviously made at least a partial recovery from the devastating effects of the Kansas-Nebraska struggle of 1854, while the Republicans, although undismayed by their recent defeat, were for the moment without a burning issue to exploit. Buchanan, as he took the presidential oath on March 4, 1857, had reason to believe that national politics might be turning into a less turbulent channel. But this was a hope soon blighted.

Two days after the inaugural ceremony, the Supreme Court issued its decision in the Dred Scott case, declaring that the Missouri Compromise line was unconstitutional because Congress possessed no power to exclude slavery from the federal territories. The President, the Chief Justice, and various other public leaders had deluded themselves with the expectation that such a decision would settle the slavery question once and for all. Instead, it only emboldened Southern extremists, infuriated the Republicans, and laid an additional burden on Northern Democrats, who dutifully applauded the Court's action, but not without apprehensive glances toward the next election.

Yet the Dred Scott decision, while it set off a furious public debate and drove another wedge between the North and the South, did not itself precipitate a major political crisis. Neither did it cause an open break in the Democratic party. Strictly speaking, the Court had merely invalidated a law already repealed by the Kansas-Nebraska Act of 1854. Still open to argument was the question of how extensively the decision would govern future legislation affecting slavery. Southerners naturally assumed that the central purpose of the Republican party had been pronounced illegal, and many of them also maintained that the Douglas doctrine of popular sovereignty was no longer tenable, since a power denied to Congress could scarcely be exercised by subordinate bodies (the territorial legislatures) which Congress had created. But Douglas, speaking at Springfield on June 12, 1857, doggedly insisted that the Supreme Court had sustained *his* "great principle" by ruling out congressional intervention while leaving the people of a territory free to protect or discountenance slavery in their local legislation.* As for the Republicans, they indignantly refused to consider the Court's word binding upon anyone except the parties in the case. It was an "erroneous" decision, based upon a false reading of history, Lincoln declared in his Springfield speech of June 26. "We know the court that made it, has often over-ruled its own decisions, and we shall do what we can to have it to over-rule this. We offer no *resistance* to it."[8] Here, then, were three emphatically different schools of thought on the scope and force of the Dred Scott decision, but before the issue could become a concrete and urgent one, the center of sectional conflict had shifted once again to Kansas.

Ambition, greed, and plain villainy produced a certain amount of disorder on nearly every American frontier, but the troubles of Kansas Territory were multiplied by its symbolic importance in the slavery controversy. Like Spain in the 1930's and Korea in the 1950's, it became the focus of a struggle between external forces, the scene of a "limited war." Proslavery elements in Kansas, with illegal help from neighboring Missourians, had gained control of the territorial government. The aggressive and rapidly growing "Free State" faction, spurred on by antislavery enthusiasts in the Northern states, had repudiated this government and organized its own, in defiance of federal authority. The result was civil war on a guerrilla scale, reaching its climax in the spring and summer of 1856 with the "sack" of Lawrence, the Pottawatomie massacre, and the assault upon Osawatomie. Thereafter, the violence was substantially checked by an energetic territorial governor, but the situation remained tense.

* In this speech, Douglas for the first time used the argument that later became famous as his "Freeport doctrine," and it is significant that he did so without serious objection from Southern Democrats. For a more extensive treatment of this subject, see Chapter Six.

Quite obviously, the simplest way to remove Kansas as a prime source of national discord was to make it a state without delay. Yet sectional rivalry in Congress had prevented the passage of an enabling act. Then, early in 1857, the territorial legislature took matters into its own hands by ordering an election of delegates to a constitutional convention. This proved to be the first in a series of decisions that renewed the sectional conflict, disrupted the Democratic party, and profoundly influenced the career of Abraham Lincoln. The other decisions may be summarized as follows: (2) The Free State forces in Kansas, continuing their policy of noncooperation with the legislature and protesting that the arrangements for the election of delegates were grossly dishonest, refused to go to the polls on June 15. A convention packed with proslavery men was consequently elected. (3) The convention met at Lecompton in the autumn and drafted a constitution which was sufficiently weighted in favor of slavery to provoke a storm of anger throughout the North. (4) Buchanan, under heavy pressure from Southern leaders, chose to endorse the Lecompton constitution in his first annual message of December 8, 1857. (5) Douglas and many other Northern Democrats promptly rose up in revolt, joining the Republicans in denunciation of the instrument. Thus the year closed with public feeling again inflamed over the slavery question and, to make matters worse, with the country mired in a severe economic depression which had crippled trade, closed most of the banks, and thrown thousands of men out of work.

*

The behavior of Douglas at this point, and the motives behind it, deserve special attention. Heretofore the Little Giant had wasted no sympathy upon the Free State men of Kansas; now he was suddenly coming to their support, even at the hazard of wrecking his party. Historians have generally been willing to grant that in opposing the Lecompton constitution he played a hero's role and "acted on principle."[9] Yet the principle at stake is somewhat difficult to identify. The Lecompton controversy, as

Lincoln repeatedly pointed out, had nothing to do with the status of slavery in a territory and so presented no test of Douglas's popular sovereignty. Instead, the quarrel concerned the procedure for admitting a state to the Union, something that Congress had never taken the trouble to regularize. Since everyone did agree, however, that the constitution of a new state should reflect the will of the people, the point at issue was whether the Lecompton document measured up to this accepted standard. "It was," said Lincoln, "a question of fact, and not of principle."[10]

Douglas launched his attack in the Senate immediately after the reading of Buchanan's annual message. The Lecompton constitution, he declared, had been written without authorization from Congress and by an unrepresentative convention. Worst of all, the convention had elected to submit only the question of slavery to the voters of the territory, denying them the opportunity to pass on the constitution as a whole. The effect would be to "force this constitution down the throats of the people of Kansas, in opposition to their wishes."[11] With these remarks, which signalized his revolt against Southern domination of the Democratic party, Douglas by no means exhausted the list of objections to the "Lecompton swindle." Republicans protested that the submission of the slavery clause was a miserable sham. Even if the usual proslavery election frauds were prevented, they complained, a popular vote against slavery would not eliminate the institution entirely, since the convention had decreed that slaves already held in the territory would not be affected by the referendum. In short, Kansas could choose only between some slavery and more slavery, despite the fact that a majority of its citizens wanted none at all.*

At the same time, Buchanan and other supporters of the Lecompton constitution, although not unembarrassed by the shab-

---

* That the Free State forces in Kansas substantially outnumbered their proslavery adversaries was clearly demonstrated on October 5, 1857, when the former took part for once in a regular territorial election and gained a decisive majority in the legislature.

bier features of the document, were able to make a strong case for its legality and utility. New states had been admitted before without congressional enabling acts and without submitting their constitutions to the people. Moreover, the convention *had* agreed to submit the one question of overwhelming importance, and, in protecting the property rights of slaveholders already residing in Kansas, it was following a precedent set in a number of states and territories where slavery had been abolished. As for the contention that a large part of the Kansas population was not represented at Lecompton, where should the blame be placed except upon the willful men who had refused to participate in the election of delegates? Besides, with admission to statehood, the people of Kansas would become their own masters, free to change any part of their constitution that displeased them. Was it not sensible, then, to accept the work of the Lecompton convention, whatever its defects, rather than precipitate another dangerous struggle over Kansas?

Such arguments naturally made no headway in Republican circles, but it is a little surprising that they also failed to satisfy Douglas or even soften his anger. In fact, the anti-Lecompton heroics of the Illinois senator were so inconsistent with his previous line of conduct that they seemed almost out of character. Hitherto a political realist interested in practical results and the expedients that would produce them, he now manifested the intransigence of a doctrinaire. Always a strong party man who had shown little mercy to insurgents, he was now leading a revolt that threatened to devastate his party. Renowned as an advocate of self-government in the territories with a minimum of interference from Congress, he now proposed to reject a constitution framed in an orderly manner under the authority of a territorial legislature. There was, to be sure, incontrovertible evidence that the Lecompton instrument did not represent the will of the majority in Kansas, but here too one finds a curiously abrupt change of heart. At Springfield, on June 12, 1857, Douglas had used the words "just and fair" to describe the approaching election of delegates to the Lecompton convention. And he had warned the Free State men of Kansas that if they stayed away from the polls and allowed the proslavery faction to win by default, the blame would rest upon them alone. Six months later, however, he told his fellow senators that the act calling the Lecompton convention had been "null and void from the beginning," and that the Free State men of Kansas, although they should have gone to the polls, nevertheless "had a right to stay away."[12] Genuine though it undoubtedly was, Douglas's indignation against the Lecompton constitution does not fully explain the remarkable change in his outlook between June and December, or the almost desperate haste with which he declared himself when Congress convened. Wounded pride and political necessity, it appears, likewise induced him to play the party rebel.

The relations between Douglas and Buchanan, never very cordial at any time, had turned completely sour by the autumn of 1857. Having acquiesced magnanimously in his rival's nomination for the presidency and given him wholehearted support during the campaign that followed, the Illinois leader was vexed to find himself an outsider in the new regime. Now plagued with money troubles in the wake of the financial panic, he had reason to regret his liberal contributions to party coffers for the election of an ungrateful President. But what annoyed him most was his inability to secure any major appointments for his friends in the Northwest. After being snubbed again and again, Douglas was all the more embarrassed by the announcement that his father-in-law, James Madison Cutts, had been named to a Treasury position. His letter of remonstrance to Buchanan and the latter's sarcastic reply were released to the newspapers in October. The country buzzed with talk of the coolness between the two men. Before he left for Washington the next month, Douglas is said to have exclaimed, "By God, sir, I made Mr. James Buchanan, and by God, sir, I will unmake him!"[13]

But if the Little Giant's spectacular fight against the Lecompton constitution was a display of personal bitterness as well as one of public virtue, it could also be called an act of self-preservation.

In engineering the passage of the Kansas-Nebraska Act several years earlier, Douglas had badly misread the temper of the North, with disastrous results for his party. He dared not make the same blunder again, especially since his own seat in the Senate was now at stake. Unlike 1853, when he had toured Europe and fallen out of touch with his constituents, the summer of 1857 found Douglas in Illinois, traveling about the state and taking a careful measure of popular feeling. He witnessed the general revulsion against the work of the Lecompton convention, saw that Republican strength was still increasing ominously, and returned to Congress knowing that the Northern Democrats could not carry another ounce of Southern weight. Behind the emotional energy of his political revolt there was shrewd calculation of its consequences.

With his slashing attack upon the Lecompton constitution Douglas brought extraordinary confusion to American politics because the strokes of his blade actually cut two ways. From one point of view, he had dealt a heavy blow to the slave power and disrupted the Democratic party; but from another, he had set out to rehabilitate himself and his party in the North by stealing thunder from the Republicans. Significantly, in many letters of encouragement that he received from Illinois Democrats, the dominant note was jubilation over the practical benefits of his anti-Lecompton stand. "Your position takes the wind clean out of the B[lack] Republican leaders," one man wrote. "You have adopted the only course that could save the Northern Democracy from annihilation at the next election," another declared.[14] Republicans, under the circumstances, were puzzled and divided by the problem of how to deal with the new Douglas. As their discussion of the subject developed into a warm argument, it became apparent that the Little Giant was not only splitting his own party but causing dissension in the ranks of the opposition.

*

On December 21, 1857, with the battle lines still forming in Congress, the referendum on the slavery clause of the Lecompton constitution took place in Kansas. Free Staters once again refused to participate, and so the clause was overwhelmingly approved. But meanwhile the new territorial legislature had boldly ordered submission of the entire constitution at a special election on January 4. This time it was the proslavery men who stayed home while the Free State party rolled up an even greater majority for outright rejection of the instrument. To Buchanan it appeared that the choice lay between immediate settlement and indefinite prolongation of the whole dangerous controversy. He therefore ignored the January vote and on February 2, 1858, presented the Lecompton constitution to Congress with a recommendation that Kansas be promptly admitted to the Union as the sixteenth slave state.

The legislative struggle that ensued was no less fierce than those of 1850 and 1854. Administration leaders, mixing promises with threats, exerted heavy pressure upon restive Democrats. In Illinois and other states of the Northwest, the heads of office-holders friendly to Douglas began to roll. After seven weeks of bitter debate, the Senate passed the Lecompton bill and sent it to the House. There, however, a coalition of Republicans and insurgent Democrats blocked the measure by pushing through an amendment that required resubmission of the constitution to the voters of Kansas. Then a conference committee was appointed, and late in April it brought forth the so-called "English compromise." This bill was cleverly fashioned to save face for the Administration and yet satisfy the opposition by giving Kansans another opportunity to vote on the constitution. The Republicans, to be sure, were outraged by certain provisions of the compromise, and Douglas too, after some hesitation, pronounced it unacceptable.* But enough anti-Lecompton Democrats did change sides to assure passage in both houses, and Buchanan signed the

* The English compromise (named for Congressman William H. English of Indiana, the wavering anti-Lecompton Democrat who served as chairman of the conference committee) indulged Southern sensitiveness by providing for submission of a proposed land grant, rather than the Lecompton constitution itself, to the voters of Kansas. But since the bill made acceptance of the grant a prerequisite for statehood, the election would

measure on May 4, thus achieving one of the hollowest triumphs in American political history. Everyone knew what would happen at the election scheduled for August 2. On that date, Kansans voted six to one against statehood and relegated the Lecompton constitution to oblivion.

From the beginning of the battle in Congress, Douglas acted openly and enthusiastically with the Republicans. Before leaving Chicago in November of 1857, he had unburdened himself to local leaders of the party and "made some of their eyes stick out at his zeal."[15] Once in Washington, he quickly established cordial relations with various Republican lawmakers and set to work forging an anti-Lecompton alliance. His conferences with men like Henry Wilson, Schuyler Colfax, and Anson Burlingame were the talk of the city. Seward, too, was ready to clasp hands with the Little Giant, and a rumor spread that these two erstwhile enemies had concluded a secret agreement looking toward the election of 1860.[16] Meanwhile, the spectacle of Douglas in revolt against the slave power had also dazzled many Republicans outside of Congress. Rank-and-file members of the party like Rutherford B. Hayes of Cincinnati wrote him letters of commendation,[17] and some of the most influential Republican newspapers were lavish in their praise. Even those editors who suspected the man's motives were forced to acknowledge his usefulness as an ally, temporary though it might be. "We are not about to embrace him as a political brother, or to canonize him as a Republican saint," declared the Chicago *Tribune*. "He is neither one or the other, but, in this cause he is an efficient co-worker, and we shall treat him accordingly."[18]

It is unlikely that Douglas, always an improviser, entered upon his political revolt with any clear idea of where it would ultimately take him. At times during the spring of 1858 he

---

actually determine the fate of the constitution. The most objectionable feature was a provision requiring a much larger population before Kansas, if it rejected this opportunity, could be considered for admission again. Republican charges that the land grant was a bribe were, however, without much foundation; for the amount of land offered was close to the standard for new states.

appeared to be on the verge of making peace with the Administration. Perhaps he also considered trying to draw moderate Republicans and anti-Lecompton Democrats into a new organization under his command. But in the early months of the year his vehemence convinced many observers that he was about to become an outright Republican. "He is as sure to be with us in the future as Chase, Seward or Sumner," wrote Henry Wilson, the radical antislavery senator from Massachusetts.[19] Schuyler Colfax, after a long parley with Douglas in February, reported that he was about ready for baptism. "We talked over the whole future that lies before us politically," said the young Indiana congressman, "and he did not attempt to deny that he did not expect to act with his old party in that future, but with us."[20] Charles H. Ray, senior editor of the Chicago *Tribune,* held similar views but found less pleasure in the prospect. Writing to Lyman Trumbull in March, he asserted: "It is my opinion from all that I see and know that he [Douglas] is coming among us; and that we have got him to deal with in our own camp. The disposal of him will be a difficult problem, unless he will remain content with the hope of a place in the Cabinet of the next Republican President."[21]

Few Republicans wanted to bar Douglas absolutely from admission to their ranks or deny him all credit for his valuable assistance in the Lecompton struggle. But there was sharp disagreement over how far the party ought to go in rewarding and accommodating him. For one thing, some Republican leaders were showing a new respect for the Douglas version of popular sovereignty. Herndon, after visiting Washington, New York, and Boston in the spring of 1858, returned home with the news that a group headed by Horace Greeley proposed to lower the party platform so that Douglas could climb onto it.[22] Lincoln listened to his partner's report with deep concern. He saw only disaster in a policy of bartering principles for recruits, and during the next two years he repeatedly warned his fellow Republicans not to "dally" with the very doctrine that had caused all the trouble in Kansas.[23]

The more urgent question, however, was whether Douglas and other anti-Lecompton Democrats should receive Republican support for re-election. Self-appointed strategists like Greeley were anxious to foster the split in the Democratic party and fairly intoxicated by the prospect of enlisting the author of the Kansas-Nebraska Act in the antislavery crusade. Such a conspicuous accession to the cause of freedom, they thought, would be worth some little sacrifice. In the columns of his New York *Tribune,* as well as in private correspondence, Greeley argued that Douglas, by opposing the Lecompton iniquity, had earned another term in the Senate, that his re-election would be a severe rebuke to the slave power, and that the Republican party of Illinois ought to join cheerfully in making it unanimous.[24] Similar views were expressed by such sound antislavery publications as the *Atlantic Monthly,* the New York *Times,* the Springfield *Republican,* and Thurlow Weed's Albany *Evening Journal.*[25]

Thus a Republicans-for-Douglas movement began to emerge from the Lecompton controversy, reaching its peak of strength in April and May after the Little Giant had taken his stand against the English compromise. Yet the promoters of the movement were more prominent than numerous, and concentrated largely in a few Eastern cities. Western Republicans, with a few exceptions, displayed little enthusiasm for the Greeley proposal, and in Illinois it provoked open resentment and protest. There the Republican party had fought Douglas year after year in bitter hand-to-hand combat and could not easily forget its accumulated wounds. Besides, the man to replace him had already been chosen. "We want no such ominous wooden horses run into our camp," wrote one small-town editor. "All eyes are turned toward Mr. Lincoln as . . . the unanimous choice of the people."[26]

*

Among Illinois Republicans, Lincoln's claim to the senatorship had been tacitly recognized long before it was publicly confirmed. Testimony to his commanding prestige and influence, this unusual consensus can also be explained in more specific terms. He had worked hard for the party without reward and had achieved some reputation as a worthy opponent of Douglas on the stump. Furthermore, since both Senator Trumbull and Governor Bissell were former Democrats, it was generally conceded that the next high office should go to a Whig. And most important of all, there was a strong feeling that Lincoln deserved support because of his "sacrifice" which had assured Trumbull's election in 1855. Trumbull himself cordially acknowledged the debt, and it was mentioned frequently in party newspapers and correspondence. John M. Palmer, for example, surpassed other Republican leaders in his willingness to work with Douglas, but considered himself bound in honor to Lincoln until the latter released him.[27]

In Illinois, the first round of Republican applause for Douglas caused more bewilderment than anger. Lincoln, seeing his own political future threatened, sent off an anxious letter to Trumbull. "What does the New-York Tribune mean by it's constant eulogising, and admiring, and magnifying [of] Douglas?" he demanded. "Does it, in this, speak the sentiments of the republicans at Washington? Have they concluded that the republican cause, generally, can be best promoted by sacraficing us here in Illinois? If so we would like to know it soon; it will save us a great deal of labor to surrender at once . . . . I am not complaining. I only wish a fair understanding."[28]

But as Greeley continued to press his unwanted advice upon Illinois Republicans, they became more indignant and rebellious. To their sensitive ears his tone sounded insufferably patronizing. "There seems to be a considerable notion pervading the brains of political wet-nurses at the East, that the barbarians of Illinois cannot take care of themselves," growled the Chicago *Tribune*.[29] Hatred of Douglas and loyalty to Lincoln were now reinforced by a determination to resist interference from treacherous "outsiders." Illinois, Herndon exclaimed, would not allow itself to

be "huckstered off" by Eastern "pimps." Other voices cried out
that the very thought of falling in behind Douglas was "an abomi-
nation" and "too much for human nature to bear."[30] By April
and early May, the chorus of protest had become thunderous,
with virtually the entire Republican press of the state screaming
its defiance of Eastern dictation.[31] Greeley admitted that he was
receiving "perfectly savage" letters from Illinois. Still convinced
that Douglas should and would be re-elected, he made repeated
efforts to persuade or at least placate the Illinois barbarians, but
finally gave up in disgust. "I am weary," he snapped, "of trying
to pound any reason into their heads."[32]

Not satisfied with presenting their case in letters and editorials, the Republican leaders of Illinois prepared to employ more
formal means of rebuffing the Greeley faction. "We must make
them understand that *Lincoln* is our man," said the prominent
German-American, Gustave Koerner. "Whether a State Convention is necessary or not, I am not yet prepared to say." Lincoln
himself had already proposed just such a step. "Let us," he wrote
on March 24, "have a State convention in which we can have a
full consultation, and till which, let us all stand firm, making no
committals as to strange and new combinations."[33] This strategy
was endorsed at a conference of party leaders held in Chicago a
few weeks later.[34] It was decided that a convention should be
called for the ostensible purpose of nominating candidates to fill
the offices of state treasurer and superintendent of public instruction. Once assembled, the delegates could then take whatever
action seemed necessary concerning the senatorship. The state
central committee subsequently announced the time and place:
June 16 at Springfield.

Meanwhile, the Illinois Democrats, now divided into Douglas
and Buchanan factions, were making preparations for their own
state convention at Springfield on April 21. A large group of
Republican leaders gathered to watch the proceedings and con-
sult with one another. They saw the Douglas men establish firm

control of the convention, while the noisy but feckless "Buchaneers" withdrew to set up a separate organization. By now it was clear that Douglas, having retained full command of his party in Illinois, would not be joining the Republicans as predicted. Yet Greeley and other Easterners still urged his re-election and sang his praises louder than ever, perhaps with the hope of fashioning a grand anti-Lecompton alliance for 1860. Thus the Illinois Republicans, although greatly encouraged by the behavior of the Buchanan Democrats, were at the same time fearful that Greeley's influence might produce similar defections from their own ranks. At a meeting of some thirty party leaders immediately following the Democratic convention, this danger was the chief subject of discussion, and again Lincoln received firm pledges of loyalty.[35]

That Lincoln expected the state convention to clear the air regarding the senatorship is indicated in a letter he wrote on June 1 :

> I suppose it is hardly necessary that any expression of preference for U.S. Senator, should be given at the county, or other local conventions and meetings. When the Republicans of the whole State get together at the State convention, the thing will then be thought of, and something will or will not be done, according as the united judgment may dictate.[36]

But public feeling was by now so intense that in one county convention after another the delegates did pass resolutions naming Lincoln as their "first, last, and only" choice for senator. In some cases they added thinly veiled rebukes to Greeley.[37] Consequently, when the state convention met, it needed only to confirm the emphatic pronouncements already made at the grass-roots level. Reviewing these remarkable expressions of party unanimity, the Chicago *Tribune* of June 14 declared: "We assure our Eastern contemporaries who have been so sorely troubled with fear that the Republicans of Illinois could not take care of their own affairs, that this action, where not spontaneous, has been provoked by their interference, though it is the result of no arrangement or concert. It is the natural and expected remonstrance against outside intermeddling."*

In the meantime, however, persistent gossip had brought the hulking figure of Long John Wentworth into the senatorial picture, to the annoyance of his fellow Republicans and the subsequent confusion of certain historians.

*

John Wentworth, owner and editor of the Chicago *Democrat,* was only forty-three years old, but he had been a power in Illinois politics for more than two decades. A veteran of five terms in Congress as a Jacksonian Democrat, he had joined the Republicans just soon enough to become the party's first mayor of Chicago. Not until the gaudy days of William Hale Thompson would the city elect another to compare with him. Despite his durable popularity with the voters, Long John probably had a longer list of enemies than any other politician in the state. A certain rude integrity saved him from being an outright scoundrel, but he was arrogant and unpredictable, a political brawler, with an abusive tongue and a cynical view of power, whose malice often outran even his restless ambition. Unruly beyond control, and yet too influential to be ignored, he was six and a half feet of trouble for anyone who got in his way.

Wentworth's feuds with the other Republican editors in Chicago were a constant threat to party unity. His election as mayor and the highhanded manner in which he proceeded to rule the city made him all the more vulnerable to their attacks, which became so fierce that Lincoln expressed alarm: "We can not afford to lose the services of 'Long John' and I do believe the unrelenting warfare made upon him, is injuring our cause."[38] The hatred that Wentworth inspired in his newspaper rivals was compounded with fear that he would somehow use the mayoralty

---

* In the same editorial, the *Tribune* asserted that resolutions for Lincoln had been passed in 95 out of 100 counties, but a sampling of convention proceedings as published in various newspapers indicates that this was an overstatement.

as a springboard to higher office. He had his eyes upon the senatorship, a *Tribune* editor warned in November of 1857. "All his moves have been made to win that darling prize. He wants to control a balance of power in the next legislature and compel the Republican members to choose between him and Douglas."[39]

Perhaps Wentworth did for a time cherish some vague hope of becoming senator. Almost anything seemed possible in the first confusing months of the Lecompton struggle, and Long John habitually canvassed every opportunity. But by April it was abundantly clear that the Republicans of Illinois had made their choice, and he wisely acquiesced. The *Democrat* joined other party newspapers in hailing Lincoln as the heir to Douglas's seat. Wentworth, on the eve of the state convention, had no support for the Senate and gave no indication of seeking it. The dramatic story of how he was thwarted in a plot to seize the nomination from Lincoln is historical fiction. Its principal author, Albert J. Beveridge, simply misread the evidence.[40]

The only plot, if there was one in 1858, originated with certain Democratic editors who wanted to undermine the formidable unity of Illinois Republicanism and neutralize Lincoln's popular appeal. By May, the putative senatorial ambitions of John Wentworth had long ceased to cause any serious concern in Republican ranks; yet the leading Democratic newspapers insisted that he was still an active and likely candidate. Long John, they repeatedly predicted, would "pack the nominating conventions" and make Republican legislators "his own creatures, pledged to vote for him through thick and thin." Lincoln might as well resign himself to being "cheated" again. "It is becoming every day more apparent," said the *State Register* early in June, "that the contest for senator lies between Douglas and Wentworth."[41]

The purpose of these absurd reports was obvious. At the polls in November, Illinois voters would indicate their preference for senator only indirectly by electing a new legislature. And if the Democrats could convince even part of the electorate that a vote for Republican legislators was a vote for the obnoxious Wentworth instead of Lincoln, they would strengthen their chances of victory. Republican editors saw through the maneuver immediately and hastened to counteract it. They assured their readers that Wentworth was a "cordial supporter" of Lincoln, that the Democrats were using him as an "ogre" to frighten the public, and that such a "stale piece of charlatanism" merely revealed the desperate state of Douglas's fortunes.[42] Delegates to the Republican state convention, already aroused over Greeley's interference, now had a second reason for giving Lincoln their explicit endorsement.

The Republicans of Cook County, meeting on June 8, appointed a large delegation to represent them at the state convention, but apparently neglected to pass a resolution about the senatorship.[43] Anxious, perhaps, to repair this omission, the Chicagoans turned their trip to Springfield into a boisterous demonstration for Lincoln. They emblazoned his name on their railroad car, and when the train stopped at the town of Lincoln, they all piled out to give three cheers for their favorite. These same enthusiasts entered the convention hall carrying a banner that read: "Cook County is for Abraham Lincoln." It was received with applause, and then a delegate from Peoria moved that the wording be changed to "Illinois is for Abraham Lincoln." That produced a deafening roar of approval, followed by a long volley of cheers. But such informality did not satisfy Charles L. Wilson, editor of the Chicago *Journal*. Toward the close of the afternoon session, he rose to offer the resolution already ratified in so many county conventions declaring that Lincoln was the party's "first and only choice" for senator. The thunderous response of the delegates compelled even the *State Register* to admit that the contest now lay "plainly and squarely" between Stephen A. Douglas and Abraham Lincoln.[44]

A good deal of misunderstanding has resulted from Lincoln's subsequent assertion that the primary purpose of the Wilson

resolution was to silence the "everlasting croaking about Wentworth." He was obviously referring to the idle gossip in Democratic newspapers, not to any actual threat from Long John, and
his explanation in any case falls far short of the whole truth.
Wilson, according to his own editorials, was furious with Greeley
for supporting Douglas, and annoyed by the Democratic chatter
about Wentworth. No doubt he nominated Lincoln with both
problems in mind. But in approving his resolution, the state convention merely brought to its climax a general uprising of Illinois
Republicans against dictation from the East. Lincoln himself
had thought of the convention as an answer to Greeley, and his
House Divided speech, as we shall see, was essentially an effort
to show why honest Republicans could not fall in behind Douglas.
The Chicago *Tribune* directed a long editorial to the same purpose
on June 15, the very eve of the convention. Whatever part the
Wentworth bugaboo played at the last moment, it was not the
major reason for the great upsurge of popular feeling that culminated in Lincoln's nomination.

*

The history of the next few years might have been much different if the Republicans of Illinois had followed the course so
obligingly marked out for them by Horace Greeley in 1858.
Their stubbornness erased some of the political confusion that
resulted from the Lecompton struggle and militated strongly
against any general transformation of party alignments in the
North. By nominating their own senatorial candidate, they vetoed partnership with Douglas and forced him to show his claws
in a desperate fight for political survival. The image of the Little
Giant as an antislavery champion melted away in the heat of his
contest with Lincoln, while Illinois, in the process, won recognition as a stronghold of untainted Republicanism.

The unprecedented nomination of Lincoln by the state convention, although it had no legal force, virtually turned the legis-

lative election into a senatorial contest and thus cleared the way for his historic debates with Douglas. Furthermore, in the course of their sturdy resistance to Eastern advocacy of Douglas, Illinois Republicans were drawn closer together, and loyalty to Lincoln became the emotional core of party solidarity. It was the great popular demonstration for Lincoln in the spring of 1858, as well as his performance in the subsequent campaign, that lifted him to pre-eminence above other distinguished Republicans in the state and set his feet on the path to the presidency.

Four

The Origins and Purpose of the
House Divided Speech

AFTER A BRIEF ADJOURNMENT for supper, the state convention of Illinois Republicans reassembled at eight o'clock in
the evening of June 16, 1858, to hear an address by the man whom
it had just acclaimed as the party's "first and only" choice for
senator. The heat of the day still clung to Representatives Hall,
and as the room became "crowded almost to suffocation," some
perspiring delegates began to plead for removal of the meeting
to the front steps of the State House. Lincoln came forward and
said that he would speak in the open air if the audience desired
it, but that he preferred to remain inside because his voice was
not in the best condition. There being general acquiescence, he
proceeded with the delivery of his memorable House Divided
speech.[1]

Although Lincoln made no mention of the resolution nominating him for the Senate, he did not neglect to discuss the unusual
state of affairs which had prompted it. His carefully prepared
address closed with a devastating criticism of the Greeley viewpoint and a solemn warning to Republicans against putting any
faith in Douglas. How, he demanded, could the fight against
slavery be led by a man who proclaimed his indifference to the
evil? "Our cause . . . must be intrusted to, and conducted by
its own undoubted friends—those whose hands are free, whose
hearts are in the work." In a direct reference to the senatorial
contest, and with more irony than modesty, he recited a pungent

sentence from Ecclesiastes: "A living dog is better than a dead lion."[2]

Still, it was another scriptural quotation that gave the speech its name. The part that became famous was neither the conclusion nor the body of the speech, but the opening passage, in which he asserted his belief that the nation could not "endure, permanently half slave and half free." And here one meets a mystery that has never been satisfactorily resolved.

Why did Lincoln choose this moment for the most provocative utterance of his career? In the long run, to be sure, the speech added appreciably to his political stature. Widely read and praised, it marked him out among party leaders in the nation and raised him to Seward's level as a Republican phrasemaker. But whether the house-divided metaphor suited the immediate needs of the day in Illinois is another question. Many of his friends considered it more eloquent than wise. A group of them, given an advance reading of the manuscript just before the convention, registered almost unanimous disapproval.[3] And there were others, like the Chicago editor John L. Scripps, who admired the speech when it appeared in print, but feared that it would be misinterpreted as a promise to make war upon slavery in the Southern states.[4] Leonard Swett, an old companion on the judicial circuit, never departed from his belief that Lincoln invited certain defeat in 1858 with the "unfortunate" and "inappropriate" doctrine which he enunciated at the beginning of the campaign.[5]

The speech caused misgivings because it seemed likely to alienate the very votes that Lincoln needed in order to unseat Douglas. With Illinois divided, like the nation, into Republican north and Democratic south, the senatorial contest would actually be decided in a belt of doubtful counties stretching across the middle of the state. The crucial zone was a stronghold of old-line Whig elements whose traditional hostility to locofoco Democracy was balanced by a deep aversion for the excesses of abolitionism. Sound political strategy seemed to require that the Republicans court the favor of this important group by striking a note of moderation and restraint as they opened the campaign. Instead, Lincoln pitched his first words to a Garrisonian key and thus exposed himself to the persistent Democratic charge that he was a dangerous radical.

The standard explanation for this apparent recklessness is the one distilled from memory and imagination by William H. Herndon. It pictures Lincoln as a man wrapped in passion like a Hebrew prophet, determined to speak his thoughts without concern for the consequences. "The time has come when these sentiments should be uttered," he is supposed to have told his faint-hearted friends, "and if it is decreed that I should go down because of this speech, then let me go down linked to the truth—let me die in the advocacy of what is just and right." As for the house-divided phrase itself, he allegedly declared: "I would rather be defeated with this expression in the speech, and uphold and discuss it before the people, than be victorious without it."[6]

It is hard to agree with the historian who detects a "ring of authenticity" in such words.[7] Direct quotations raked out of dim remembrance—a kind of retrospective ghostwriting—are questionable sources at best, and certainly less than conclusive as evidence of motivation. This pretentious talk does not sound at all like the flesh-and-blood Lincoln of 1858, but rather like the legendary figure subsequently evoked from the ashes of martyrdom. The real Lincoln was a man of flexibility and discretion as well as conviction. A seat in the Senate had long been his fondest personal ambition, and he knew that the Republican cause would benefit immensely from the overthrow of Douglas. It is unlikely that the uttering of a few dramatic phrases could have seemed more important to him than victory at the polls—or than life itself.

Here another familiar interpretation of Lincoln's conduct may be noticed. It is often asserted or suggested that by 1858 he had already fixed his eyes upon the White House, and that more than once during the contest with Douglas he seemed ready to compromise his chances of becoming senator in order to improve his prospects of becoming president. This idea turns up frequently in accounts of the Freeport debate, and the House Divided speech, with its apparent disregard of urgent political realities, can also be explained as a gambler's throw for the highest stakes. "It was . . . his most important move in the game for the Presidency," says Beveridge, "a game Lincoln meant to win."[8] Similarly, Richard Hofstadter believes he "was making the great gamble of his career at this point."[9]

And yet there is little in the contemporary record to support such theories. No one who follows Lincoln's campaign trail back and forth across the hot prairies of Illinois in 1858 will find reason to doubt that he was concentrating all his attention upon the task immediately before him. Besides, even if a vagrant thought of the presidency did cross his mind, it could only have strengthened his determination to carry the day against Douglas. Repeated failure in one's own state was not the customary path to national leadership. History would have combined with logic to counsel Lincoln that if he expected to be taken seriously in 1860, he must win, not lose, in 1858.

There is an eight-page manuscript in Lincoln's hand which clearly reveals the intensity of his concentration upon the senatorial contest. Using the election returns for 1856, he carefully estimated his chances in each of the doubtful counties, with particular attention to the critical problem of capturing the Whig-American vote.[10] These businesslike calculations were made in the early part of July, only a few weeks after the state convention. Did his outlook change in that short time? Or is it possible that the practical purposes which Lincoln had in mind when he delivered the House Divided speech have been obscured by its historical consequences? A satisfactory answer must take into account the *full* text of the speech, the circumstances surrounding its composition, and the general background of Lincoln's thought on slavery and politics.

*

It was actually a rather short address, judged by the oratorical standards of the day, and the famous opening passage was crisply spoken in about two minutes. After only one prefatory sentence,[11] Lincoln plunged into an attack upon the Kansas-Nebraska policy, which instead of putting an end to sectional controversy had greatly intensified it. Agitation of the slavery question would not cease, he declared, until a crisis had been "reached and passed."

[1] "A house divided against itself cannot stand."

[2] I believe this government cannot endure, permanently half *slave* and half *free*.

[3] I do not expect the Union to be *dissolved*—I do not expect the house to *fall*—but I *do* expect it will cease to be divided.

[4] It will become *all* one thing, or *all* the other.

[5A] Either the *opponents* of slavery, will arrest the further spread of it, [B] and place it where the public mind shall rest in the belief that it is in course of ultimate extinction; [C] or its *advocates* will push it forward, till it shall become alike lawful in *all* the States, *old* as well as *new*— *North* as well as *South*.

[6] Have we no *tendency* to the latter condition?

Here, reproduced in its entirety, with Lincoln's own emphases and paragraphing, is the doctrine of the house divided.* These are the lines which Douglas denounced as a "revolutionary" effort to incite "warfare between the North and the South," which historians have often linked with Seward's Rochester speech as an expression of militant Republicanism, and which later generations have found "heavy with awful prophecies."[12] Yet when the passage is studied as a whole, with the more eloquent phrases confined to their context, it becomes apparent that much of the provocative quality inheres in the vigor of Lincoln's rhetoric rather than in the substance of his argument. Nowhere in these sentences does he reproach the South or suggest a program of aggressive action against slavery. Like many of his countrymen, he sees another "crisis" approaching, but there is no mention here of "irrepressible conflict," no apocalyptic vision of the bloody years ahead.[13]

---

* Numbers and letters have been added to facilitate subsequent references to the passage.

Instead, Lincoln considers four possible terminations of the sectional struggle, and in the process offers a series of predictions. It was, to be sure, disingenuous of him to protest a few weeks later: "I did not say that I was in favor of anything . . . I only said what I expected would take place."[14] For his expectations must have been based in part upon the assumption that the Republican party would pursue a certain course—one that he sanctioned and was helping to determine. What he favored was therefore an understood element of what he predicted, and it is not surprising that to Southern ears such predictions should sound like threats. The house-divided passage was more than a prophecy. It must also be read as a declaration of purpose. But even then its total effect is less than incendiary, and certain qualifying words reveal the essential reasonableness of its author.

There is probably no better example of Lincoln's ability to order and compress his thoughts than these six sentences. The first two constituted a clear-cut rejection of the *status quo* as a final answer to the slavery question. This might be considered revolutionary doctrine if it were not for the insertion of the word "permanently," which lends special emphasis to the fact that the speaker was scanning a distant horizon, not just the proximate ground of sectional controversy. In the third sentence, he examined the alternatives to a divided house, dismissing one and accepting the other. Here his repetition of the verb "expect" was no doubt purely rhetorical, for on the subject of disunion his mind was already firmly set. He curtly rejected partition of the nation as an ultimate arrangement, not because it seemed utterly improbable, but because it was impermissible.* The house could not stand if it remained divided; yet it would not be allowed to fall; therefore, it must—some day, somehow—cease to be divided.

This line of reasoning had merely led Lincoln to another pair of alternatives, stated in the fourth sentence and elaborated in

---

* "But the Union, in any event, won't be dissolved," Lincoln had declared in a speech at Galena during the campaign of 1856. "We don't want to dissolve it, and if you attempt it, *we won't let you.*" *Collected Works,* II, 355.

the fifth. But now he was ready, it seemed, for a final prediction. If he had indeed resolved, as Allan Nevins believes, to place the Republican party upon "more advanced ground," he needed only to brush aside as an absurdity any design to make slavery national, then clinch his case with "a statesmanlike examination of the necessity for facing all that was implied in 'ultimate extinction.' "[15] Yet he did not take this last, obvious step. Perhaps his courage failed him, as Nevins implies; but a more reasonable explanation is that Lincoln's entire argument had simply been directed toward a different conclusion.

"Ultimate extinction," although it would ever afterward be singled out as one of the main points of the speech, actually received only the briefest mention. In the first half of the long fifth sentence, Lincoln presented his own definition of Republican objectives: (A) The further spread of slavery was to be prevented, and (B) the institution was to be placed where the public could rest assured that it would eventually disappear. The clause marked "A" obviously amounted to nothing more than an iteration of the most familiar and basic tenet of Republicanism. Part B, taken by itself, seemed to go further; for by introducing the concept of "ultimate extinction," Lincoln was presumably stepping across the line that divided free-soil principles from the "more advanced ground" of abolitionism.

But the point is that B cannot be taken by itself without distorting its meaning, because it was not offered as a separate proposition, requiring separate implementation. The bright promise of ultimate extinction was one of the consequences expected to flow naturally from a settled policy of restriction. The achievement of B required nothing beyond the achievement of A—or so Lincoln believed, and quickly affirmed when his words were misinterpreted. Writing to John L. Scripps only a week after the speech, he denied having any wish to interfere with slavery in the Southern states, and then added: "I believe that whenever the effort to spread slavery . . . shall be fairly headed off, the institution will then be in course of ultimate extinction; and by

the language used I meant only this."[16] He made the same assertion in five of the seven debates with Douglas. Here, for example,
is what he said at Ottawa: "Now, I believe if we could arrest the
spread, and place it where Washington, and Jefferson, and Madison placed it, it *would be* in the course of ultimate extinction, and
the public mind *would,* as for eighty years past, believe that it was
in the course of ultimate extinction."[17]

And Lincoln maintained that once this belief had become
firmly implanted, "the crisis would be past." Slavery might continue to exist in the South for "a hundred years at least," because
abolition would come only "in God's own good time," but the
Northern conscience would be satisfied without invading Southern constitutional rights, and the Union would be safe.[18] These
benefits were all to accrue from the simple act of confining slavery
to the area where it already existed. Moreover, Lincoln repeatedly insisted that the goal of ultimate extinction, far from being
new and radical, had been established by the founding fathers.
Openly disapproving of slavery, they had "restricted its spread
and stopped the importation of negroes, with the hope that it
would remain in a dormant condition till the people saw fit to
emancipate the negroes."[19]

These subsequent amplifications, which are consistent with
the entire record of Lincoln's public and private observations
upon the slavery issue, make it clear that he did not intend, by
his introduction of the phrase "ultimate extinction," to propose
any course of action going beyond the exclusion of slavery from
the territories. He did deliberately affirm, however, that exclusion was more than an end in itself, that it implied a moral judgment against slavery and a commitment to freedom. Republicanism, as Lincoln defined it, embraced a belief (that slavery was
wrong), a program of action (federal legislation preventing its
extension), and an ultimate objective or hope (complete extinction of the institution at some distant date and by some peaceful
means not yet discovered). Such a definition was bound to invite trouble; yet Lincoln returned to it again and again, with

mounting emphasis, as the campaign progressed.[20] His reasons
for doing so were not quixotic but practical, and can be understood
only against the background of unusual circumstances which had
already produced his nomination for the Senate.

*

Remote as it may seem in retrospect, the possibility that the
Republican party—or a considerable portion of it—might become
a tail fastened to the Douglas kite loomed up before Lincoln's eyes
as a real and imminent danger in the spring of 1858. The Lecompton controversy, besides making Douglas a hero to many
antislavery leaders, had also softened their opposition to his
"great principle." Popular sovereignty now wore a more benign
aspect. Recent events in Kansas tended to support the argument
that a policy of nonintervention, if honestly applied, would be
sufficient (along with the iron necessities of climate) to prevent
the extension of slavery into the remaining Western territory.
No less a Republican than William H. Seward had recently announced on the Senate floor that the battle for freedom in the
territories was already substantially won.[21] Why then, it was
asked, should the South be antagonized and the Union endangered by insistence upon a superfluous policy of congressional
restriction?

Such arguments were especially persuasive as long as attention was narrowly centered upon the Kansas crisis and the issue
of slavery in the territories. But Lincoln regarded the territorial
problem as just the point of contact in a larger and more fundamental struggle.* To him, the Douglas-Republican convergence
on the Lecompton question seemed superficial and transient because it had not resulted from agreement on basic principles. It
was also dangerous because it threatened the unity and purpose

---

* In a speech to Chicago Republicans on March 1, 1859, Lincoln said:
"Never forget that we have before us this whole matter of the right or
wrong of slavery in this Union, though the immediate question is as to its
spreading out into new Territories and States." *Collected Works,* III, 369.

of the Republican party. In response to this threat, Lincoln laid down a definition of Republicanism which, while merely articulating what everyone knew, served to emphasize the doctrinal gulf that still yawned between Douglas and the Republicans. The concept of "ultimate extinction" could thus be used as a touchstone for separating the true from the casual or pretended opponents of slavery. His object, it appears, was not to lead a Republican advance to higher, more radical ground, but rather to check an ill-considered retreat to the lower ground of popular sovereignty.

The brevity with which he treated the subject in the House Divided address was not necessarily a mark of diffidence. A convention composed exclusively of party leaders needed no elaborate instruction in the meaning of Republicanism. Later, for the mixed political audiences attending the debates, he would explain, qualify, and vigorously defend the proposition that slavery should be restricted *because* it was wrong, and *in order to* anchor national policy upon the expectation of its ultimate demise. Now, however, he proposed to consider the sinister alternative: progressive legalization of slavery everywhere in the United States (5C in the house-divided passage). This was the major theme to which his historic opening sentences had led. He proceeded to spend nearly three-fourths of the entire speech detailing a solemn charge that the Kansas-Nebraska Act and the Dred Scott decision were part of a maturing Democratic plot to nationalize slavery. The leading conspirators, he said, were Douglas, Pierce, Taney, and Buchanan. Having first repealed the Missouri Compromise restriction upon slavery in the territories, and then denied the power of Congress to impose such a restriction, they needed only one more victory, namely: "another Supreme Court decision, declaring that the Constitution of the United States does not permit a *state* to exclude slavery from its limits." That decision was soon coming, he predicted. "We shall lie down pleasantly dreaming that the people of Missouri are on the verge of making their State *free*; and we shall awake to the *reality*, instead, that the *Supreme Court* has made *Illinois* a *slave* State."*

Modern scholars, however much they may admire Lincoln, are inclined to see in this sweeping accusation and somber warning only the extravagance of partisanship.[22] There is, it appears, no evidence of any organized movement in 1858 to push slavery into the free states, or of any disposition among members of the Supreme Court to attempt such folly. In short, the conspiracy that Lincoln described did not exist; the danger that he professed to fear was extremely remote. And so this, the major part of the House Divided speech, is commonly dismissed as "an absurd bogey," unworthy of intensive scrutiny.[23] But political rhetoric is a response to historical developments, not a record of them, and circumstances can sometimes make the most erroneous statement credible, even justifiable, thus giving it a kind of temporary validity. The conspiracy charge may have been absurd, but the real problem is to explain why Lincoln, certainly a reasonable man, insisted that it was true.

In the setting of 1858, the charge carried conviction. It is not surprising that even reasonable men should have seen an ominous pattern in the sequence of events which had begun four years earlier with the Kansas-Nebraska Act. Nor was it hard for them to believe that behind such a pattern there must be some kind of concert. Lincoln, to be sure, was exercising the politician's privilege of overstating his case. In later speeches he admitted that the existence of a plot could only be inferred, not proved, and he conceded that Douglas might have been playing the role of dupe instead of conspirator. But the effects were what mattered, he argued, not the motives. A trend toward the nationalization of slavery had become manifest; it was more than mere

---

* Lincoln was by no means the first person to voice this fear, which was a part of the general Republican reaction to the Dred Scott decision. On March 10, 1857, for example, the Bloomington *Pantagraph* warned, "One little step only remains, to decide all *State* prohibitions of Slavery to be void."

accident; and the advocates of popular sovereignty, whether intentionally or not, were contributing to it.[24]

Yet even if there was some basis for suspecting a design to make slavery national, how could a reasonable man, knowing the strength of the antislavery forces in the North, have had any fear of its success? It is precisely at this point that Lincoln's argument is often misconstrued, and the error usually stems from a failure to observe the close connection between the "conspiracy" section of the speech and the "house divided" passage which preceded it. In that passage he had asserted that one of two opposing policies must eventually prevail. The triumph of either would obviously have to begin with the disablement of the other. Just as the first step toward ultimate extinction of slavery was the thwarting of efforts to extend it, so the first step toward nationalization of slavery was the blunting of the moral opposition to it. Lincoln thought he detected signs of the latter. His warning that slavery might become lawful everywhere was therefore not absolute but conditional, and, within its context, far from absurd. He was describing what would happen *if* the existence of slavery should become a matter of general indifference—*if,* in other words, the Republicans should allow themselves to be deflected from their purpose.

And this was where Douglas fitted into the picture with his enunciated philosophy of not caring whether slavery was "voted down or voted up."[25] His function, Lincoln maintained, was to instill a complaisant attitude toward slavery in the minds of Northerners and thus prepare the way for new advances, new court decisions which would make the institution universal and permanent. Here was the burden of Lincoln's case against Douglas and popular sovereignty, and to no other argument did he return more persistently and eloquently in his later speeches. He repeated it in ever stronger terms to the crowds attending the debates, to Ohio audiences in 1859, and to New Englanders in 1860. The proslavery conspiracy, he said, could not succeed without Douglas, its indispensable advance agent—its "miner and

sapper." The "don't-care" policy was "just as certain to nationalize Slavery as the doctrine of Jeff Davis himself." They were
"two roads to the same goal," and the Douglas road, if somewhat
less direct, was "more dangerous."[26] These and similar amplifications support the conclusion that Lincoln aimed the conspiracy
charge of the House Divided speech primarily at Douglas and
those who imitated him in "groping for some middle ground between the right and the wrong."[27]

The third—or "living dog"—section of the speech followed
logically. Here Lincoln considered and firmly rejected the Greeley proposition that Douglas, by his stand against the Lecompton
constitution, had qualified himself as a leader of the antislavery
forces. If not quite a dead lion, Douglas was "at least a caged
and toothless one" in the battle for freedom. "Clearly," Lincoln
declared, "he is not *now* with us—he does not *pretend* to be—he
does not *promise* to *ever* be." The Republican cause, therefore,
should be "intrusted to, and conducted by its own undoubted
friends." With these remarks, justifying the decision to fight
Douglas in Illinois, Lincoln had brought his argument down to
the business immediately at hand. He then concluded with a brief
plea for Republican perseverance and this final prediction:

> The result is not doubtful. We shall not fail—if we stand
> firm, we shall not fail.
> *Wise councils* may *accelerate* or *mistakes delay* it, but,
> sooner or later the victory is *sure* to come.

The House Divided address, which probably required about
thirty or thirty-five minutes to deliver, can thus be divided into
three main parts: the introductory "house divided" section (constituting approximately 7 per cent of the entire speech), the "conspiracy" section (72 per cent), and the "living dog" section (21
per cent). It is the fashion to treat everything that Lincoln said
after the first two or three minutes as anticlimax, to look upon his
argument as running downhill from high principles to low partisanship. Yet the careful reader will discover that from beginning

to end the speech is dominated by a single, coherent theme. It opens with an attack upon Douglas's Kansas-Nebraska policy. The house-divided doctrine has the effect of eliminating the middle ground upon which Douglas stands. The concept of "ultimate extinction" defines Republicanism in terms that exclude Douglas. The conspiracy theory links Douglasism with the onward march of slavery. And the last part of the address demolishes the image of Douglas as an antislavery champion. Whatever judgment may be passed upon Lincoln's rhetorical effectiveness, or upon the soundness of his reasoning, or upon the accuracy of his particulars, the immediate *purpose* of the House Divided speech seems abundantly clear. As a matter of practical politics, it was an attempt to minimize the significance and impact of Douglas's anti-Lecompton heroics and to demonstrate the folly of diluting Republican convictions with the watery futility of popular sovereignty—in short, to vindicate the nomination of a Republican candidate for the Senate in Illinois.

*

There is, however, another way of probing for the meaning of the House Divided address which ought not to be neglected. Herndon's assertion that Lincoln spent about one month preparing it is probably true so far as the final draft is concerned,[28] but the basic ideas were formulated over a longer period. Rudiments of the speech appear in some of Lincoln's earlier writings and utterances. An examination of the circumstances which produced them should throw light upon the progress of his thought.

Such a study was made a number of years ago by the historian Arthur C. Cole, who reported his findings in an address titled "Lincoln's 'House Divided' Speech: Did It Reflect a Doctrine of Class Struggle?"[29] Cole's point of departure is his reluctance to take at face value Lincoln's warning that slavery might spread to all the states. That danger, his argument runs, was simply not serious enough in itself to arouse such apprehension. "Another factor was present, lurking in the background, perhaps, but influencing Lincoln, consciously or subconsciously, in his presentation of the struggle between slavery and freedom." Cole thus undertakes to rationalize the warning by uncovering a deeper meaning beneath the literal one. His explanation, briefly put, is as follows : Lincoln had come to believe that the theories of proslavery extremists like George Fitzhugh endangered the "white man's charter of freedom." In their idealizing of slave society without regard to race, in their contempt for the doctrine that all men are created equal, in their advocacy of a "defensive and offensive alliance of the forces of capitalism, North and South," he read the beginnings of an assault upon the entire working class. The evil that he feared was therefore more monstrous than the mere expansion of Negro servitude ; it was the progressive degradation of all white men who earned their living by toil.[30]

This line of reasoning, although it hardly tends to absolve Lincoln of raising up an "absurd bogey," has a certain limited validity. That is, Lincoln did assert more than once that the defense of slavery in the abstract posed a threat to the theoretical foundations of human liberty.[31] However, he did not present it as a pressing problem demanding attention in the realm of political action. His concern for the white man's "charter of freedom" served to reinforce his belief that slavery was wrong, but that belief was the assumption with which most of his arguments began, not the conclusion toward which they were directed. The central problem to which he addressed himself in his speeches was *how* the widespread belief that slavery was wrong could be implemented within the framework of the American constitutional system. Convinced that the program of the Republican party offered the best solution, he regarded the Douglases, rather than the Fitzhughs, as the major obstacle to its success. Cole's elaborate inquiry consequently ends more or less in frustration. He is forced to concede that the class-struggle theme does not manifest itself either in the House Divided address or in Lincoln's other recorded speeches of the campaign. He acknowledges that most of the address was "directed, in its formal logic, against the leadership of Douglas." But, adhering to the erroneous view that the house-divided passage stands in "comparative isolation" from the rest of the text, he suggests that "a sense of the larger conflict between slavery and freedom served as a subconscious factor in Lincoln's historic statement."[32] This cautious conclusion scarcely constitutes an affirmative answer to the question posed in his title. Not without value, perhaps, as an insight into the general course of Lincoln's thought, it nevertheless adds little to our understanding of what he said on June 16, 1858.

The search for the origins of the House Divided speech leads back to the year of the Kansas-Nebraska Act and even beyond. Before 1854, according to Lincoln's own testimony, he had been opposed to slavery, but had believed that it was in the course of ultimate extinction, and had therefore looked upon it as "a minor question."[33] Thus the expectation that the "house" would some day "cease to be divided" was virtually native to his thinking. The Kansas-Nebraska Act, from his point of view, amounted to a revolution. It impaired the hope for ultimate extinction, opened the way for slavery's unlimited expansion, and made this corrosive issue paramount in American politics. From the beginning, too, Lincoln objected to popular sovereignty as a doctrine of moral evasion. The germ of the conspiracy theory can be detected in a sentence from his famous Peoria speech of October 16, 1854: "This *declared* indifference, but as I must think, covert *real* zeal for the spread of slavery, I can not but hate."[34] The disruptive effects of the Kansas-Nebraska policy soon confirmed his fears and inspired the analogy of the divided house. "This nation is to become a nation of slaves or a nation of freemen," said an editorial in the *Illinois [State] Journal* two days after the Peoria speech. If Beveridge is correct in his judgment, it was written by Lincoln.[35]

The surprising strength of the anti-Nebraska coalition in the elections of 1854 heartened Lincoln and, indeed, almost carried him into the Senate, but he still saw only uncertainty in the future. Writing to George Robertson, a Kentuckian, on August 15, 1855, he declared that there was no prospect of a peaceful extinction of slavery. Then he added: "Our political problem now is 'Can we, as a nation, continue together *permanently—forever*—half slave, and half free?' The problem is too mighty for me. May God, in his mercy, superintend the solution."[36] Other men, North and South, were of course asking the same question. Lincoln himself later disclaimed credit for originating the concept of the absolute incompatibility of slave and free society.[37] But in other hands the concept tended to be merely descriptive, or, in the case of Southern radicals, to point toward dissolution of the Union. Lincoln's unique contribution was not the invention of, but the use to which he put, the house-divided doctrine. He was apparently the first to couple it with an adamant rejection of disunion, thus formulating the major premise of a disjunctive syllogism which presented a choice between uniform freedom and uniform slavery, but eliminated all mediative positions, all obscuring evasions, in between.

The obscuring force in 1858 was Douglas and the anti-Lecompton Democrats. During the middle years of the decade, however, it was primarily the Know-Nothing movement that stood in the way of the emerging Republican party and a clear-cut decision on the slavery question. In the presidential campaign of 1856, much of Lincoln's energy was expended in efforts to convince the followers of Fillmore in Illinois that by deflecting votes from Frémont they were actually aiding Buchanan and the cause of slavery.[38] Here, it would seem, was a situation inviting use of the house-divided doctrine. Did Lincoln give utterance to it that year? There is a tradition that he did, perhaps several times, but especially in a speech at Bloomington on September 12. Lincoln shared the platform that evening with his friend T. Lyle Dickey, a moderate antislavery Whig. It was Dickey's story, written down only a number of years later, that Lincoln on this occasion "proclaimed it as his opinion that our government could not last—part slave and part free." Dickey further recalled that in their hotel room after the meeting he remonstrated with Lin-

coln, and that the latter, while defending the truth of his statement, admitted it might have a harmful effect and promised not
to use it again during the campaign.[39]

Since there is no precise corroboration of Dickey's assertion,
it must be viewed with appropriate caution. Nevertheless, his
veracity is to some extent endorsed by testimony from Lincoln's
own pen. This can be demonstrated more conveniently on a
later page. At the moment, it is necessary to examine the brief
summary of Lincoln's remarks which appeared in the local newspaper. Bloomington, it should be noted, was in strong Whig
territory where the Know-Nothing appeal met with a favorable
response. Lincoln therefore centered part of his attack upon the
American ticket:

> He showed up the position of the Fillmore party in fine style,
> both as to its prospects of success, and as to the propriety of
> supporting a candidate whose greatest recommendation, as
> urged by his supporters themselves, is that he is *neutral* upon
> the one only great political question of the times. He pointed
> out in regular succession, the several steps taken by the Ad-
> ministration in regard to slavery in the Territories, from the
> repeal of the Missouri Compromise down to the latest Border
> Ruffian invasion of Kansas, and the inevitable tendency of
> each and all of them to effect the spread of slavery over that
> country; . . . contrasting all this with the assertion of our
> Northern Democratic speakers, that they are not in favor of
> the extension of slavery.[40]

Here, beyond any doubt, was a framework suitable for the introduction of the house-divided doctrine; for in it one finds not only
rudimentary traces of the conspiracy theory, but also condemna-
tion of that same moral neutralism (here represented by both the
Northern Democrats and the Fillmore party) which was to be
the primary target of his historic address in 1858.[41]

It was not, however, until a decision had been rendered in
the Dred Scott case that the house-divided argument could be
used with full force. The Supreme Court's pronouncement, coming only two days after the inauguration of Buchanan, provided

the materials still necessary for manufacture of the conspiracy charge. Now, for the first time, Lincoln could specify the means by which slavery might be extended into the free states—a "second Dred Scott decision"—and thus confront his listeners with a categorical choice between policies leading toward ultimate extinction and policies promoting nationalization of the institution. Yet, with all the pieces of his argument ready for assembling by March of 1857, he waited another fifteen months before enunciating the house-divided doctrine. Opportunities to introduce it earlier were admittedly few, because this was a relatively fallow period in local politics. Nevertheless, he did discuss the Dred Scott decision at length in a major address at Springfield on June 26, 1857. He rejected the Court's assumptions, ridiculed its logic, and defended the Republican refusal to accept its judgment as final. But at the same time, he said nothing about the possibility of a second decision legalizing slavery everywhere. He did not allege a conspiracy to accomplish that purpose. Nor did he advance the proposition that the nation could not endure permanently half slave and half free. The speech, in short, contained scarcely a hint of the one that he would make on the same spot one year later.*

These interesting omissions may mean nothing more than that Lincoln's thinking along house-divided lines had not yet fully crystallized in the summer of 1857. It is equally likely, however, that they reflect the current political situation, which was to change so abruptly before the end of the year. With the Democratic party ostensibly united behind a new president, with Douglas defending the Dred Scott decision, with the lines of battle clearly drawn, there was less need for the house-divided doctrine, as Lincoln used it. Only when the Lecompton controversy blurred the political picture, exalted Douglas, and confused many

---

* The editors of the *Collected Works,* II, 452 n, maintain that Lincoln's belief in the house-divided doctrine was "implicit" in his 1857 Springfield speech, but this is true only in so far as the belief was implicit in everything he was saying and doing by that time. The striking thing about the 1857 speech is the absence of any *explicit* reference to the ideas and arguments that dominated the House Divided address.

Republicans, did Lincoln decide to advance his provocative argument as a means of clearing the air and preserving the integrity of his party. There is no escaping the simple chronological fact that it was the revolt of Douglas, not the Dred Scott decision, which called forth the House Divided speech.

*

The foregoing explanation would carry more weight if it could be shown that Lincoln actually began to compose the speech soon after Douglas first announced his opposition to the Lecompton constitution—that is, in December 1857 rather than in May 1858 (as Herndon leads us to believe). There is good evidence that Lincoln did just this, but it has long been obscured by the persistent misdating of an important document. In their *Complete Works of Lincoln,* Nicolay and Hay grouped several undated manuscripts together and marked them "October 1, 1858?" One of these, obviously a draft of a speech, is about three-quarters the length of the House Divided address and contains the basic ideas, as well as some of the phraseology, of the latter document.[42] For convenience, it may be labeled the "House Divided fragment." The editors of the *Collected Works,* pointing out that the fragment must have been written considerably earlier than October 1, chose to date it "c. May 18, 1858." But their reasons for doing so are unpersuasive, and it seems almost certain that in this instance they have committed one of their rare mistakes.[43]

With a single reading it becomes clear that the fragment was written while certain events of December 1857 were still fresh. For example, referring to Buchanan, Lincoln says: "And now, in his first annual message he urges the acceptance of the Lecompton constitution." The annual message was read to Congress on December 8. But it was Buchanan's special message of February 2, 1858, submitting the constitution for approval, that set off the real legislative battle, and Lincoln does not mention it at all. Then there is the attention that Lincoln devotes to a bill sponsored by Douglas in the Senate. This measure, authorizing the people of Kansas to frame another constitution, was introduced on December 18 and quickly buried in committee. It remained a subject of public interest for no more than a few weeks. Yet Lincoln treats it as a live issue and gives it his endorsement. Furthermore, at one point he uses the words "last year" in what is obviously a discussion of the campaign of 1856. These and other clues lead to the conclusion that the House Divided fragment was probably written during the last ten days of December 1857.* And it was on December 28, significantly, that Lincoln sent off his fretful letter to Lyman Trumbull, demanding: "What does the New-York Tribune mean by it's constant eulogising, and admiring, and magnifying [of] Douglas?"⁴⁴

If Lincoln drafted the House Divided fragment with the intention of using it immediately in a public address, there is no record of his doing so. Perhaps, in anticipation of a strenuous campaign, he was beginning to put thoughts down on paper— even as he was working hard to make money at his law practice— for expenditure in the months ahead. In any case, there can be little doubt that his composition of the fragment was provoked by the signs of Republican infatuation with Douglas, and that it was a preliminary draft of the speech he delivered the following June.

The first and major part of the fragment is a vigorous argument against Republican coalition with Douglas on his terms. It is thus analogous to the third—or "living dog"—section of the House Divided speech. Lincoln warns that if the Republicans drop their own organization and "fall in" with Douglas, they may end up "haltered and harnessed," ready to be "handed over by him to the regular Democracy, to filibuster indefinitely for additional slave territory,—to carry slavery into all the States, as well

---

* The early part of January 1858 should perhaps be included as a possibility because Lincoln speaks of "having seen the noses counted, and actually knowing that a majority of the people of Kansas are against slavery." This could be a reference to the Kansas election of January 4. However, the first clear proof of a Free State majority in Kansas had been furnished by the territorial elections of October 5, 1857, and it was probably this event that Lincoln had in mind.

as Territories, under the Dred Scott decision, construed and en-
larged from time to time." After several more pages of attack
upon "Nebraskaism" and its author, he broadens the scope of his
argument with the assertion that "Kansas is neither the whole
nor a tithe of the real question." Then follows this passage:

A house divided against itself cannot stand.[45]

I believe the government cannot endure permanently half
slave and half free. I expressed this belief a year ago; and
subsequent developments have but confirmed me. I do not
expect the Union to be dissolved. I do not expect the house
to fall; but I do expect it will cease to be divided. It will become all one thing or all the other. Either the opponents of
slavery will arrest the further spread of it, and put it in course
of ultimate extinction; or its advocates will push it forward
till it shall become alike lawful in all the States, old as well
as new. Do you doubt it? Study the Dred Scott decision, and
then see how little even now remains to be done.

The eye-catching clause, "I expressed this belief a year ago,"
loses much of its mystery when a proper date is assigned to the
fragment. Lincoln is probably referring to his use of the house-
divided doctrine during the campaign of 1856, thereby lending
support to Dickey's account of the Bloomington incident.*

* This clause, which is the only clue to the date of the fragment in its
later pages, tends to justify the belief that all parts of the manuscript were
written at about the same time and that it is indeed to be regarded as a
single document. The belief is strengthened by the logical coherence of
Lincoln's argument and by the fact that Nicolay and Hay, who presumably
had the entire manuscript in their hands, came to the same conclusion. But
an alternative possibility must be acknowledged, namely, that the latter
part of the fragment, beginning with the house-divided passage, was written
in 1859 and erroneously linked with the earlier pages by Nicolay and Hay.
During his Ohio speeches of September 1859, Lincoln indicated more than
once that he had uttered the house-divided doctrine for the first time in
1858. This appears to contradict the Dickey story, but Lincoln may have
meant the first time deliberately for publication. Moreover, the house-
divided passage in the fragment is followed by an analysis of the Dred Scott
decision which seems more appropriate for 1857 than for 1859. In summary, the first and major portion of the House Divided fragment was
almost certainly written sometime near the end of December 1857; the

In the final pages of the manuscript, Lincoln briefly discusses the ominous implications of the Dred Scott decision and the dangerous futility of a "don't-care" attitude. "Welcome, or unwelcome, agreeable or disagreeable," he declares, "whether this shall be an entire slave nation, *is* the issue before us. Every incident—every little shifting of scenes or of actors—only clears away the intervening trash, compacts and consolidates the opposing hosts, and brings them more and more distinctly face to face." The conflict, he concludes, will be severe, and it will be fought through by "those who *do* care for the result." But victory can be won, under the Constitution, with *"peaceful ballots,"* rather than *"bloody bullets."*

Verbally, the House Divided fragment bears only an occasional resemblance to the House Divided speech, but in substance the two documents are remarkably similar. The fragment, like the finished speech, may be divided into three parts: the rejection of Douglas (constituting approximately 72 per cent of the whole), the house-divided passage (5 per cent), and a conclusion, which contains the core of the conspiracy theory (23 per cent). Between December and June, Lincoln shortened the first section, recasting the phraseology but not the meaning, and moved it to the end of the address. At the same time, he greatly expanded the conspiracy argument, making it his major theme. These modifications no doubt reflected the changing political situation. With each passing month, the possibility of a permanent alliance between Douglas and the Republican party became more remote, but the danger of losing potential Republican votes to his magnetic leadership and plausible doctrine remained as serious as ever. Lincoln was shifting his emphasis to meet the needs of the hour.

In addition, there were several incidents which may have encouraged Lincoln to elaborate the conspiracy charge. Cole suggests, for example, that he was influenced by editorials in the

---

latter part, including the house-divided passage itself, raises some doubt, but the available evidence tends to support the assumption that it was written at the same time.

Mattoon *National Gazette* advocating the legalization of slavery in Illinois.[46] Perhaps he was even more impressed by the widely discussed decision of the California Supreme Court on February 11, 1858, in the case of the slave Archy, who was held to be still the property of his master even though the latter had settled down to more or less permanent residence in the state.[47] Also, since Lincoln usually kept a watchful eye upon proceedings in Congress, he could have drawn inspiration from a speech enunciating the conspiracy theory which was delivered in the Senate on February 8, 1858, by William P. Fessenden of Maine.[48] Most important of all, Douglas himself, at one point in the desperate Lecompton struggle, came close to accusing the Buchanan administration of conspiring to nationalize slavery.* Lincoln seized upon these remarks and, in the debates at Ottawa and Freeport, quoted them to show that his rival had "made substantially the *same charges* against substantially the *same persons,* excluding his dear self from the category."[49]

Whatever influences prompted him to recast it, Lincoln's December draft is highly revealing as a stage in the development of his thought, and it tends to reinforce certain conclusions already

* The Washington *Union,* generally regarded as the organ of the Administration, had published an article on November 17, 1857, in which it argued that state laws forbidding slavery were a violation of constitutional rights. Douglas, speaking in the Senate on March 22, 1858, linked this article with the philosophy of the Lecompton constitution and asserted that together they represented a "fatal blow" at state sovereignty. Later, he insisted that his criticism had been leveled only at the *Union,* not at the Buchanan administration. As Lincoln pointed out, however, the Little Giant more than once labeled the article "authoritative," thus implying that the *Union* spoke for the President and his advisers. In the famous article which he wrote for *Harper's Magazine* in 1859, Douglas maintained that the Southern interpretation of the Dred Scott decision would legalize slavery everywhere in the United States. This bore a striking resemblance to Lincoln's warning in the House Divided speech, and during a debate in the Senate on May 22, 1860, Judah P. Benjamin of Louisiana accused Douglas of adopting the very argument advanced by his Illinois adversary. *Congressional Globe,* 35 Cong., 1 sess., Appendix, pp. 199–200; 36 Cong., 1 sess., p. 2238; Stephen A. Douglas, "The Dividing Line Between Federal and Local Authority: Popular Sovereignty in the Territories," *Harper's Magazine,* XIX (1859), 530–31.

advanced, namely : that the different parts of the House Divided speech were intimately related to one another and constituted a cohesive whole; that the speech was a direct response to the peculiar political conditions created by the revolt of Douglas; and that it was written not only as a statement of principle, but with a practical purpose in mind.

*

The House Divided speech represents one of those moments of synthesis which embody the past and illumine the future. Lincoln, who revered his country's historical tradition, believed that the cause he embraced pointed the way to a fuller realization of the ideals upon which the republic had been built. Enjoying an advantage which accrues especially to founders of new political movements, he experienced little difficulty in squaring his partisan commitments with his moral convictions. He was confronted with no painful choice between expediency and principle.

At the level of practical politics, Lincoln was defending his own candidacy for the Senate and trying to save his party from disintegration. He never doubted that the decision to oppose Douglas in Illinois had been absolutely crucial. Speaking in Chicago on March 1, 1859, he said: "If we, the Republicans of this State, had made Judge Douglas our candidate for the Senate of the United States last year and had elected him, there would to-day be no Republican party in this Union."[50] And he continued to issue warnings against "the temptation to lower the Republican Standard in order to gather recruits."[51]

But if Lincoln had satisfied himself that his personal ambition accorded with the welfare of his party, he was equally certain that nothing other than unadulterated Republicanism could rescue the nation from the peril into which it had fallen. Although his language in the House Divided speech contained echoes of old-line abolitionism, he was adapting Garrisonian rhetoric to a more conservative purpose. In his view, the Republican program offered the only solution to the problems of slavery and sectionalism because it alone recognized the tension between moral conviction and constitutional guarantees, and yielded as much to either as the other would allow. Douglas insisted, to be sure, that the concept of ultimate extinction conflicted with the promise not to attack slavery in the Southern states.[52] And so it did, from the viewpoint of 1858. To Lincoln, however, the two propositions were like lines extending into the future, seemingly parallel, but capable of being brought together gradually and gently. Convinced that slavery was wrong, yet willing to settle for a promise of ultimate extinction, he believed that an established policy of restriction would incorporate that promise and bring peace to the nation.

It is at this point that his argument becomes, in retrospect, especially vulnerable. The house-divided doctrine was essentially an effort to polarize public opinion and to elicit a clear-cut decision upon the most critical aspects of the slavery issue. Lincoln maintained that such a decision would terminate controversy and terminate it peaceably. He assumed, in other words, that the South would acquiesce in a Republican accession to power. But events soon proved that he had misread the Southern mind and seriously underestimated the threat of disunion.

Yet it is unlikely that even a revelation of the future would have changed Lincoln's thinking. Civil war was not, in his opinion, the worst disaster that could befall the American people. Behind his expectation that the South *would* submit to a verdict at the polls was a conviction that it *must* submit; for if majority rule, based on popular elections and bounded by constitutional restraints, could be set aside at the will of a dissatisfied minority, what remained of democratic government?[53] Furthermore, Lincoln had constructed his political philosophy upon the belief that public policy should reflect an ethical purpose which was not itself subject to the daily barter of politics. "Important principles," he said, in the last speech of his life, "may, and must, be inflexible."[54] These words were, in a sense, his final postscript to the House Divided speech.

Five

A New Look at the Great Debates

THE GREAT BATTLE of the next Presidential election is now being fought in Illinois," said the Richmond *Enquirer* on August 10, 1858. This was shortly after the seven debates between Lincoln and Douglas had been announced, but eleven days before their first encounter at Ottawa. The editorial writer, unaware of the hidden prophecy in his statement, was thinking only of Douglas and the latter's enormous stake in the senatorial contest. Already facing bitter opposition from the South, the Little Giant could scarcely hope to obtain the Democratic presidential nomination if he were defeated for re-election in Illinois. On the Republican side, meanwhile, Seward appeared to have a commanding lead over other potential candidates, among whom no one had yet thought to include Lincoln.

The full significance and the irony of the Lincoln-Douglas debates was not revealed until 1860, when Fortune whimsically bestowed her generous consolation prize upon the man who had been denied the senatorship. Lincoln's election to the presidency rounded off the history of his dramatic rivalry with Douglas— and at the same time seriously distorted it; for the debates, although held in 1858, have been interpreted and evaluated in the light of what happened two years later. In retrospect, the tall form of Lincoln dominates the scene; Douglas, originally the star of the show, is relegated to second billing; and the hard-fought battle for a Senate seat shrinks to the proportions of a dress rehearsal. Historiography thus inverts history and makes yesterday the determinant of the day before.

The primary significance of the Lincoln-Douglas contest must indeed be sought in its consequences, but with due precaution, always, against the *post hoc* traps and other hazards that are scattered over the ground of inquiry. The House Divided speech, for example, undoubtedly contributed to Lincoln's emergence as a presidential contender; yet there is not the slightest evidence that any objective beyond the senatorship was in his mind when he drafted it. Retrospection runs riot in the assertion of Henry C. Whitney (quoted with approval by Beveridge) that "while . . . his political friends were training him for the Senate he was coaching himself for the Presidency, two years thereafter."[1] The tendency to explain motives by consulting results, and to mistake mere sequence for cause and effect, has cast a veil of legend over a well-documented historical event. Despite all that has been written about the Lincoln-Douglas campaign of 1858, certain aspects of this familiar story can still be examined with profit.

*

The seven formal debates beginning on August 21 and ending on October 15 provided the ceremonial framework for a campaign that would have been unique and exciting even without them. The spectacle of a stump contest between two avowed candidates for the United States Senate—one of them already the central figure in national politics—could not fail to attract wide attention all across the country. Very often, however, the out-of-state interest was haphazard and spasmodic. Newspapers, with a few exceptions, were still limited to four pages, and local politics had first claim upon their meager space, not to mention such events as the laying of the Atlantic cable, the championship prize fight between John Morrisey and John Heenan, the burning of the famous Crystal Palace in New York, and the dispatch of the first overland mail to California. Some editors printed frequent reports on the campaign in Illinois, while others completely ignored it. The total effect was a fragmentary national coverage which nevertheless greatly exceeded that given most state elections.*

---

* In its chronology of some two hundred events occurring in 1858, the *American Almanac* did not even mention the Lincoln-Douglas debates.

Southerners showed little interest in Lincoln as an individual. He fitted the odious stereotype of a black Republican, and nothing else mattered. It was Douglas whom the slaveholders watched intently, knowing that they would soon have to reckon with his bid for leadership of the Democratic party. The question debated extensively by Southern newspapers as the campaign in Illinois progressed was whether the South would suffer more from the re-election of a powerful renegade or from the triumph of a Republican nonentity. Many editors insisted that Douglas should be beaten whatever the cost. Others argued that in spite of his defection on the Lecompton issue he was still preferable to Lincoln. A third group washed its hands of the Illinois contest, agreeing with the Jackson *Mississippian* that the South could have no choice between a "pair of depraved, blustering, mischievous, lowdown demagogues."[2]

Elsewhere in the nation, there was greater curiosity about Lincoln. "You are like Byron, who woke up one morning and found himself famous," wrote Charles H. Ray on July 27 from his old home in Chenango County, New York. "I have found hundreds of anxious enquirers burning to know all about the newly raised-up opponent of Douglas—his age, profession, personal appearance and qualities, etc."[3] Lincoln, as he proved himself a match for his formidable adversary, won increasing admiration from Eastern Republicans, although Greeley and the other editors who had supported Douglas remained aloof and almost neutral. Interest in the campaign became more pronounced as one traveled westward, and Illinois itself seemed like bedlam to many visitors. There, the newspaper accounts were unusually full and fiercely partisan. The decision of the Chicago *Times* and the Chicago *Press and Tribune** to print complete stenographic reports of the seven debates constituted a landmark in political journalism. It was also something new to have a corps of paid correspondents trailing the two candidates wherever they went.

---

* This new name resulted from the consolidation of the *Tribune* and the *Democratic Press* in July 1858. The word *Press* was dropped in October 1860.

The historic contest between Lincoln and Douglas actually began in Chicago on July 9, 1858, when an uproarious celebration welcomed the latter home from Washington. That evening, with Lincoln by invitation sitting near him, the Little Giant addressed a huge crowd from the balcony of the Tremont House. The speech, besides lifting the morale of local Democrats, had two other significant effects. In it, Douglas renewed his quarrel with the Buchanan administration at the very moment when a truce was being arranged. He also undertook an extensive refutation of the House Divided speech, thereby publicly recognizing Lincoln as his rival for the senatorship. Lincoln spoke in reply from the same balcony twenty-four hours later. Then Douglas, traveling southward, delivered speeches at Bloomington on July 16 and at Springfield in the afternoon of July 17. He again centered much of his fire upon the House Divided address, but now added a rejoinder to Lincoln's remarks at Chicago. Lincoln, having heard Douglas at Bloomington, responded at Springfield in the evening of the 17th.[4]

And so, before any formal arrangements were made, a brisk running debate had been launched, as much on Douglas's initiative as on Lincoln's. Left to his own devices, Lincoln might have been satisfied to continue in just this manner. "My recent experience shows," he wrote later in the summer, "that speaking at the same place the next day after D[ouglas] is the very thing— it is, in fact, a concluding speech on him."[5] Some Republicans were afraid, however, that Lincoln would lose face if he kept on following Douglas about the state, especially since Democratic newspapers had begun to jeer at the strategy. The obvious solution was a series of joint discussions in which the two men would appear as equals. An editorial in the Chicago *Press and Tribune* broached the subject on July 22: "We have a suggestion to make ... Let Mr. Douglas and Mr. Lincoln agree to canvass the State together, in the usual western style .... If Mr. Douglas shall refuse to be a party to such arrangement, it will be because he is a coward." Lincoln, who had just arrived in Chicago for talks with party leaders, was quickly persuaded. On the 24th, he wrote to Douglas proposing that they "divide time, and address the same audiences during the present canvass."[6]

It is inaccurate to say, as so many historians do, that the Little Giant "accepted" this challenge. Lincoln's plan, if agreed to, would have meant at least fifty debates, an exhausting thing even to contemplate. Douglas dared not respond with an outright refusal, but he had no intention of going through the entire campaign yoked to Lincoln. Explaining that his speaking schedule precluded such a comprehensive arrangement, he offered instead to "accommodate" his rival by meeting him seven times. Lincoln, with some unseemly grumbling about the terms, accepted this wholesale revision of his original proposal.* Republican papers in the state left no doubt that they considered the challenge declined. The *Press and Tribune* exclaimed: "The little dodger shirks, and backs out, except at half a dozen places which he himself selects." In Springfield, the *State Journal* maintained that about one hundred debates ought to have been scheduled, and that Douglas, by his "inglorious retreat from a public discussion," had stamped himself as only "seven hundredths of a candidate for the Senate."[7]

For the most part, then, each man went his own way, and the debates, although they were the dramatic high points of the campaign, represented only a small fraction of its total oratory. Lincoln, according to his own count, made a total of sixty-three speeches. Most of them were at scheduled meetings and averaged about two hours in length. Douglas, who followed an even more

---

* The number seven was fixed upon by subtracting two from nine. Douglas proposed one debate in each of the nine congressional districts, counting the discussions already held at Chicago and Springfield. Since Lincoln had followed him at both of those places, he claimed the right to speak last four times out of the remaining seven. Lincoln acquiesced, but complained that he had actually been the more "concluded on." The places and dates of the seven debates were as follows: Ottawa, August 21; Freeport, August 27; Jonesboro, September 15; Charleston, September 18; Galesburg, October 7; Quincy, October 13; Alton, October 15. On an alternating basis, one man spoke for an hour, the other replied for an hour and a half, and the first then had a half-hour rejoinder.

strenuous schedule, later asserted that he had delivered "just one hundred and thirty speeches" during the senatorial contest, but he was apparently including all his impromptu responses to welcoming addresses, serenades, and other demonstrations.[8] In addition, the political battle was waged by the hundreds of lesser candidates who took their turns on the stump, by volunteer orators from within and without the state, by newspaper editors and their reporters, and by the countless enthusiasts of all ages and both sexes who contributed to the pageantry of the campaign by making banners, decorating halls and platforms, organizing parades, playing in bands, preparing feasts, firing cannon, and filling the air with their cheers.

Both Lincoln and Douglas concentrated their efforts in the middle of the state, where the contest would be won and lost. Yet together they covered nearly ten thousand miles in about a hundred days, traveling by train, river boat, and carriage, enduring intense heat and sudden rain storms, snatching food and sleep at odd hours, riding in processions, waving, smiling, shaking hands, conferring with swarms of local party leaders, and making hasty notes for the next speech that was always in the offing.[9] So killing was the pace that, as Paul M. Angle says, "it would not have been surprising had both men broken under the strain." Lincoln's voice stood up better than that of his opponent, which dwindled almost to a whisper near the end of the canvass, but neither warrior seems to have missed a single scheduled engagement.[10]

Even stripped of all its folklore, the Lincoln-Douglas campaign was a remarkable chapter in American political history, full of homespun vivacity and colorful incident, revealing the youthful exuberance of a still youthful nation. "The prairies are on fire," wrote the correspondent of a New York newspaper. "It is astonishing how deep an interest in politics this people take."[11] In every community favored with a visit from one or both of the senatorial candidates, there were weeks of preparation, spurred by a fierce resolve to outdo the enemy in numbers, noise, and display. Clouds of dust, raised by wagons approaching from all points of the compass, ushered in the great day. At eight o'clock in the morning of the Ottawa debate, we are told, "the streets and avenues leading from the country were so enveloped with dust that the town resembled a vast smoke house."[12] The din of the gathering crowd was usually swelled by band music, booming cannon, and the cries of peddlers hawking their wares. Adults mingled to gossip, children to romp, and great quantities of food, brought from home or served at long tables by a local committee, fortified the multitude against its long wait. As the hour appointed for the festivities drew near, there was often a rush to secure positions close to the speaker's stand. Bolder spirits sometimes swarmed upon the platform itself and, like true squatters, rebuffed all efforts to dislodge them. Then, when the speakers and other dignitaries arrived, they had to fight "a hand-to-hand conflict for even the meagerest . . . standing room."[13]

Despite the wearisome length of most such meetings, the audiences were generally attentive and responsive, but not always courteous. The stump speaker, no matter how well he pleased his partisans, usually had to contend with a certain amount of heckling from the opposition. At Freeport, where Douglas was in unfriendly territory, his repeated use of the phrase "Black Republicans" brought so many roars of anger from the crowd that he finally exclaimed: "I wish to remind you that while Mr. Lincoln was speaking there was not a Democrat vulgar and black-guard enough to interrupt him."[14] When he spoke at Joliet a few days later, the Little Giant was pestered with interruptions not only from Republicans in his audience but from the abolitionist congressman, Owen Lovejoy, who had seated himself uninvited on the speaker's platform.[15]

Democrats welcomed Lincoln to Rushville on October 20 by flying a black flag from the top of the courthouse steeple. While he was speaking, a gang of boys climbed into the steeple and tried to drown out his voice with cheers for Douglas. And several ladies looking down on the stand from upper rooms in the courthouse annoyed him with laughter and offensive remarks until he stopped his speech and asked them to be silent.[16] Entering the Mississippi town of Dallas City on October 23, Lincoln found the main street decorated with a huge banner which pictured a Negro and bore the single word "Equality." Here again, his address was punctuated with hostile interruptions.[17] Neither Rushville nor Dallas had been included in Douglas's itinerary, and so the local Democrats could show their mettle only in such counterattacks against the enemy invasion.

At Sullivan, on the other hand, both candidates were scheduled to speak the same day (September 20), and a general brawl almost ensued when parading Republicans descended in force upon the Douglas meeting.[18] From Sullivan, Douglas moved on to Danville and there received the campaign's most eloquent token of disrespect when the carriage waiting for him at the station was smeared with "loathsome dirt," or, as another reporter put it, "in a manner unmentionable."[19]

The extreme bias of most contemporary observers makes it impossible to determine whether one of the two candidates was appreciably superior to the other as a campaigner. Each man was a conquering hero in the newspapers of his own party and a pitiful failure in the opposition press. His audiences were large and spirited or small and listless, his arguments were wonderfully persuasive or wretchedly futile, depending upon the political allegiance of the sheet in which they were described. Lincoln's awkward appearance drew much ridicule. His gestures, said the Chicago *Times,* seemed "positively painful," like those of a man "suffering from an attack brought on by an imprudent indulgence in unripe fruit."[20] Douglas was equally vulnerable because of the characteristic vehemence with which he spoke, and Republican editors, knowing his convivial habits, did not hesitate to suggest that much of his fierceness came out of a bottle. At Ottawa, according to the *Press and Tribune,* the face of the Little Giant was "livid with passion"; he resembled "a wild beast in looks and gesture, and a maniac in language and argument."[21]

Lincoln had the underdog's advantage. For him, as the election was to prove, there could be moral victory in a stand-off with his illustrious rival. Furthermore, Lincoln surpassed Douglas as an orator. His ear was better tuned to the rhythms and subtleties of language. He used words more consciously and with greater versatility, passing easily from wit to sarcasm, from homely analogy to solemn eloquence. Deliberation and revision improved his style, whereas Douglas, for whom speech was but a mode of action, needed the thrust of spontaneity and often became dull with preparation. Neither a storyteller nor a phrasemaker, and seldom very original in his thought or expression, Douglas is among the least quoted of major American statesmen. Yet in debate he was a formidable antagonist, and the anti-Lecompton Douglas of 1858, fighting enemies on two fronts, was an especially attractive figure. Printed speeches reveal the man's alertness, fluency, and intelligence, but not his enormous vitality, not the dynamic quality of his platform presence. The truth seems to be that these two adversaries, so different in appearance and temperament, were exceedingly well matched, each having his peculiar sources of strength. There is perhaps no better estimate of their achievement than the one written by an editor in Portland, Maine: "Without regard to politics the contest in Illinois is taking magnificent proportions. Douglas and Lincoln are both giants, and the way they discuss political questions before immense crowds of people is an admirable illustration of the workings of our institutions."[22]

*

It has been the fashion at times to belittle the actual content of the Lincoln-Douglas debates.[23] They are, admittedly, burdened with tiresome repetition and trivial dispute. Douglas jabbed repeatedly at his opponent's stand on the Mexican War. Lincoln took full advantage of an honest mistake which Douglas made at Ottawa when he quoted a set of Republican resolutions and attributed them to the wrong convention. More than half of the time at the Charleston meeting was occupied with a tedious re-hashing of Douglas's part in framing the Toombs bill, an enabling act for Kansas passed by the Senate in 1856.[24] Yet the worst faults of the debates derive from the circumstances of their presentation, which did not encourage compactness, strict relevancy, or logical progression. Intended for the ears of clamorous partisans in seven separate meetings, not for the eyes of one reader, these twenty-one hours of oratory deserve to be judged by their superior passages, rather than by the average level of the discussion.

From the text of the seven debates it appears that Lincoln expected the argument to be somewhat different in each new encounter, whereas Douglas had the skeleton of a set speech which he intended to use, with suitable variations, at every meeting. The Little Giant's primary purpose, besides defending his own political record, was to persuade uncommitted moderates that Lincoln's views were those of a dangerous radical. The house-divided doctrine therefore continued to be his point of departure. Lincoln, he declared, was not only preaching sectional warfare, but advocating an oppressive uniformity that would be repugnant alike to the principle of state sovereignty and to the cultural diversity which had made America great. The nation *could* endure half slave and half free, Douglas insisted, if each state and territory were allowed to regulate its own domestic institutions in accordance with local needs and customs.[25]

The moderate platform adopted by Illinois Republicans in 1858 was less vulnerable than the House Divided speech, and Douglas consequently paid little attention to it. Instead, he endeavored to identify his rival with the more radical Republicanism of 1854, at which time, he charged, Lincoln had joined Trumbull in a plot to "abolitionize" the Whig and Democratic parties of the state. Douglas found the true spirit of the Republican movement most starkly revealed in the militant antislavery resolutions that emanated from many northern counties during the Kansas-Nebraska excitement. Such resolutions, besides demanding the exclusion of slavery from the territories, usually

called for repeal of the Fugitive Slave Law, abolition of slavery
in the District of Columbia, and various other assaults upon the
outer defenses of slave society. The seven questions that Douglas
reeled off at Ottawa were designed to measure the extent of Lincoln's concurrence with these aggressive proposals and to expose
the inherent radicalism of his sympathies.[26]

Another weapon upon which Douglas relied was the exploi-
tation of race prejudice. He scornfully rejected Lincoln's contention that the philosophy of the Declaration of Independence
embraced Negroes as well as white men. If this belief ever won
general acceptance, he warned, an inferior race, utterly incapable
of self-government, would be elevated to a position of absolute
equality, and the nation would experience all the degradation and
misery that had accompanied racial amalgamation in the countries
of Latin America. "I do not question Mr. Lincoln's conscientious
belief that the negro was made his equal, and hence is his brother,"
Douglas sneered, "but for my own part, I do not regard the negro
as my equal, and positively deny that he is my brother or any
kin to me whatever."[27] When Lincoln emphatically disclaimed
any desire to confer political and social equality upon Negroes,
Douglas accused him of hypocrisy, complaining that he offered
one set of principles in northern counties and another to audiences farther south.[28] The cry of Negro equality pursued Lincoln, despite all his protestations, throughout the campaign and
no doubt affected its outcome. White supremacy, a doctrine that
scarcely needed defending in nineteenth-century America, was
not the central theme of Douglas's argument, but he used it with
great effectiveness to buttress his plea for a multiform society,
resting on sturdy local autonomy, as the alternative to sectional
strife.

For Lincoln, it was vitally necessary to throw off the impu-
tation of radicalism. Hence he dissociated himself from the in-
cipient Republican movement of 1854, renewed his pledge to
support recovery of fugitive slaves and to oppose interference with
slavery in the Southern states, disavowed racial equality, and

rejected the invidious inferences which Douglas drew from the House Divided speech.[29] But it was not enough merely to defend himself against the thrusts of his opponent. As the challenger, Lincoln needed to mount a vigorous offensive. His greatest task was, in the apt words of Harry V. Jaffa, to "destroy Douglas' credentials as a free-soil champion," credentials won in the fight against the Lecompton constitution.[30] This meant accentuating the fundamental differences that still separated Douglas from the Republican party despite their recent collaboration in Congress. Such strategy, already embodied in the House Divided speech, was not entirely compatible with Lincoln's efforts to absolve himself from antislavery extremism; for the latter required conservative utterances that actually reduced the distance between him and Douglas. The resulting ambivalence in his argument exposed him to the charge of being inconsistent and inspired conflicting historical interpretations of his essential outlook and purpose.

Lincoln's case against Douglas may be summarized as follows: The divisive influence of slavery was the one great threat to the American union, and the policy inaugurated in the Kansas-Nebraska Act had only intensified the sectional conflict. On the moral issue posed by slavery there could be no middle ground; the neutralism preached by Douglas was calculated to dull the Northern conscience and thus clear the way for legalization of the institution everywhere in the nation. Only the Republican program, which accorded with the views of the founding fathers, offered a feasible alternative to this grim eventuality. Slavery must be recognized as an evil and, within the bounds of the Constitution, treated as an evil. Specifically, it must be confined to its existing limits and marked for ultimate extinction.*

There were obvious risks attached to this line of argument, but Lincoln had good reason for accepting them. The territorial

---

* Lincoln, of course, exaggerated the extent and intensity of antislavery feeling among the founders of the Republic, who dealt equivocally with the institution and excluded it from only part of the Western wilderness. There was much historical truth in Douglas's assertion that the house-divided doctrine ran counter to the judgment of the fathers.

question by itself simply did not present enough contrast between Douglas and the Republicans, especially since their joint anti-Lecompton effort. A much sharper distinction could be drawn if the discussion were shifted to the more expansive domain of moral principles. And so, as the debates progressed, Lincoln laid increasing emphasis upon the fundamental conflict between those who believed, and those who did not believe, that slavery was wrong. "That is the real issue," he said at Alton. "That is the issue that will continue in this country when these poor tongues of Judge Douglas and myself shall be silent. It is the eternal struggle between these two principles — right and wrong — throughout the world."[31]

Along with his main assault upon Douglas's position, Lincoln was quick to undertake any collateral maneuver that promised advantage. For example, the first two questions that he asked at Freeport were designed to aggravate the quarrel between Douglas and the Buchanan-Southerner wing of the Democratic party. One of them forced the Little Giant to repudiate a significant provision in the English compromise. The other elicited his famous "Freeport doctrine," summed up in the phrase "unfriendly legislation," with which he proposed to rescue popular sovereignty from the effects of the Dred Scott decision.[32] Both replies aroused anger in the South, but since the slaveholders had by now written off Kansas as a lost cause, the Freeport doctrine soon became the primary focus of their hostility to Douglas. Here, then, was the raw material for a familiar legend: that Lincoln, with a single well-placed blow, split the Democratic party and deprived Douglas of the presidency.

This second Freeport question was actually tangential to Lincoln's principal line of attack, which, after all, stressed the *affinity* between Douglas and the slave interest, not their disagreements.*

* In so far as it exposed the precariousness of Douglas's medial position, the second Freeport question no doubt reinforced the house-divided doctrine. But Lincoln's third and fourth questions at Freeport (dealing with the possible establishment of slavery in the free states and in newly acquired territories) were far more relevant to his main argument.

Yet because of the prodigious consequences attributed to it, the question has come to be regarded as the very crux of the debates and as a major turning point in American history. An utterance invested with such importance commands special attention, and will receive it in the chapter that follows.

The vigor with which Lincoln and Douglas belabored one another tended to magnify the distance separating their respective points of view. Neither man was an extremist; both offered reasonable solutions to the slavery problem; and they were frequently closer to agreement than either would admit. But these are facts that should qualify, not dominate, any description of their relationship. The distortion that results from emphasizing consensus instead of conflict in the Lincoln-Douglas debates can be seen in the writings of James G. Randall. A biographer who fully appreciated Lincoln's greatness, but whose sympathies, as a "revisionist" historian, were primarily with Douglas, Randall found his way out of an awkward dilemma by minimizing the differences between the two rivals. Lincoln and Douglas, he was fond of repeating, had "much in common." They thought alike on many problems that went unmentioned throughout the debates, and even in their discussion of slavery they *"seemed to differ* while actually agreeing on many points." Indeed, a reading of Randall leaves one with the impression that no vital principles were at stake in the campaign, that the candidates, merely to satisfy the demands of partisanship, put on an exciting show which obscured the underlying similarity of their aims and methods.[33]

What Randall seemed to overlook was that differences may be far from absolute and yet historically important. The debates do not reflect the ultimate conflict between abolitionist and slaveholder. They embody instead the principal cleavage in Northern thought, which, though narrower, had its own profound influence upon the course of events. A brief review will show that Lincoln's disagreement with Douglas was broad enough and deep enough to be significant.

1. *Negro slavery in the territories.*—Here, beyond any question, the debaters supported different policies. It is the contention of Randall and others, to be sure, that the difference was inconsequential because freedom would have been as well served by popular sovereignty as by the Republican program of restriction. But this argument ignores certain compelling facts. First, the recent history of Kansas had demonstrated that popular sovereignty could easily be perverted to the service of slavery. Second, many Northerners feared that the Douglas doctrine would be combined with new annexations—of Cuba, for instance—to enlarge the domain of slavery.* And finally, the territorial issue was not separable from the larger problem; for the legal status of slavery in the federal territories had become a measure of its moral acceptability in the nation as a whole.

2. *Negro slavery.*—The great difference here was not in the category of immediate objectives but in certain general commitments which would surely influence future action. Lincoln, holding that slavery was a "moral, social and political wrong," proposed to yield it only the minimum protection guaranteed by the Constitution and looked forward to its eventual abolition. Douglas refused to pass any judgment upon slavery and would let it compete for public approval in every locality on an equal basis with the antislavery principle. He professed indifference to the ultimate fate of the institution, but saw no reason why the republic could not "exist forever divided into free and slave states, as our fathers made it." Furthermore, whereas Douglas maintained that the problem was one to be dealt with exclusively by the states, Lincoln contended that the presence of slavery affected the whole nation and was therefore a proper subject of concern to the federal government, within the limits of its powers.[34] Whatever contemporary merit there may have been in

---

* An exchange of questions on this subject at Ottawa and Freeport revealed that the two debaters were far apart in their attitudes. Douglas favored acquiring new territory "without reference" to slavery. Lincoln said that he would weigh any proposed acquisition against the aggravation that it might cause in the sectional controversy.

Douglas's argument, history has vindicated Lincoln's nationalism, as well as his verdict against slavery.

3. *The Negro.*—According to Randall, the debaters "did not fundamentally differ" in their views on racial relations.[35] The accuracy of this assertion must be challenged, however, because it was when they discussed fundamentals that the two men disagreed most sharply. For one thing, Douglas subscribed unequivocally to the belief that the Negro race was innately inferior to the white, but Lincoln never went beyond the acknowledgment that the belief might be true. In speaking of Negroes, moreover, the Little Giant did not attempt to hide a strong personal repugnance which contrasted noticeably with Lincoln's tone of detachment. The fact remains, it is true, that Lincoln explicitly approved all the social arrangements of his day (except slavery) that were based upon the theory of Negro inferiority. In words that grate harshly upon the modern ear, he declared his opposition to Negro citizenship, Negro suffrage, and racial intermingling. "I have no purpose," he protested under Douglas's goading, "to introduce political and social equality between the white and black races. There is a physical difference between the two, which . . . will probably forever forbid their living together on the footing of perfect equality."[36]

The whole texture of American life compelled such a pronouncement in 1858, and the Lincoln of history would not exist if he had failed to comply. But it is what Lincoln *claimed* for the Negroes, not what he was willing to *deny* them, that retains significance, namely: "all the rights enumerated in the Declaration of Independence."[37] No doubt Lincoln failed to see everything that was implied in confirming the Negro's inalienable right to life, liberty, and the pursuit of happiness. His eyes were fixed upon the problem of slavery. Yet he must have known that for Negroes, no less than white men, the Declaration promised much more than freedom from bondage. The first steps toward fulfillment of that larger promise were taken during his presidency. Lincoln's first principle of racial relations—that the Declaration of Independence belongs to all Americans—was actually subversive of the existing order which he endorsed. It has become increasingly meaningful in the twentieth century, while the doctrine embraced by Douglas is on its way to the scrap-heap of error. There was that difference, if none other, between the two debaters.

*

Not the least curious feature of this extraordinary campaign was the fact that neither candidate had the full support of party leaders outside the state. In Lincoln's case, the defection of certain Eastern Republicans went no further than periodic declarations of neutrality regarding the Illinois contest. The New York *Post* of July 13, for instance, said that the cause of freedom would benefit substantially from either man's election. Such impartiality, exasperating to Illinois Republicans, was prompted largely by the desire to court anti-Lecompton Democrats in several critical states. It implied no disparagement of Lincoln, whom Republican newspapers everywhere treated with the utmost respect. Douglas, on the other hand, faced the venomous opposition of the Buchanan administration, which, not satisfied with editorial assaults and patronage reprisals, attempted to undermine his strength in Illinois by setting up a rival Democratic organization there.

The separate Buchanan party in Illinois began to take shape during the spring of 1858 when it became apparent that Douglas would retain firm command of the regular Democratic machinery. Invested with control of federal patronage in the state, and warmly supported by Administration newspapers like the Washington *Union,* this motley group of political castoffs, misfits, and placemen proposed to enter its own slate of candidates in the contest for legislative seats. Even a few victories might give the "Buchaneers" a decisive voice in the balloting for senator and thus assure the defeat of Douglas. Illinois Republicans were naturally delighted at the prospect of facing a divided opposition.

More than that, they found it desirable to foster the schism by lending encouragement to the weaker faction. The result was one of the strangest situations ever to develop in American politics. At the very time that an alliance of Republicans and Douglas Democrats in Washington was waging a desperate fight against the Administration and the Lecompton constitution, the Republicans of Illinois were entering into collaboration with pro-Lecompton Democrats for the purpose of unseating Douglas.

The Little Giant repeatedly denounced this "unholy and unnatural combination" of his adversaries, but Republican spokesmen met all such complaints with protestations of innocence. "There is not now, has not been, and will not be, any union . . . expressed or implied, between the Republicans of Illinois and the Lecomptonites here or elsewhere," declared the Chicago *Tribune*. Lincoln's own disclaimers were equally emphatic. "I have no objection to the division in the Judge's party," he said at Galesburg, "but I defy the Judge to show any evidence that I have in any way promoted that division."[38] Yet it is a matter of record that Lincoln held several consultations with John Dougherty, the Buchaneer candidate for state treasurer,[39] and that negotiations produced at least a working agreement, if not a formal alliance, between Republicans and Administration Democrats.

"It is our true policy to nurse the Buchanan men," Joseph Medill informed Trumbull in April. From the editor of the *State Journal* came a similar report: "All along, as you are aware, we have been encouraging the Buchanan men as much as possible and stimulating them to organize."[40] Republicans not only conferred and corresponded with the Buchaneers but wrote editorials praising them, published notices of their meetings, and augmented the size of those meetings by attending them in force. In Chicago, John Wentworth worked openly with the Administration men, filling columns of his newspaper with exhortations and advice.[41] Republicans of the Springfield area kept in close touch with Buchaneer activities through William Herndon, whose father and brother were local leaders of the movement. The latter served

on the editorial staff of the *Illinois State Democrat,* a newly established Administration organ which apparently expected financial help from the Republicans and hired a Republican journalist
in Chicago to write some of its political articles.[42]

Hoping to promote mass desertions from Douglas by predict-
ing them, Republican newspapers published fantastic estimates of
Buchaneer strength in the state. The *Press and Tribune* said that
a "general stampede" of Democrats to the Buchanan side was
developing. Douglas would be "driven from the field" or left with
less than ten supporters in the new legislature. On October 7,
less than four weeks before election day, the same sheet described
the Administration forces as "hopeful, enthusiastic and defiant,"
with "flattering prospects of success" in many of the Democratic
strongholds. When the election was over and the Buchaneers had
polled a miserable 2 per cent of the popular vote, *Tribune* editors
sourly confessed the truth: "There is not now and never has
been a Buchanan party in Illinois . . . . every shrewd politician
in the state has known it for a month at least."[43]

The spectacle of Republicans cooperating with Lecompton
Democrats offended Horace Greeley, and James G. Randall has
called it "one of the least inspiring aspects" of the 1858 campaign.[44] Whether the Illinois strategy was reprehensible or justified by circumstances must remain a matter of opinion, but the
results certainly failed to vindicate its wisdom. Douglas lost only
a few thousand votes to the Buchaneers, and for this cheap price
he freed himself from much of the burden that the slavery issue
had placed upon Northern Democrats. The fierce hostility of the
Buchaneer faction was his best answer to the conspiracy charge in
Lincoln's House Divided speech. By exploiting the break between
Douglas and the Administration, Illinois Republicans weakened
their case against him as a tool of the slaveholding interest.

*

Although a heavy rain fell over much of the state on November 2, more voters went to the polls than in the presidential

contest two years earlier. The election proved to be so close that even the losers could claim a measure of victory. With a popular plurality of about four thousand votes in a quarter of a million (but not quite a majority, since the Buchanan faction polled five thousand), the Republicans elected their candidates for state treasurer and superintendent of public instruction.* The Democrats carried off the major prize, however, by winning enough seats in the legislature to ensure Douglas's re-election, fifty-four to forty-six. Just a few hundred votes in several critical counties had made all the difference.[45] For Lincoln and his disappointed followers there was frustration as well as comfort in having come so near. And while the exultant Democrats, like most victors, hailed the outcome as a simple triumph of virtue, Republicans mournfully catalogued every specific factor that might have tipped the scales against them. Their list included such items as the rainy weather and the malign influence of the Catholic church, but according to the three most common complaints, Lincoln had been victimized by dishonesty at the polls, treachery from abroad, and an unfair apportionment of legislative seats.

Lax enforcement of defective laws permitted much trickery and fraud in the election procedures of the 1850's. There were, for example, no official ballots. Local party organizations usually printed their own, and it was common practice to run off, in addition, a supply of spurious opposition tickets for distribution in the enemy camp. More serious was the lack of a general registration law, which made it relatively easy to evade the residence requirement. As a consequence, voters were frequently "colonized," that is, moved on the eve of an election from safe or hopeless districts into doubtful ones. Here the Democratic party had a distinct advantage because it commanded the loyalty of Irish railroad workers, whose semi-transient existence fitted them admirably for such maneuvers.

---

* The popular vote can be tabulated in several ways, but the simplest and most significant figures are those for state treasurer: Republicans, 125,430; Douglas Democrats, 121,609; Buchanan Democrats, 5,071.

During the final weeks of the Lincoln-Douglas campaign, Republican leaders became increasingly alarmed about reports of Irish movements into the central counties. Newspapers described the invasion in detail and issued frantic warnings against a plot to steal the election for Douglas with "border ruffian tactics." Late in October, the state central committee sent out a circular letter with careful instructions on how to prevent illegal voting. Charles H. Ray proposed that a secret army of vigilantes be organized to guard the polls with revolvers protruding from their pockets. Herndon, almost beside himself, confided to Theodore Parker that bloodshed might be necessary to "maintain the purity of the ballot-box." "What shall we do?" he demanded. "Shall we tamely submit to the Irish, or shall we rise and cut their throats?"[46]

The trouble was that an illegal voter, even when challenged, could swear to his eligibility and cast a ballot. He ran the risk of prosecution for perjury, of course, but convictions were hard to get. Lincoln, who had himself encountered at Naples "about fifteen Celtic gentlemen, with black carpet-sacks in their hands," suggested an additional piece of strategy. To Norman B. Judd, the state chairman, he wrote:

> When there is a known body of these voters, could not a true man, of the *"detective"* class, be introduced among them in disguise, who could, at the nick of time, control their votes? Think this over. It would be a great thing, when this trick is attempted upon us, to have the saddle come up on the other horse.[47]

With his usual prudence, Lincoln did not specify the means by which the "control" was to be established.

Despite Republican precautions, some "colonized" Irishmen undoubtedly did vote on election day, but whether their number was large enough to affect the outcome is impossible to determine. The Republicans, in their post-election grumbling on the subject, were far less frenzied, however, than they had been a few weeks earlier. Their fears, though not groundless, had apparently been exaggerated.

Lincoln men reserved their bitterest reproaches for the Eastern Republicans who had given aid and comfort to Douglas. "I say d—n Greely & Co.," exclaimed an Edgar County leader. "They have done more harm to us in Ills. than all others beside not excepting the d—n Irish." From Quincy, Lincoln's friend Jackson Grimshaw reported that it had rained "rain and rail road Irish and Pro Slavery K.N.'s and worse than all Seward and Greely Republicans who voted for Douglas."[48] Similar expressions of anger issued from David Davis, John M. Palmer, Ebenezer Peck, and other prominent Republicans, as well as from the party press.[49] Whatever its merits as a diagnosis of Lincoln's defeat, this renewed outcry against betrayal from the East had important consequences, primarily because the Illinoisans were disposed to blame William H. Seward almost as much as they did Greeley.

Seward, unlike Greeley, had never openly advocated the re-election of Douglas, but at the same time he had not lifted a finger to help Lincoln. Many Illinois Republicans resented his aloofness and, more than that, mistrusted it. Remembering his cordial relations with Douglas during the Lecompton struggle, the rumors of a personal alliance, and the course followed by Thurlow Weed's newspaper, they were convinced that the New York senator had been covertly hostile to their cause. More than one looked ahead to 1860 as a time of reckoning and echoed the sentiments of the Chicagoan who declared: "If the vote of Illinois can nominate another than Seward, I hope it will be so cast."[50] This was an abrupt change from the situation at the beginning of 1858, when Seward had been, to all appearance, the favorite choice for the presidency among Illinois Republicans.[51] The decline of his popularity in the state left an empty space which Lincoln soon filled. That at least one Illinoisan nursed his grudge for two years is revealed in a congratulatory letter addressed to Lincoln on

May 28, 1860. "It is a double satisfaction to me," wrote the Chicago banker, J. Young Scammon, "that you should have been nominated over Seward and New York dictation; and when I recollected how much Seward did to favor Douglas and prejudice you and us in Illinois, I could but feel that it was a very righteous retribution that he should be defeated by you."[52]

In the opinion of some Illinois Republicans, however, the worst blow had been struck by the respected Whig-American leader, Senator John J. Crittenden of Kentucky, with help from Lincoln's old friend, T. Lyle Dickey. The latter, having persuaded himself that the Republican party was falling into radical hands, went over to the Democrats in the summer of 1858 and campaigned actively for Douglas. He managed to draw a letter from Crittenden praising the Little Giant and, after waiting for the most favorable moment, published it shortly before election day. The maneuver undoubtedly hurt Lincoln most in the very places where he was beaten—that is, in the old Whig strongholds of central Illinois. Lincoln himself bluntly told Crittenden that the use of his name had "contributed largely" to the Republican defeat.[53]

Pointing to their plurality in the popular vote, Republicans also charged that Lincoln had been cheated by an unjust distribution of legislative seats. It had required four votes in the northern counties, they complained, to offset three in the south, and the new General Assembly would have forty-six Republicans who represented a larger total population than the fifty-four Democrats. Douglas, the advocate of popular sovereignty, had been re-elected under a system that thwarted the will of the majority.[54]

Historians tend to agree. With uncritical vehemence they label the apportionment "unfair," "antique," "gerrymandered," and even "infamous."[55] Yet the statute in question actually dated back only to the "antiquity" of 1852 and was based upon the latest federal census. True, a state census taken in 1855 supplied fresher data, but a Republican bill deriving from it had been killed in the Democratic legislature, and a Democratic bill had been vetoed by the Republican governor. The word "gerrymander" is singularly inappropriate because the Republican party did not even exist when the law was passed, and Illinois politics had not yet become thoroughly sectionalized. Any gerrymandering undertaken in 1852 would have had little force by 1858.* Furthermore, even though Lincoln did unquestionably labor under some disadvantage, the Illinois law, compared with other apportionments past and present, was actually somewhat better than the average.

One thing often overlooked is that not every legislative seat was at stake in the 1858 contest. There were thirteen state senators holding over, eight of them Democrats, and so the Republicans needed more than a minimal victory to place Lincoln in the United States Senate. Altogether, the voters elected 87 legislators: 46 Democrats and 41 Republicans. This means that Lincoln, whose party polled about 50 per cent of the popular vote, received only 47 per cent of what we may call the electoral vote, while Douglas, with just 48 per cent of the popular vote, was given 53 per cent of the electoral vote—an inequity, to be sure, but hardly an unusual or outrageous one. If the results had mirrored the popular vote exactly, the Republicans would have won 44 seats instead of 41, still two less (counting their holdovers) than the number necessary to elect Lincoln.

As an additional test, however, let us suppose that the Republican apportionment bill had become law. When the 1858 votes are redistributed according to its provisions, Lincoln naturally fares better, but the issue is still in doubt. With the total number of seats increased by the bill to 105, it appears that the Republicans would have controlled 53, the barest possible majority.[56] It is therefore less than certain that the popular will of 1858 was thwarted by the apportionment of 1852. The closeness

---

* For example, a number of Whig strongholds in the middle of the state had become Democratic between 1852 and 1858, while Cook County shifted from the Democratic to the Republican column during the same period.

of the race made a relatively minor injustice seem decisive. But under that same law, after all, a Republican named Lyman Trumbull twice won election to the Senate.

*

The Lincoln-Douglas campaign of 1858 proved to be a contest without a real loser. Lincoln, despite his defeat, emerged as a national figure; Douglas with a hard-won victory preserved and consolidated his leadership of Northern Democrats. The most obvious consequence of this anomalous election, in which the voters of a state virtually appropriated the power to choose a senator, was that it produced not one, but two nominees for the presidency. The startling swiftness with which Lincoln rose to party leadership by 1860 should not obscure the fact that Douglas, too, climbed higher than ever before. Both men profited immensely from their strenuous efforts in 1858.

It is often said, however, that Douglas paid a high price for his re-election—that in order to win he was compelled to take a position which alienated the South and widened the split in the Democratic party. The statement is true, and yet it is not the whole truth; for a politician must choose from possible alternatives. Election results in other Northern states, where the Democratic party met nothing but defeat, testified eloquently to the soundness of Douglas's judgment in 1858. No one realized better than Lincoln that the Little Giant had adopted the strategy best calculated to prevent a Republican victory in 1860. His ultimate failure only verified the fact that in some circumstances even the best strategy is not good enough. The momentum gathered in their contest for a Senate seat carried both Lincoln and Douglas to the threshold of the White House, but only one could enter.

Six

The Famous "Freeport Question"

ONE OF THE FASCINATIONS of the Lincoln-Douglas debates is the pattern of paradox that can be traced in their consequences. Lincoln, the loser, did not sink back into the obscurity which ordinarily awaits a twice-defeated candidate for the Senate, but emerged instead as a serious presidential contender. Douglas's victory, on the other hand, is generally thought to have been gained at a ruinous cost, primarily because of what he was compelled to say in response to Lincoln's second question at Freeport. Few tableaux of American history are more familiar or striking than this famous exchange of August 27, 1858. The tall, awkward prairie lawyer cleverly pins his distinguished opponent upon the horns of a dilemma; the pugnacious Little Giant, his back to the wall, unhesitatingly chooses to risk the displeasure of slaveholders rather than that of his constituents:

LINCOLN: Can the people of a United States Territory, in any lawful way, against the wish of any citizen of the United States, exclude slavery from its limits prior to the formation of a State Constitution?

DOUGLAS: It matters not what way the Supreme Court may hereafter decide as to the abstract question whether slavery may or may not go into a territory under the constitution, the people have the lawful means to introduce it or exclude it as they please, for the reason that slavery cannot exist a day or an hour anywhere unless it is supported by local police regulations. Those police regulations can only be established by the local legislature, and if the people are opposed to slavery they will elect representatives to that body who will by unfriendly legislation effectually prevent the introduction of it into their midst.[1]

Momentous results are customarily attributed to this "Freeport doctrine," which retained the husk of the Dred Scott decision while saving the core of popular sovereignty. To put the matter in its bluntest terms, the Douglas pronouncement is said to have (1) secured his re-election to the Senate, but (2) destroyed much of his support in the South, and (3) divided the Democratic party, thus (4) contributing decisively to Lincoln's victory in 1860. The various qualifications and refinements that careful scholars usually add to this primitive causal analysis have not materially altered its effect. In the mainstream of American history-as-record, the Freeport question has become one of those pivots upon which great events turn. Lincoln, by one brilliant maneuver, "outgeneraled Douglas and split the Democrats."[2]

The skeptical investigator must deal not only with a sturdy folklore tradition but also with a certain amount of undeniable fact. The unfriendly legislation doctrine did indeed grate upon Southern ears and contribute to the disruption of the Democratic party. But to determine the *weight* of that contribution is the real historical problem and the aim of this chapter. In so far as a dissent is registered in the pages that follow, it is to the undue emphasis commonly put on the Freeport question and to the inflated estimate of its influence. Such emphasis tends to throw the debates themselves out of focus and to magnify the importance of finespun doctrinal differences in the breakup of the Democrats.

*

Before studying Douglas's *reply,* it will be well to take some notice of the legend that has grown up around the *question.* At Freeport, Lincoln began by answering the seven questions previously posed by his adversary at Ottawa and then countered with four of his own. The story goes that when he submitted

the latter to the scrutiny of certain advisers, they shook their
heads at number two. It would give Douglas a chance to increase
his popularity in antislavery circles, they warned. It might easily
cost Lincoln the election. But Lincoln, we are told, waved the
protests aside and declared, "I am after bigger game. The battle
of 1860 is worth a hundred of this."

Although the more extravagant aspects of this tale have won
only partial acceptance, the tradition that Lincoln asked the second Freeport question against the advice of several leading Republicans has never been seriously challenged.[3] At the very least
he is made to appear wiser and bolder than those around him,
with the result that one more colorful thread is woven into the
fabric of the Lincoln myth. Yet no part of the story can be sub-
stantiated by contemporary testimony. It turned up first as an
undocumented assertion in one of the 1860 campaign biographies
and was retold many times during the years that followed.[4]

In 1892, Horace White published his version, adding that he
had learned all the details from one of the men involved in the
attempt to dissuade Lincoln. This was Charles H. Ray, long
since dead, but in 1858 the chief editor of the Chicago *Tribune*.[5]
White chose the wrong witness, however; for there is ample
proof that Ray was on a business trip to New York at the time
of the alleged conference. Furthermore, he was in no mood to
preach caution. On the eve of his departure, he wrote as follows
to Congressman Elihu Washburne: "When you see Abe at Freeport, for God's sake tell him to 'Charge Chester! charge!' Do
not let him keep on the defensive . . . . We must not be parrying
all the while. We want the deadliest thrusts. Let us see blood
follow any time he closes a sentence."[6] So White's evidence is
not even good hearsay.

William H. Herndon had made no reference to the incident
in the first edition of his biography of Lincoln, published in 1889.
His memory was apparently jogged, however, by conversations
or correspondence with White, and he wrote out approximately
the same story in a letter to Jesse W. Weik, dated October 2,

1890. According to Herndon, he had received his information from Norman B. Judd, but there is good reason to believe, as we shall see, that Judd actually favored the asking of the second Freeport question. Herndon's account is therefore secondhand, based on a dubious source, and heavily influenced by White.[7]

Finally, in 1895, an eyewitness offered his belated corroboration. Joseph Medill's description of the Freeport episode, first published in his own Chicago *Tribune*, requires special attention because it was reprinted in the Sparks edition of the debates and has been relied upon by scholars of the first rank like Beveridge and Nevins.[8] Medill's recollection was that Lincoln showed him the questions on the train to Freeport and that he objected to the second one because it would enable the Little Giant to escape from a "tight place." Lincoln stubbornly insisted, however, that he would "spear it at Douglas" that afternoon. Before the debate, other prominent Republicans, at Medill's urging, argued the point with Lincoln, but to no avail. Two years later, just after the presidential election, Lincoln reminded Medill of their disagreement and asked, "Now don't you think I was right in putting that question to him?" "Yes Mr. Lincoln," Medill responded, "you were, and we were both right. Douglas' reply . . . undoubtedly hurt him badly for the Presidency but it re-elected him to the Senate . . . as I feared it would." Then Lincoln with a broad smile said, "Now I have won the place that he was playing for."

Medill had undoubtedly read White's version of the incident, published three years before. And now, by amplifying it and making himself the central figure along with Lincoln, he had constructed a delightful anecdote—in which, however, there was scarcely a word of truth. Having safely outlived all the men who might have contradicted his story, the *Tribune* editor, oddly enough, contradicted himself in the end. What really happened has become fairly clear with the discovery of two documents, one of them from Medill's own hand.

On August 23, two days after the Ottawa debate, Lincoln

sent letters to Ebenezer Peck and Norman B. Judd, Chicago Republican leaders who were both members of the state central committee. The Judd letter has never been found. The one to Peck, which has come to light only recently, reads as follows:

> I have just written Judd that I wish him and you to meet me at Freeport next Friday to give me the benefit of a consultation with you. Douglas is propounding questions to me, which perhaps it is not quite safe to wholly disregard. I have my view of the mode to dispose of them, but I also want yours and Judd's. I have written more at length to Judd, and would to you, but for lack of time. See Judd, you and he keep the matter to yourselves, and meet me at Freeport without fail.[9]

Peck and Judd had not planned to attend the Freeport debate, however, because a central committee meeting required their presence in Springfield the same weekend. Instead, they met with several other Republicans in Chicago on Thursday evening, the 26th, to discuss the strategy that Lincoln should follow at Freeport the next day. Medill attended the conference and was apparently detailed to report its conclusions. The Robert Todd Lincoln Collection, opened in 1947, contains a long letter which he wrote Friday morning and probably handed personally to Lincoln at Freeport. From the letter it is obvious that the primary concern of the Chicago conference had been to help Lincoln with his answers to the seven questions posed by Douglas at Ottawa. But along with advice on this subject, Medill transmitted the recommendation that Lincoln "put a few ugly questions" of his own. He went on to list some examples, including:

> Will you stand by the adjustment of the Kansas question on the basis of the English bill Compromise[?]
> Having given your acquiescence and sanction to the Dred Scott decision that destroys popular sovereignty in the Territories will you acquiesce in the other half of that decision when it comes to be applied to the states by the same court?
> What becomes of your vaunted popular sovereignty in [the] Territories since the Dred Scott decision?

Here, differently phrased, are not only the first and third, but finally the *second* question that Lincoln asked at Freeport. Judd, Peck, Medill, and the other Republican leaders were urging him to exploit the incompatibility of Douglas's principle and the verdict of the Supreme Court. In addition, Medill echoed Ray's plea for more aggressiveness. "Employ your best hour in pitching into Dug," he exhorted. "Make your assertions dogmaticall and unqualified. Be saucy . . . in other words give him h—l."[10]

*

The story of all the apprehensive talk about the dangerousness of the second Freeport question lacks both proof and credibility. The fact is that Lincoln did not decide to ask *the* question, but to ask *questions*—partly as a matter of *quid pro quo*,[11] and partly as a way of taking the offensive. Many of his friends thought that he had done too much backpedaling in the Ottawa debate.[12] Far from advocating restraint, they were, like the managers of a sluggish prize fighter, imploring him to "open up" in the next round, to "Charge Chester! charge!"

Once Lincoln made up his mind to fire a return volley of questions, it was hardly a display of "uncanny skill"[13] to select one that was already being asked on all sides. He himself had raised the point in an earlier speech,[14] and Republican newspapers had been hammering away for many months at the conflict between popular sovereignty and the Dred Scott decision. To cite an example, the Bloomington (Illinois) *Pantagraph* of July 15, 1858, printed eight questions directed at Douglas, and the first one read: "Do you believe that the people of a Territory, whilst a Territory, and before the formation of a State constitution, have the right to exclude slavery?" Shortly before the Freeport debate, Lincoln received from Charles L. Wilson of the Chicago *Journal* a newspaper clipping containing this same query.[15] It had also been suggested to him a few weeks earlier by a Quincy lawyer.[16] And Medill, as we know, included the substance of it in his list of last-minute instructions. Lincoln's final phrasing was an improvement, but otherwise it might be said that the celebrated question was virtually shoved into his hands as he stepped onto the platform. Since the celebrated reply, too, had been enunciated by Douglas on several previous occasions, not much was really new or surprising in the exchange at Freeport.

Not only evidence but logic is against the view that Lincoln deliberately courted defeat in order to deprive Douglas of Southern support for the presidency. Well before the debates began, Douglas's fight against the Lecompton constitution had alienated large numbers of slaveholders—so many, in fact, that Lincoln wrote late in July: "He cares nothing for the South—he knows he is already dead there."[17] Why, then, would this man who wanted so badly to become senator jeopardize his chances in order to kill something he considered "already dead"? Besides, if Lincoln did propose to knock Douglas out of the presidential race, there was scarcely a better way of doing it than by ousting him from the Senate; for such a defeat on his home grounds would have been a staggering blow to the Little Giant's prestige. It must be remembered also that whatever course Southern politicians took, the Republican party could capture the presidency in 1860 only by sweeping the North, and in Illinois, which was one of the most doubtful states, any strategy that hurt or helped Lincoln in 1858 would have been expected to exert a similar influence upon Republican prospects two years later. There was, in short, no observable conflict between Lincoln's personal ambition and the welfare of his party, hence no reason for the sacrifice often attributed to him.

Although Lincoln and his advisers apparently did not anticipate any ill effects from the asking of the second Freeport question, one must still consider the possibility that such effects did in fact ensue. Numerous historians have joined Medill in asserting that Douglas's reply at Freeport procured his re-election to the Senate.[18] Close examination reveals, however, that the assertion is demonstrably true only to the extent that it is pointless. By his anti-Lecompton heroics, Douglas had projected a new and attractive image of himself upon the public consciousness in the free states. Had he chosen at Freeport to smash that image, then the day would indeed have marked a turning point. Yet such a decision was beyond the realm of possibility because Douglas fully realized that any attempt to crawl back into the good graces of the slaveholders and the Buchanan administration would invite almost certain defeat. In other words, no one is likely to deny that Lincoln would have profited immensely if his opponent had elected to commit political suicide, but historical consequences are not ordinarily ascribed to improbable events that never happened.

The pertinent question, surely, is whether the things that *did* happen at Freeport actually changed enough votes to cause the defeat of no less than four Republican candidates for the state legislature. Since lack of data rules out an answer based on empirical investigation,[19] one can only rummage through the possibilities and take one's choice. Douglas, we must remember, was already in good standing with many moderate antislavery men as a result of the Lecompton struggle. Perhaps the Freeport doctrine won some additional voters to his side and perhaps the number was large enough to be important, but there is not the slightest evidence with which to prove it. Furthermore, in an election so close that a switch of a few hundred votes in the right places would have reversed the outcome, any one among scores of factors can be made decisive by definition. Republicans blamed their narrow defeat upon such things as the inequitable apportionment, the editorial antics of Horace Greeley, the influence of John J. Crittenden, the inclement weather on election day, and illegal voting by peripatetic Irishmen. Nobody at the time ventured to add the Freeport question to the list.

*

But now the more significant problem claims attention. What part did the Freeport doctrine play in the disruption of the Democratic party and the election of Lincoln? Beginning at the far end of the subject, it must be pointed out that the connection between the two latter events is by no means clear. That a united Democratic party could have retained the presidency in 1860 is possible, but hardly presumable. The election figures indicate that the division of Lincoln's opposition did not give him the victory but merely increased his electoral majority.[20] Yet there are good reasons for studying the Democratic split at Charleston. It severed one of the strongest bonds of union and helped prepare the South emotionally for secession. In the words of Roy F. Nichols, it was like "the bursting of a dike which unloosed an engulfing flood."[21] And there is no denying that the subject of bitterest dispute in the final hour of crisis was the issue raised by Lincoln at Freeport.

The dispute had roots that went much deeper than Lincoln's question, however; for the Freeport doctrine was of course the post–Dred Scott remnant of popular sovereignty. Throughout the previous decade, Democrats had been discussing the power of a territorial government to prohibit slavery, with no more definite results than some periodic agreements to camouflage their disagreement. What needs to be explained is why the issue should have become a matter of such deadly concern after 1858, when it was of less practical importance than ever before.

Although Douglas became its greatest champion, popular sovereignty had been broached in 1847 by Lewis Cass as a middle way between the Wilmot Proviso and the Calhoun-inspired proposition that slaveholders possessed an indefeasible right to take their property into any territory.* At first the principle was more commonly called "nonintervention." The two terms, while roughly equivalent, were in a sense also complementary. Nonintervention meant that Congress, whether as a matter of policy or because of constitutional inability, should not interfere with the "domestic institutions" of a territory.[22] Popular sovereignty

---

* Cass drew upon the ideas of other men in formulating his doctrine, but for practical purposes it may be said to have originated with his Nicholson letter of December 24, 1847.

lodged the control of those institutions with the territorial populations and their authorized governments. The practical result, it was thought, would be to banish the most dangerous of political issues from the halls of Congress—all in the name of local democracy. Introduced first as a piece of campaign strategy for the election of 1848, this formula was incorporated (in its nonintervention sense, at least) into the Compromise of 1850, established as official territorial policy by the Kansas-Nebraska Act, and acknowledged in the Democratic platform of 1856. In all of these applications, however, the principle retained a basic ambiguity which proved to be its most viable characteristic.*

The Cass-Douglas doctrine, which Northern Democrats assumed to mean territorial home rule on the slavery question, was imprecise enough to allow the shaping of a Southern interpretation that differed little from the views of Calhoun. Specifically, the principle of nonintervention implied congressional passivity and repudiated restrictive measures like the Missouri Compromise, but it in no way impaired the assertion of a Southern right, under the Constitution itself, to take slave property into the territories. And as long as the right was asserted, only a truncated version of popular sovereignty could be admitted into the Southern scheme of things; that is, a territory might establish or prohibit slavery when it framed a constitution in preparation for statehood, but not before. To construe the doctrine in this way was obviously to eviscerate it. Yet Northern Democrats, realizing the practical advantage of having different constructions under a cover of verbal accord, prudently avoided forcing the issue and even cooperated in the perpetuation of the ambiguity. Thus when Cass was confronted with an equivalent of the Freeport question in 1848, he flatly refused to clarify his Nicholson letter.[23] Two presidential elections later, Buchanan talked

---

* The phrase "squatter sovereignty" was often used interchangeably with "popular sovereignty," but it sometimes had other meanings: (1) the assumption of governing powers by settlers before they were authorized to do so, and (2) in the South, the unacceptable Northern interpretation of popular sovereignty.

out of both sides of his mouth as he interpreted the popular sovereignty plank in the Democratic platform.[24] And in a committee report the same year, Douglas made a remarkable attempt to run with both hares and hounds on this subject which was supposedly dear to his heart.[25]

But if the double meaning of popular sovereignty enabled Northern and Southern Democrats to keep up a thin pretense of unity on a divisive issue, it also served as a ready target for political opponents. Before Lincoln took up the Freeport question, it had been asked and answered many times—especially during the year 1856. For example, Lyman Trumbull challenged Douglas on the Senate floor to say whether the territorial legislature of Kansas had a right to exclude slavery.[26] In the other house, Humphrey Marshall of Kentucky chided the Democrats for peddling two contradictory explanations of the Kansas-Nebraska Act, and Galusha Grow of Pennsylvania demanded to know whether the Democratic platform meant that "previous to the formation of a State constitution the people of a Territory could prohibit or permit slavery."[27] In Georgia, meanwhile, an American candidate for presidential elector named Cincinnatus Peeples was badgering his Democratic opponent, Junius Hillyer, with the very same query.[28]

Douglas's reply to Trumbull was the standard one being offered by Democrats in 1856. The Kansas-Nebraska Act, he said, had conferred upon the territorial governments all the control over their domestic institutions that the Constitution allowed. But whether that included the power to deal with slavery was strictly a legal question and had been left to the judiciary. Douglas, in other words, plainly conceded that his brand of popular sovereignty might be unconstitutional and agreed to accept a decision of the Supreme Court in the matter.[29] This idea of dumping the whole problem into the lap of the Court, which can be traced back to the abortive Clayton compromise of 1848, was about as far removed as possible from the idea of leaving it to the people of a territory. Yet the two solutions had been more or less wrapped up together in the Utah and New Mexico Acts of 1850 and in the Kansas-Nebraska Act.[30] Thus the Democratic party, under pressure to enunciate a coherent territorial policy and incapable of doing so, could evade the consequences of its internal disunity by proposing to convert a political issue into a courtroom case. But of course if the Supreme Court ever rendered a definitive decision, this escape valve would cease to function.

There were some Democrats, however, who, instead of evading the issue, sought to minimize its seriousness. Buchanan, for instance, took note in his inaugural address of the difference between Northern and Southern versions of popular sovereignty and then pronounced it "a matter of but little practical importance."[31] It was as a contribution to this strategy of depreciation that the Freeport doctrine first appeared on the scene. Junius Hillyer in Georgia and James L. Orr of South Carolina, responding to Humphrey Marshall's taunts in Congress, were among those who anticipated Douglas's reply to Lincoln. So was Samuel A. Smith of Tennessee, who answered Galusha Grow as follows:

> I regard this as a question of no practicability. I have held that in a territorial capacity they had not the right to exclude slavery. Yet the majority of the people in the Territory will decide this question after all. In a Territory we must have laws, not to establish, but to *protect* the institution of slavery; and if a majority of the people of a Territory are opposed to the institution, they will refuse to pass laws for its protection.[32]

And what was the remedy if protection were refused? "None, sir," declared Orr, adding that slavery would then be "as well excluded as if the power was invested in the Territorial legislature, and exercised by them, to prohibit it."[33]

These statements were not entirely new. Upon other occasions, Southerners had conceded that even a full confirmation of their constitutional rights could accomplish only so much—that a certain residue of popular sovereignty would always survive as one of the extralegal facts of life.[34] Orr and Smith resorted to the Freeport doctrine in the hope of quieting controversy and mollifying the opponents of slavery. They soothingly implied that the North could safely yield the South its theoretical rights because in practice slavery would never go where it was not wanted. Later, when Douglas appropriated it, this unguent became an irritant, but the effects were still primarily cutaneous.

*

Before March 6, 1857, then, Northern and Southern Democrats were substantially united upon a negative principle of congressional nonintervention in the territories and had implemented it by repealing the Missouri Compromise. At the same time, they differed sharply over what positive principle should operate in the vacuum thereby created. But this disagreement had been muted by the obscurity of party pronouncements and an informal understanding that the whole problem was deposited with the Supreme Court. The Dred Scott decision put an end to the period of dissimulation, however, and compelled a redefinition of the Democratic party's position on the subject of slavery in the territories.

Southerners could see no room for further argument. Slavery had won its case in court, and Democrats of both sections were pledged to accept the verdict. The Northern wing of the party must therefore abandon popular sovereignty, except in its innocuous Southern version. This is precisely what James Buchanan proceeded to do. Yet for Douglas and others like him who were already hard pressed by Republicans at home, an abject surrender to the doctrines of Calhoun would mean disaster. Somehow the old face-saving ambiguity must be restored. If party loyalty dictated a formal assent to the Dred Scott decision, political necessity required that its teeth be drawn in the process of interpretation.

Actually, the Court had ruled only that Congress was without constitutional authority to bar slavery from the territories.

The Chief Justice, to be sure, had implied that territorial governments were similarly inhibited, and there was logic in the Southern argument that a power denied to Congress could not be delegated by it to a subordinate legislative body.[35] Nevertheless, Douglas was prepared to insist that the decision itself had no direct bearing upon territorial regulation of slavery; thus he could treat the Freeport question, when it came, as purely hypothetical.* His major resource, however, was bound to be the Smith-Orr doctrine of residual popular sovereignty. Speaking at Springfield on June 12, 1857, he delivered a powerful defense of the Buchanan administration, white supremacy, and the Dred Scott decision, but then added:

> While the right [to carry slaves into a territory] continues in full force under the guarantees of the Constitution, and cannot be divested or alienated by an act of Congress, it necessarily remains a barren and worthless right, unless sustained, protected and enforced by appropriate police regulations and local legislation prescribing adequate remedies for its violation. These regulations and remedies must necessarily depend entirely upon the will and wishes of the people of the Territory, as they can only be prescribed by the local Legislatures. Hence the great principle of popular sovereignty and self-government is sustained and firmly established by the authority of this decision.[36]

This speech received national attention, and, far from provoking a storm or splitting the party, it was highly praised in the Democratic press North and South. The Washington *Union,* which would lead the attack upon the Freeport doctrine in 1858, printed the address in full and said that it deserved "unqualified commendation."[37] Consequently there is reason to suspect that as long as Douglas remained loyal in other ways, Southerners were willing to view with tolerance his use of the Freeport doctrine as a sop to public opinion in Illinois.

The storm broke when Douglas took his stand against the

* This is why Douglas used the word "hereafter" in his reply to Lincoln at Freeport.

admission of Kansas with the Lecompton constitution; for here he was levying open war against the President and the South on a concrete issue of major importance—something that could not be tolerated. It was bad enough that he should bring about the defeat of the Lecompton measure and refuse to approve even the English compromise, but the Little Giant's worst offense in Southern eyes was his intimate collaboration with the Republican enemy throughout the legislative struggle. The man who had given aid and comfort to the Sewards, Wilsons, and Wades, who had become a special favorite of Horace Greeley, could never again command the full trust of the slaveholding states. In the volume and intensity of recrimination heaped upon him by the Southern press during the early months of 1858 there is adequate proof that Douglas had already sacrificed much of his standing in the South before he entered upon the contest with Lincoln. With scarcely an exception, the newspapers that denounced the Freeport doctrine had been denouncing its author for the better part of a year, while Southern editors who defended or tolerated Douglas before the Freeport debate maintained the same attitude afterward.*

During the Lecompton battle in Congress from December 1857 to May 1858, Douglas betrayed a curious reluctance to defend the constitutionality of popular sovereignty in the light

---

* Consulting numerous files of Southern newspapers for 1858, I found that Douglas's Chicago speech of July 9 had a much greater effect upon editorial opinion than did the Freeport doctrine. Denunciation of the latter was confined almost entirely to newspapers already bitterly inimical toward him like the Washington *Union,* the *North Carolina Standard,* the Charleston *Mercury,* the Mobile *Register,* and the Jackson *Mississippian.* A few journals which had either condoned or only mildly reproved Douglas's anti-Lecompton stand actually defended the Freeport doctrine. Among them were the Louisville *Democrat,* the Richmond *Enquirer,* and the Augusta *Constitutionalist.* A surprising number of Southern newspapers, furthermore, took little or no notice of the doctrine in the weeks after its enunciation, and some, like the Memphis *Appeal* and the Montgomery *Confederation,* even became more friendly toward Douglas after the debates began. Thus, Southern press opinion concerning Douglas in 1858 was both varied and variable, but one conclusion appears to be sound: the Freeport doctrine produced no significant change.

of the Dred Scott decision. Trumbull, in effect, raised the Freeport question on the Senate floor in February, but Douglas brushed it aside.[38] At one point, he even seemed on the verge of retreating to the sterile Southern definition of his cardinal principle.[39] He obviously wanted to avoid giving Administration leaders additional grounds for charging him with apostasy. Not until his return to Illinois in the summer did he resume use of the Freeport doctrine, and then it was more the progress of events than pressure from Lincoln that induced him to do so.

Douglas came home to a hero's welcome in Chicago on July 9, 1858, and made a speech that carried him past the point of no return in his relations with the Buchanan administration. During the final weeks of the congressional session, with the thorny Kansas problem temporarily resolved, the breach in the Democratic party had begun to heal. Douglas had left Washington in a conciliatory mood, knowing that his friends were negotiating a truce with the Administration. But as he traveled westward, Nichols says, the Illinois senator realized that the temper of the people would not permit the slightest backward step.[40] At Chicago, therefore, he renewed his attack upon the "Lecompton fraud" and the "arrogant" attempt to force it through Congress.[41] That ended all hope of reconciliation. The Administration continued its patronage reprisals, and pro-Lecompton newspapers redoubled their abuse of the party "traitor." Douglas, with the last bridge burned behind him, now had little reason to suppress his extenuating corollary to the Dred Scott decision. He gave the subject a prominent place in his very next speech, but not, it must be acknowledged, without some prompting from Abraham Lincoln.

It has escaped general notice that Lincoln actually posed the Freeport question when he spoke in reply to Douglas at Chicago on July 10, six weeks before the debates began. What was left of popular sovereignty since the Dred Scott decision, he demanded. "Can you get anybody to tell you now that the people of a territory have any authority to govern themselves in regard to this mooted question of Slavery, before they form a State Constitution?"[42] Douglas, although under no formal obligation to respond, was evidently eager to speak his mind. In speeches at Bloomington and Springfield, he not only reaffirmed the doctrine that he had enunciated the year before, but made it more aggressive by introducing the words "unfriendly legislation."[43] This went beyond the Smith-Orr version, which contemplated only a refusal to pass friendly laws, and bore a striking resemblance (as Lincoln later pointed out) to the principle of nullification.[44]

At Freeport, then, Douglas merely followed the course that he had already marked out for himself in adjusting to political circumstances which Lincoln exploited but in no way produced. The latter did tighten the screws a little when he attached the phrase "in any lawful way" to his famous question. But Douglas, if he had wished, could have skirted the legal issue by confining his attention to the inevitable fact of ultimate popular control.[45] Instead, he boldly declared that the people of a territory had the "lawful means" to exclude slavery. To legalistic Southerners the difference between means and lawful means was important, and such a statement could not fail to bring added censure upon its author. Only in this very restricted sense, however, is there any substance to the legend that Douglas walked into a trap at Freeport.

*

The Freeport doctrine, which had originated in offhand remarks of various Southerners, thus became more dangerous in the hands of Douglas and was at last angrily repudiated by the South. It is usually said that the doctrine made Douglas obnoxious in Southern eyes. Yet the reverse was perhaps equally true; that is, the doctrine was to some extent rendered repulsive by its association with Douglas. A case in point is the strange behavior of Jefferson Davis.

Fifteen days after the Freeport debate, the Mississippi senator, who had been vacationing in New England, addressed a

Democratic meeting at Portland. Anxious to disclaim his reputation as a narrow sectionalist, and apparently not yet aware of
Douglas's reply to Lincoln, he offered the following observations
on the territorial problem.

> If the inhabitants of any territory should refuse to enact such
> laws and police regulations as would give security to their
> property . . . it would be rendered more or less valueless, in
> proportion to the difficulty of holding it without such protec-
> tion. In the case of . . . slave property, the insecurity would
> be so great that the owner could not ordinarily retain it.
> Therefore, though the right would remain, the remedy being
> withheld, it would follow that the owner would be practically
> debarred . . . from taking slave property into a territory where
> the sense of the inhabitants was opposed to its introduction.
> So much for the oft-repeated fallacy of forcing slavery upon
> any community.[46]

Here Davis was unmistakably subscribing to the Smith-Orr version of the Freeport doctrine, using it in the customary way as
a formula of reassurance to those who feared the aggressiveness
of the slave power. Later, however, when he found himself quoted
in support of Douglas and fiercely criticized at home, he hastened
to belie the clear meaning of his words. Territorial governments,
he told a Mississippi audience, had the naked power but not the
legal authority to exclude slavery. The dependence of the institution upon local law conferred no "right to destroy," but rather
created "an obligation to protect."[47] With this explanation, which
was a brazen transposition of his Portland utterance, Davis sought
to purge himself of doctrinal affiliation with the renegade from
Illinois.* And during the next two years he continued to atone
for his slip by leading the Southern assaults upon Douglas in the
Senate.

---

* The difference between Davis in Maine and Davis in Mississippi is
essentially the difference between Douglas and his Southern critics. In
each case the legal right of the slaveholder is contrasted with the effective
power of the territorial population, and one's final judgment depends upon
which is given primacy.

The distinction between power and right was the key to the next phase of the controversy. There were really two parts to the Freeport doctrine: a statement of fact (that slavery could not survive without local protection) and an inference (that it therefore could not be forced upon an unwilling people). But the Southern leadership now proceeded to stand the doctrine on its head by conceding the fact and then drawing an entirely different conclusion. The Richmond *Enquirer* pointed the way in what purported to be a defense of Douglas. With an irony that may or may not have been intended, it characterized him as an honest observer who had done the South the distinct service of demonstrating a need for federal protection of slavery in the territories.[48] Thus the Freeport doctrine was to be converted into an argument for a territorial slave code.

This handful of dust obscured no one's vision, however, for it was obvious that the *Enquirer* had misrepresented Douglas's position. At Jonesboro, on September 15, Lincoln cleared the air when he propounded what might be called the second half of the Freeport question:

> If the slaveholding citizens of a United States Territory should need and demand Congressional legislation for the protection of their slave property in such territory, would you, as a member of Congress, vote for or against such legislation?[49]

Douglas responded rather vaguely by reaffirming the principle of nonintervention, but in a subsequent debate he explicitly declared his opposition to a congressional slave code for the territories.[50]

And so Northern and Southern Democrats were at last brought face to face over the paltry remnant of an issue that had long been troublesome but never a sufficient reason for breaking up the party.* Back in the Senate, Douglas was greeted with

---

* There is no need here to enter into a detailed description of Lincoln's powerful assaults upon the Freeport doctrine, that "bare absurdity," as he called it, which maintained that "a thing may be lawfully driven from a place where it has a lawful right to stay." Unlike most Southern critics of the doctrine, Lincoln rejected as "historically false" its basic premise that

hostility by many of his colleagues and removed from the chairmanship of the Committee on Territories. Then, in February of 1859, Albert G. Brown of Mississippi issued a demand for the protection of slavery in the territories and set off a bitter debate which ended with Davis and Douglas snarling defiance at one another. The embattled Illinoisan continued the controversy in his provocative *Harper's* article later that year, and Davis renewed the Southern attack with a series of resolutions early in 1860. The running battle finally carried over into the Charleston Convention, where the rejection of a slave-code plank was used by Southern delegates as the excuse for their withdrawal.[51]

In retrospect, the whole quarrel seems utterly senseless because nothing of practical value was at stake. Douglas and his Southern adversaries were agreed that a slaveholder had the legal right to take slaves into any territory. They agreed also that such a right would be barren without the protection of local laws. They disagreed as to whether unfriendly local legislation should be offset by federal intervention. But on the other hand, it was more or less agreed that a test case for the issue could not be produced. Although challenged to put their demands in the form of specific bills, the Southerners refused to go beyond hollow generalities. "We want a recognition of our right, because it is denied," said Judah P. Benjamin of Louisiana, "but we do not want to exercise it now, because there is no occasion for exercising it now." Asked about Kansas, where the territorial legislature had passed a law prohibiting slavery, Benjamin replied that he was not interested because there was no hope of its becoming a slave state.[52] Thus he frankly admitted that congressional intervention would be futile in the one place where it was needed.

---

slavery required police protection in order to enter new country. On the other hand, Lincoln agreed with Southerners that *if* the Dred Scott decision was a sound construction of the Constitution (which he, of course, denied, but which Douglas affirmed), then the slaveholders had every right to full protection, and the Freeport doctrine was a "monstrous" invitation to lawlessness. (*Collected Works,* III, 130–32, 278–79, 316–18, 417–19, 449–50.) For an enlightening discussion of Lincoln's views and of the Freeport doctrine as "a calculated indoctrination in incontinence," see Jaffa, *Crisis of the House Divided,* pp. 352–59.

The obtrusion of the slave-code question makes sense only in the way that a chip on the shoulder makes sense—as a pretext for fighting, as the symbol of deep-seated antagonisms. The conduct of the Douglas Democrats is easy enough to understand. Losing ground steadily to Republicans at home, they simply could not yield another inch to the slaveholders. But why did the South press its hopeless pursuit of an almost useless prize? A satisfactory answer is difficult to find. Though some Southern leaders may have desired to break up the Democratic party as a step toward secession, the motives of the majority were too complex and variable to be explained with the convenient word "conspiracy." Among the influences at work, there was a feeling that it would be humiliating to be cheated of the Dred Scott victory, however little it might actually be worth; a bitter aftertaste of anger and frustration from the Lecompton struggle; a knowledge that the presidential nomination would be wide open if Douglas could be sidetracked; and, of course, a fierce personal animosity toward the recreant Illinois senator.

The most fundamental factor of all, however, was a vague and perhaps unreasoning sense of apprehension which was something more than the specific fear of abolitionism. Southerners could see the walls closing in upon them, and the defection of Douglas vividly dramatized the growing isolation of slave society. Above everything else, the South wanted security for the future. It was fighting dangers that had not yet fully materialized, and the battlefields available for such phantom warfare were neither numerous nor spacious. In the end, as Nichols says, the Southern leaders "sought refuge in a formula."[53] They drew an arbitrary line on the ground and took their stand behind it. But there was much more on either side of that line than an interpretation of the Dred Scott decision; for the rending of the great Democratic party was caused by the same massive, complex, and persistent forces that were dividing the nation itself. In the total picture, the Freeport question appears as one of the rivulets contributing to a mighty stream.

Furthermore, emphasis upon the Freeport episode has tended

to obscure the real significance of the Lincoln-Douglas debates. In 1860, there were actually two presidential elections, and the one in the South between Bell and Breckinridge proved to be irrelevant. It was the decision of the free states (well-nigh unanimous in terms of electoral votes) that determined the subsequent course of events. And every element of that fateful choice was embodied in the Illinois contest of 1858, as the same candidates and same opposing principles competed for supremacy in one of the most critical states. It is in the representative appeals of both men to the Northern voter, not in any side maneuvers directed toward Southern opinion, that one finds the main themes of the debates. The results of this Illinois election in 1858, revealing that the most powerful Northern Democrat, in spite of his praiseworthy stand against the Lecompton constitution, could not command a majority of the popular vote in his own state, foreshadowed the political revolution of two years later.

*

In summary, it seems reasonable to suggest that the famous exchange at Freeport is not the key to the historical significance of the great debates; that no unusual amount of cleverness or originality was required to draft the question; that Lincoln included it among his queries at the urging of his friends, rather than against their advice; that there was nothing very decisive about Douglas's reply at Freeport because he had already fully committed himself on the subject, and his earlier pronouncements were easily available to Southern critics; that the Freeport doctrine was elicited more by the logic of circumstances than by Lincoln's questioning; that Douglas's opposition to the Lecompton constitution was the principal reason for his loss of standing in the South; and that the Freeport doctrine, for all the talk about it, was only a superficial factor in the disruption of the Democratic party.

Seven

The Path to the Presidency

TALK OF LINCOLN as a presidential possibility began in a modest way immediately after the election of 1858. Some of it was no doubt complimentary and consolatory—a tribute to his performance in the hard, close fight with Douglas. It came for the most part from small-town editors and other obscure persons who were indulging in the national sport of president-making. Their feeble voices mingled with a chorus of countless sponsors offering dozens of names for consideration.[1] Yet the results of the Illinois election compelled Republicans everywhere to take a respectful look at this new party leader who had arisen on the Western prairie. The popular vote indicated that the state hung in the balance for 1860 and would require special attention, perhaps even a place on the national ticket. And Lincoln had proved himself a match for the leading Democratic contender.

As the months passed, scattered support for Lincoln continued to manifest itself, chiefly but not exclusively in Illinois. With increasing frequency his name appeared on the long lists of potential candidates that editors liked to compile. He himself at first refused to take the idea seriously and more than once protested that he was not "fit for the Presidency."[2] But a change gradually came over Lincoln during 1859; this was his year of self-discovery. With a new confidence gained from the contest with Douglas, he began to assume the role of a national leader, even intervening discreetly in the politics of other states.[3] His horizon had widened, and within a four-month period from August to December he delivered political speeches in Illinois, Iowa,

Ohio, Indiana, Wisconsin, and Kansas. By autumn he was fast
becoming, without acknowledging it, a presidential candidate in
earnest.

State pride and the measure of fame that he had achieved
in the senatorial campaign gave Lincoln his first push toward the
presidency, but a host of other factors contributed to his ultimate
success on the third ballot at Chicago. The dramatic story of that
triumph has often been told and need not be repeated here in all
its complex detail. It is enough, perhaps, to point out and briefly
examine three aspects of Lincoln's spectacular rise to power: his
own skillful work in building upon the reputation acquired from
the debates with Douglas; the firm and united support that he
managed to obtain from Illinois Republicans; and the peculiar
political conditions that made him, on the eve of the national
convention, something more than a favorite son.

*

Having spent more than usual, and earned less, for nearly half
a year, Lincoln at the end of the 1858 canvass was, in his own
words, "absolutely without money now for even household purposes." The time had come once again to set politics temporarily
aside and concentrate upon the practice of law. "This year I must
devote to my private business," he declared.[4] At first it was not
difficult to abide by the resolution, but when various state campaigns got under way late in the summer of 1859, Lincoln began
receiving invitations to participate and found several of them
irresistible.[5]

His most important expedition of the season was into Ohio
during the third week of September. Republican leaders there
had summoned his aid after learning that Douglas intended to deliver a series of speeches in the state, and Lincoln was delighted to
resume hostilities with his old adversary. He spoke at Columbus
(nine days after Douglas), at Dayton, and at Cincinnati (eight
days after Douglas), then stopped off in Indianapolis for a fourth
address on his way home.[6] The tour proved to be virtually an

extension of the great debates, for Lincoln made every speech a slashing rebuttal to the Little Giant's recent public utterances, and especially to his essay in *Harper's Magazine*. Douglas, on the other hand, had two battles to fight; he divided his time between denouncing the Republicans and bidding defiance to his enemies within the Democratic party. As a visiting dignitary Lincoln was something less than a match for Douglas. The local fame that followed him from Illinois suffered in contrast with the other's national reputation. Yet the Ohio speeches brought Lincoln once again to the attention of the whole country, and when the Republicans swept the state in October, he was awarded a share of the credit.

Eight days after his return from Ohio, Lincoln set out for Milwaukee, where he delivered a nonpartisan address before the Wisconsin Agricultural Society and then followed it with three political speeches in the area. During the next two months his public appearances were confined to the vicinity of Springfield, but the first day of December found him in Kansas for a round of speeches on the eve of the territorial election. Warmly received, Lincoln went home a serious entrant in the presidential race, if he had not been one before. Soon he was dispatching an autobiographical sketch to the corresponding secretary of the state central committee, completing arrangements for publication of the debates with Douglas, and drafting the speech which he had agreed to make in New York near the end of February.[7] Just before Christmas, too, there came the good news that Chicago had been chosen as the site of the national convention. Meanwhile, support for Lincoln and resistance to Seward were growing in Illinois and various other states, as the effects of the John Brown raid strengthened the argument of those Republicans who wanted a relatively conservative candidate.

By the time Lincoln boarded a train for New York on February 23, 1860, his candidacy was more or less out in the open. He had authorized a group of party managers in the state to work for his nomination and was now counting upon nothing less than the full support of the Illinois delegation, especially since the influential *Press and Tribune* had recently given him an emphatic endorsement.[8] At Cooper Institute four days later, with eloquence and dignity he brought his preconvention efforts to an impressive culmination and in effect measured himself against Seward on the latter's home ground. Encouraged by the abundant praise awarded the address, he proceeded into New England and before a succession of enthusiastic audiences completed the most strenuous two weeks of campaigning (twelve major speeches in thirteen days) of his entire career.[9] Weary, but in high spirits, he arrived home on March 14, having gained not only the respect of many Eastern Republicans but a firmer hold upon the loyalty of Illinois. Before the end of the month, a pamphlet edition of the Cooper Institute address was in wide circulation, and the first copies of *Political Debates between Lincoln and Douglas* were coming off the press. Lincoln, although not yet a major contender, had already risen above the status of a mere favorite son. Writing to an Ohio friend on March 24, he explained his position and strategy: "My name is new in the field; and I suppose I am not the *first* choice of a very great many. Our policy, then, is to give no offence to others—leave them in a mood to come to us, if they shall be compelled to give up their first love."[10]

In Lincoln's speeches, correspondence, and general conduct after 1858, some historians discern a pronounced shift toward conservatism. Perhaps the most emphatic expression of this viewpoint comes from Reinhard H. Luthin, whose contributions to Lincoln scholarship include the latest full-scale biography and an important monograph on the campaign of 1860. According to Luthin, the House Divided address was Lincoln's only display of antislavery radicalism—a document "unique among his state papers"—which he thereafter endeavored to "explain away." In his strategy for 1860, Luthin maintains, Lincoln was inclined to put expediency ahead of principle. He "muffled the slavery issue," advised that radical tendencies be "toned down," and wisely followed a "conservative course." The theme of his Cooper Institute and New England speeches was "conservatism, caution, and conciliation." Victory came to him at Chicago because he was "vastly more moderate" than Seward on the slavery question.[11]

Although not without an element of truth, this interpretation of Lincoln's behavior during the eighteen months preceding his nomination is neither adequate nor accurate. In the first place, the word "conservative" can have only a very restricted meaning when it is used to describe a man whom 60 per cent of the American electorate considered too radical for the presidency. Within the Republican party, to be sure, Lincoln exercised a restraining influence upon the more aggressive opponents of slavery. He had done so from the beginning, guided by conviction no less than political discretion. But at the same time he took a firm stand against the disposition in some quarters to compromise Republican principles for the sake of attracting conservative votes. His letters and speeches of the period indicate that he was more worried about backsliding and excessive opportunism than about antislavery extremism. They embody no retreat whatsoever from the views expressed in 1858. Lincoln's position in the Republican party remained the same. He was neither on the left wing nor the right, but very close to dead center.

Like all practical-minded Republicans, Lincoln gave much thought to the problem of carrying the five free states that had helped elect Buchanan in 1856 and, accordingly, to the necessity of winning over the Whig-Americans who had voted for Fillmore in those states. Some apparent ways of accomplishing this purpose received his approval; others did not. He was willing, for instance, to accept a conservative antislavery man, even a Southerner, as the Republican standard-bearer.[12] He also deprecated militant flourishes likely to alarm moderates and warned Salmon P. Chase in particular that a resolution demanding repeal of the Fugitive Slave Law would "explode" the national convention if it were introduced.[13] On the other hand, Lincoln stood resolutely opposed to lowering the Republican platform by so much as a "hair's breadth," and he doubted the wisdom of broadening it with planks not directly related to the issue of slavery extension.[14]

In Lincoln's speeches after 1858, there was the same ambivalence that had characterized his earlier discussions of slavery. Neither conservative nor radical, but a combination of both, he favored slow, firm progress toward a revolutionary goal. The Republicans, he said again and again, had no aggressive intentions toward the South, no wish to establish racial equality, in fact, no purpose except "to place this great question of slavery on the very basis on which our fathers placed it."[15] Yet in other passages Lincoln reaffirmed the house-divided doctrine, even identifying it with Seward's "irrepressible conflict." At Cooper Institute, he declared that Southerners would be satisfied with nothing less than Northern approval of slavery by word and deed. He frequently repeated his warning that the course advocated by Douglas would lead inevitably to nationalization of the institution. And most important, he insisted that there must be a national policy which recognized and dealt with slavery as a wrong. Such policy was authorized, he argued in reply to the Dred Scott decision, by the general welfare clause of the Constitution.[16] Thus for Lincoln the restriction of slavery continued to be not only an immediate objective in itself, but the means of determining the moral status of slavery in a nation that had been dedicated to human liberty.

*

In Decatur, on May 10, 1860, the Republican state convention instructed Illinois delegates to "vote as a unit" for Lincoln at Chicago and "use all honorable means to secure his nomination."* This, his first formal step toward the presidency, gave Lincoln not only twenty-two convention votes but a psychological advantage over candidates like Chase of Ohio and Simon Cam-

---

* It was at Decatur, too, that Lincoln's frontier background was shrewdly dramatized with a display of fence rails that he had allegedly cut thirty years before. He promptly became, and would remain forevermore, the "Rail Splitter" from Illinois.

eron of Pennsylvania who were unable to command unanimous support in their respective states. Some such endorsement had been expected for months and was a foregone conclusion by the time the delegates assembled at Decatur. Yet Lincoln did not obtain it without effort. Indeed, considering all the hazards and alternative possibilities, his success was in some ways extraordinary.

For one thing, the Illinois Republican organization was plagued with dissension in the early months of 1860. Rivalry for the gubernatorial nomination and a bitter feud among party leaders at Chicago revived much of the old factional jealousy and distrust that had been submerged in the battle against Douglas. The chief troublemaker was John Wentworth, editor of the Chicago *Democrat,* whose political career and newspaper, to his intense dissatisfaction, had both entered a period of decline. Wentworth blamed his eclipse primarily upon the *Press and Tribune* and its allies, especially Norman B. Judd. In his fight for survival against these powerful enemies, he hoped to enlist the aid of Lincoln and perhaps even install himself as the latter's political manager.[17]

During 1859, therefore, Wentworth launched a series of violent editorial attacks upon Judd, whom he accused of mismanaging the 1858 campaign, wasting party funds, betraying Lincoln, and using his power as state chairman to promote Trumbull for the presidency and himself for the governorship. Coming from Long John alone, these charges might not have carried much weight, but they were quickly taken up and repeated by other Republicans, including Lincoln's close friend, David Davis, and his law partner, William Herndon. Stung to a fury, Judd struck back at Wentworth with a libel suit for huge damages, and on the same day (December 1, 1859) he dashed off a reproachful letter to Lincoln demanding vindication. Wentworth, in turn, with characteristic brashness asked Lincoln to serve as his counsel. Republican leaders throughout the state, although divided in their sympathies, agreed that the quarrel must be smothered before it caused serious damage. More than one urged Lincoln to step in as mediator.[18]

Lincoln knew the hazards of peacemaking and was reluctant to give any appearance of taking sides in the heated gubernatorial contest, since the three leading candidates—Judd, Leonard Swett, and Richard Yates—were all personal friends whose support he needed. Yet justice, self-interest, and party welfare all seemed to require his intervention. Accordingly, he first proceeded to write for publication a letter warmly praising Judd's loyalty and skill, but at the same time affirming his own neutrality with regard to the governorship. Later, he also attempted to patch up a truce between Wentworth and Judd, even drafting terms for the settlement of their lawsuit.[19]

There were some disturbing repercussions when the letter defending Judd appeared in print near the end of January, but Lincoln cleverly used them as an excuse for asking a favor in return. Writing to Judd on February 9, he confessed that it would "hurt some . . . to not get the Illinois delegates," and then added:

> Your discomfitted assailants are most bitter against me; and they will, for revenge upon me, lay to the Bates egg in the South, and to the Seward egg in the North, and go far towards squeezing me out in the middle with nothing. Can you not help me a little in this matter, in your end of the vineyard?[20]

It was just one week later that the *Press and Tribune,* which had been sternly noncommittal on the subject of the presidency, came out enthusiastically for Lincoln. Judd, who had close ties with the newspaper, probably influenced its decision. At least he wrote a few days later: "You saw what the Tribune said about you. Was it satisfactory?"[21]

Meanwhile, the feud between Wentworth and Judd was coming to a climax in Chicago. Long John had entered the mayoral race and won the Republican nomination in spite of savage opposition from the Judd forces. The latter were now torn between hatred for the nominee and dismay at the thought of turning the city over to the Democrats just before it played host to the Republican National Convention. In the end, they yielded to heavy pressure from party leaders. The *Press and Tribune* gave Wentworth its sullen support, and Judd himself, perhaps at Lincoln's urging, went through the motions of advocating his enemy's election. The libel suit was quietly put aside, and on March 7, Long John swept to an easy victory at the polls.[22] Republican newspapers hailed the outcome as a portent of success in the approaching national contest.

During the next two months, while Lincoln moved steadily forward as a presidential candidate, the fierce struggle over the governorship continued to cause bad feeling among Illinois Republicans. Judd appeared to be the strongest contender, but he ultimately met the same fate that awaited Seward. In addition to his personal enemies, many Republicans were persuaded that he could not carry the middle counties and thus lacked "availability." At the Decatur convention, Judd led on the early ballots, only to see his opponents combine and nominate Yates. Grievously disappointed, he nevertheless delivered a generous speech of acquiescence, and the delegates, with tension relaxed, were all the more ready to demonstrate their unity in an emphatic endorsement of Lincoln. Throughout the entire affair, Lincoln had displayed the ability to act forcefully and yet impartially as the leader of his party, holding its disparate elements together.

In sharp contrast with the spirited competition for the gubernatorial nomination, only one presidential candidate emerged in Illinois. Lincoln had no serious rival for the position of favorite son, and this, on the surface, seems a little odd, since he was nominally outranked by at least two Republican leaders in the state, Governor William H. Bissell and Senator Lyman Trumbull. Bissell, who had been only a middling success as governor, was in declining health by 1860 and succumbed to pneumonia on March 18. But with Trumbull it was a different story. A man of intellectual vigor and no little oratorical ability, he had won a reputation as one of the stronger Republicans in the Senate.

During 1859 and 1860, there was talk in various southerly counties about placing him on the national ticket.[23] Trumbull apparently did not encourage the movement, and it eventually subsided. At the same time, he remained aloof from the Lincoln boom, while offering no open resistance to it. Opposed to Seward, he favored John McLean, the seventy-five-year-old Supreme Court Justice who had given Frémont his only competition for the presidential nomination in 1856. Any explanation of Lincoln's success in obtaining a firm endorsement at the Decatur convention is incomplete without some consideration of Trumbull's failure to either challenge or support him.

Until 1858, Trumbull had been the state's most prominent Republican, but the debates with Douglas pushed Lincoln to the fore. Besides, with the advantage of being at home and in close contact with local leaders, Lincoln from the beginning had played a more active part in the management of the state organization. Whether or not his national prestige surpassed Trumbull's by 1860, he unquestionably exercised greater power in Illinois. The key to Trumbull's conduct, however, was his own vulnerability. Having entered the Senate more or less by accident in 1855, he now faced a stiff fight for re-election, especially in the central counties where Lincoln had been beaten two years before. The legislative contest, with the apportionment unchanged, would be the hardest for Republicans to win. Lincoln pledged his full support and explicitly disclaimed any thought of competing for the seat himself, thus giving Trumbull a clear field. But an open struggle with Lincoln over the presidency would no doubt divide the party in Illinois and jeopardize the Senator's chances of re-election. Wisely, he chose to settle for the bird in hand. And Lincoln, as the national convention drew near, virtually warned him to walk carefully:

> You better write no letters which can possibly be distorted into opposition, or quasi opposition to me. There are men on the constant watch for such things out of which to prejudice my peculiar friends against you. While I have no more sus-

picion of you than I have of my best friend living, I am kept in a constant struggle against suggestions of this sort. I have hesitated some to write this paragraph, lest you should suspect I do it for my own benefit, and not for yours; but on reflection I conclude you will not suspect me.[24]

Wanting, above all, a presidential nominee who would strengthen the party's appeal in central Illinois, Trumbull aligned himself with the opponents of Seward and to that extent aided Lincoln's cause. His preference for McLean reflected an emphasis on availability, but it may also have sprung from a vague hope of becoming the aged Justice's running mate.[25] Lincoln, however, was anything but disturbed by the injection of McLean's name into discussion of the presidential contest. In fact, he encouraged it, confident that the Republicans would not nominate anyone so old, and asking nothing better than that they should go looking for a younger man with similar qualifications.

Lincoln's biggest obstacle in Illinois was the inability of many Republicans to take him seriously as a rival of men with far more illustrious records of public service. State pride, which encouraged allegiance to a favorite son, was in some degree offset by the desire to be an "original" supporter of the candidate who won the nomination. Cameron, Chase, McLean, and various lesser figures had scattered backing in Illinois at the beginning of 1860, and there were stronger movements for Seward and Edward Bates of Missouri. Seward, although fallen in popularity since his alleged cooperation with Douglas, remained the first choice of many Germans and antislavery militants of Whig background.[26] Bates, on the other hand, was well liked by conservatives in the southern half of the state. None of these elements displayed much hostility toward Lincoln, but they regarded his candidacy in its earlier stages with courteous skepticism. Governor Bissell, for example, wrote to Chase in February explaining that he really favored the Ohioan, but could not say so publicly because it would seem "ungracious" to Lincoln. Then he added: "Still, I do not suppose that many of our friends seriously expect to secure his nomination . . . In fact they would be very well satisfied, probably, if he could secure the second place on the ticket."²⁷

It was undoubtedly Lincoln's Cooper Institute address and impressive tour of New England that convinced many Illinoisans of his presidential stature. Furthermore, with Seward's name anathema in one part of the state and Bates unacceptable in the other, Lincoln proved to be about the only man upon whom Illinois Republicans could unite. Thus even in his own state he was to some extent a compromise candidate—an embodiment of availability.

In spite of all the enthusiasm that accompanied it, there was a tentative quality in the demonstration for Lincoln at Decatur. Delegates talked a good deal about their "second choice," indicating, says William E. Baringer, that they "did not expect to vote for Lincoln very long when the balloting began at Chicago."²⁸ It seems likely that his Illinois managers went to the national convention hoping for a miracle, but anticipating nothing better than the vice-presidential nomination. Lincoln, the realist, probably shared their views.²⁹ But when they arrived on the scene and sounded out certain key delegations, the Lincoln men discovered that their prospects were brighter than anyone had dreamed.

*

The Republican delegates who converged on Chicago in the middle of May were well aware that their party, having no strength in the South, needed almost a clean sweep of the North to capture the presidency. More specifically, of the four Northern states that had voted for Buchanan in 1856 (New Jersey, Pennsylvania, Indiana, and Illinois), the Republicans would have to carry at least two, including Pennsylvania, or the other three if Pennsylvania were lost. The delegates from these states had favored McLean instead of Frémont at the 1856 convention, and there was a widespread feeling that their judgment must be deferred to in choosing the nominee for 1860. This, in turn, meant that special attention must be given to satisfying the conservative Whig-Americans who held the balance of power in each of the four critical states, and who had voted in large numbers for Fillmore at the previous election. The difficult problem confronting the Republican party was that its most prominent and deserving candidate did not seem to meet the peculiar needs of the hour.

Lincoln's victory at Chicago came as a corollary to the rejection of William H. Seward. A tested veteran of many political battles, Seward stood first in Republican ranks and was the logical choice for the presidential nomination. But his reputation as an antislavery radical (by no means entirely merited), his open record of opposition to Know-Nothingism, and his long feud with the Fillmore wing of New York Whiggery all counted heavily against him in the very regions where the election would be decided. So the cry was raised that Seward could not win, that a more available candidate must be found.

Yet most of the other leading contenders also had serious shortcomings. Chase was considered more radical than Seward; Cameron's record did not inspire much confidence in either his honesty or his devotion to the antislavery cause; Bates, an elderly, lackluster figure who had supported Fillmore in 1856, was especially objectionable to the Germans and could hardly be called a Republican at all. Some of the lesser candidates in the field were more suitable, but their opportunity would come only if the leaders faltered. In addition, there was Lincoln, whose qualifications, when scrutinized, proved to be impressive.[30]

Lincoln's attitude toward slavery was actually similar to Seward's and in some respects more inflexible. Yet he managed to appear conservative in comparison with the New Yorker, primarily because he had been less prominent in the antislavery wars. Personally opposed to nativism, he had never attacked it publicly and was reasonably acceptable to Know-Nothings as well as foreigners. His lack of experience and standing in national politics had been partially remedied by the debates with Douglas, and besides, there was a certain advantage in the very freshness of his fame. His Kentucky birth and frontier background would be campaign assets. As a Westerner and former Whig, he could be trusted to sustain homestead, tariff, and internal improvements legislation. And he was the favorite son of Illinois, third behind Pennsylvania and Indiana on the list of critical states. These were the considerations that ultimately made Lincoln the rallying point of the anti-Seward forces.

The growing emphasis upon moderation and availability in Republican talk about the presidential nomination did not spring entirely from the memory of defeat in 1856. The John Brown raid, which Southerners held up as the natural consequence of antislavery agitation, had thrown the party on the defensive. Democratic gains in certain New England spring elections caused some anxiety. The entry of John Bell in the presidential race as the nominee of the Constitutional Union party darkened prospects of absorbing the Whig-Americans. And finally, the spectacular disruption of the Democratic party at Charleston early in May, while highly encouraging to the Republicans, was not regarded as an unmixed blessing; for the expected nomination of Douglas by Northern Democrats when they reassembled at Baltimore would bring a popular and persuasive campaigner into competition for the moderate vote in the free states. A contest between Seward and Douglas, it was argued, might well throw the election into the House of Representatives, where a Republican victory seemed most unlikely.[31]

The Republican platform written at Chicago reflected some of the same opportunism that was to influence the choice of a candidate. The slavery planks were a little more moderate and flexible than those of 1856,* and a variety of special interests were

---

* Many historians exaggerate the "conservatism" of the Republican platform for 1860, however. The statement is sometimes made that less than one-third of it dealt with slavery, whereas five-sixths of the one written in 1856 had done so. This is utterly inaccurate, as any reading of the two documents will reveal. It is true that the platform committee in 1860 deleted the earlier reference to "those twin relics of barbarism, polygamy and slavery," and it added a section which in effect condemned the John Brown raid. Moreover, the cardinal principle of Republicanism was restated in

courted with resolutions opposing anti-foreigner legislation and endorsing internal improvements, a homestead law, a Pacific railroad, and some degree of tariff protection. Opposition to slavery obviously was still the primary, but no longer the only purpose of the Republican party. The platform received a unanimous and enthusiastic vote of approval at about six o'clock in the evening of May 17, the second day of the convention, and the delegates, after some hesitation, chose to adjourn until the next morning, instead of proceeding immediately to the nomination of a presidential candidate. This proved to be a decision of immense importance because it gave opponents of Seward additional time in which to mobilize.

Already there were clear signs that Lincoln was becoming the main obstacle in the New Yorker's path. Perhaps the turning point of the whole convention was the decision of the Indiana delegation, which had no candidate of its own, to vote for Lincoln on the first ballot. This commitment, a magnificent gain in itself, also influenced the Pennsylvania delegates, most of whom now agreed to accept Lincoln as their second choice. Accordingly, when the hour arrived for placing names in nomination, a two-man race had already begun to take shape, with Seward in the lead but Lincoln possessing the greater momentum.

The first ballot had scarcely begun before it became apparent that Seward was weaker and Lincoln stronger than anyone had

---

more pliable terms. Instead of insisting upon "positive legislation" prohibiting slavery in every territory, the party promised to enact such legislation whenever it should become "necessary." But later passages specifically denied the power of a territorial legislature to "give legal existence to slavery" and denounced popular sovereignty as a "deception and fraud." The net effect was to offer a territory the choice of excluding slavery itself or having it done by Congress. Also, the 1860 platform contained a section strongly condemning threats of disunion as an "avowal of contemplated treason"—something that had not been present in the earlier document. (The one-third and five-sixths comparison was apparently first made by Emerson David Fite in his *The Presidential Campaign of 1860* [New York, 1911], p. 124. It is repeated in Luthin, *The First Lincoln Campaign,* p. 149. The platforms of 1856 and 1860 are printed in Edward Stanwood, *A History of the Presidency from 1788 to 1897* [Boston, 1912], pp. 271–73, 291–94.)

expected. Leading off in the roll call, the New England states with 82 votes at their disposal gave Seward a disappointing 32, Lincoln a surprising 19. In this, as in each of the succeeding ballots, New England reflected with considerable accuracy the will of the entire convention. The tabulations revealed that Seward had 173½ votes and Lincoln 102, while ten other candidates were scattered far behind. With a total of 465 votes being cast,* Seward needed only 60 more to win, but there was little room in which to maneuver for them because a sectional wall had been raised against him. The states of the lower North, stretching from New Jersey to Iowa, had given Seward only 3½ votes out of 170, whereas Lincoln had received 62, with promises of more to come.

On the second ballot, New England cast 33 votes for Seward, 36 for Lincoln, and in the convention as a whole, Pennsylvania led a shift to Lincoln which brought him almost even with Seward, 184½ to 181. Excitement was intense as the clerk began to call the roll of states once more. Now Seward's New England total fell to 31, while Lincoln's rose prophetically to 42—more than half. And as the balloting proceeded, the sectional wall remained intact; for Seward could still muster only 7 votes from the entire lower North, compared with Lincoln's 142½. The doubtful states had spoken with thunderous emphasis.† When

---

* Actually, 466 votes were authorized, but on each of the three ballots one delegate (from Massachusetts, Kentucky, and Virginia, in order) did not vote.

† The following table of the balloting shows that Lincoln's nomination, like his election, followed a sectional pattern. The delegations are reduced to three groups: (1) the upper North from New England to Minnesota; (2) the lower North from New Jersey to Iowa; (3) the miscellaneous collection of delegates from six slave states, the District of Columbia, the Territories of Kansas and Nebraska, and the two Pacific states, California and Oregon.

	1st Ballot			2d Ballot			3d Ballot		
	Seward	Lincoln	Other	Seward	Lincoln	Other	Seward	Lincoln	Other
Upper	132	19	30	133	36	13	131	42	9
Lower	3½	62	104½	8½	115	46½	7	142½	20½
Misc.	38	21	55	43	30	40	42	47	24
Totals	173½	102	189½	184½	181	99½	180	231½	53½

the totals were finally announced, Lincoln stood within 1½ votes of victory. Four delegates from Ohio scrambled aboard the band wagon, and the deed was done. The rail splitter from Illinois had been nominated for the presidency.[32]

Why Lincoln won is a question of unending interest that can be answered in many ways. It did his cause no harm, for example, to have a partisan gallery cheering every gain that he made. In addition, much has been written about the shrewd tactics of Lincoln's managers, led by David Davis, and particularly about the lavish promises regarding cabinet posts and other appointments with which they drew delegates to their side. The extent and significance of these transactions is a matter of dispute among historians,[33] but in any case it should be remembered that the Seward forces had just as many offices to peddle and something else besides—financial support in the various state elections. Fundamentally, it was neither the roar of the crowd nor the promise of spoils that brought the delegates to their choice. The very pattern of voting reveals a hardheaded decision that the leading candidate could not win and must give way to someone who could. Yet in nominating the more "available" Lincoln, the Republicans did not compromise themselves or their principles. In fact, without fully realizing it, they had selected a man whose moral fiber was tougher than Seward's.

*

Lincoln received less than 40 per cent of the votes in the presidential election of 1860. Yet since nearly all of them were cast in the Northern states, he won a clear and constitutional majority in the electoral college.* Desperate last-minute efforts

---

* Total votes for the four candidates were as follows:

	Popular Vote	Electoral Vote
Lincoln	1,865,593	180
Douglas	1,382,713	12
Breckinridge	848,356	72
Bell	592,906	39

to unite his divided opposition did not succeed, except for some fusion tickets in a few states. Nor is it likely that such a union would have made any difference. If the popular votes given Douglas, Bell, and Breckinridge had been concentrated on one candidate, the Republicans would have lost only eleven electoral votes and retained their majority. Thus in order to win, the hypothetical single nominee would have had to poll more votes than all three of Lincoln's opponents put together, and, more specifically, he would have had to carry several free states while wearing the endorsement of the entire South—something which, in the circumstances, was very nearly impossible. Actually, the Democrats divided were in some ways more formidable than if they had been united, because a Douglas untainted with the support of the slaveholders probably had a better chance of winning enough electoral votes in the North to prevent Lincoln's election. It is therefore reasonable to argue that Lincoln became president in spite of the split in the Democratic party, rather than because of it.

Observing the custom of the time, Lincoln refrained from active campaigning as a presidential nominee. And during the critical months that followed the election he continued to say little for the public's enlightenment, insisting that his views were on display in his printed speeches. Americans wanting to know more about the man who had so suddenly risen from semi-obscurity to become their chief executive were heavily dependent upon the campaign biographies and newspaper sketches which poured from Republican presses. With these eulogistic writings began the creation of the idealized Lincoln—humble, ingenuous, and almost insufferably virtuous—who made the great American journey from log cabin to White House, realized a lifelong ambition in freeing the slaves, and passed through martyrdom to national sainthood. It was a portrait that turned Herndon's stomach and that historical scholars were bound to modify if not reject. To Albert J. Beveridge, who had absorbed the Lincoln legend in childhood, intensive study of the pre-presidential years brought severe disillusionment. Where was the gifted leadership, the moral purpose? When would they begin to come prominently into view? The earlier Lincoln, he sadly concluded, "showed few signs of the Lincoln of the second inaugural."[34] Beveridge, like James G. Randall, found his true hero for the 1850's in Stephen A. Douglas. That greatness was wrung from Lincoln almost entirely by his ordeal in the presidency is a common, although by no means universal, historical judgment. His most recent biographer, Reinhard H. Luthin, declares that Lincoln up to 1860 had demonstrated "few, if any, signs of the great qualities that he was to reveal in future years," had left "no record of achievement, except the quest for office."[35]

But if greatness is the response of inner strength to an extraordinary challenge, Lincoln had first met such a challenge and begun to show such strength in 1854, after the repeal of the Missouri Compromise. Never in the presidency did he surpass the political skill with which he shaped the Republican party of Illinois, held it together, and made himself its leader. In his relations with other Illinoisans one finds the same patience and respect for human dignity that characterized the wartime president. Ambition drove him hard in these years of preparation, and yet it was an ambition notably free of pettiness, malice, and overindulgence. It was, moreover, an ambition leavened by moral conviction and a deep faith in the principles upon which the republic had been built. The Lincoln of the 1860's was much the same man under greater challenge.

BIBLIOGRAPHICAL NOTE

Bibliographical Note

This brief essay, an introduction and supplement to the documentation that follows, will first present a survey of the sources relied upon most heavily by the author and then conclude with some comments upon interpretative trends.

The core of material for any Lincoln study is, of course, Roy P. Basler, Marion Dolores Pratt, and Lloyd A. Dunlap, eds., *The Collected Works of Abraham Lincoln* (8 vols. plus Index; New Brunswick, N.J., 1953–55); and the Robert Todd Lincoln Collection, Manuscript Division, Library of Congress, which contains the bulk of Lincoln's incoming correspondence. Among other manuscript collections, the most valuable are the Lyman Trumbull Papers and the Elihu B. Washburne Papers, Library of Congress; the Ozias M. Hatch Papers, Illinois State Historical Library; and the Stephen A. Douglas Papers, University of Chicago. Especially useful because of their introductory essays and because they contain speeches by Douglas not easily available are Paul M. Angle, ed., *Created Equal?: The Complete Lincoln-Douglas Debates of 1858* (Chicago, 1958); and Harry V. Jaffa and Robert W. Johannsen, eds., *In the Name of the People; Speeches and Writings of Lincoln and Douglas in the Ohio Campaign of 1859* (Columbus, Ohio, 1959). Reminiscences, although they must be used carefully, are sometimes the only source of information. The Herndon-Weik Collection, Library of Congress, falls into this category, as do the most valuable portions of Paul M. Angle, ed., *Herndon's Life of Lincoln* (New York, 1961); and Thomas J. McCormack, ed., *Memoirs of Gustave Koerner, 1809–1896* (2 vols.; Cedar Rapids, Iowa, 1909). The list of newspapers used in this study is a long one, headed by the *Illinois*

State Journal (Springfield) and the Chicago *Tribune*. Others deserving mention here are the *Illinois State Register* (Springfield), the Chicago *Times*, the Chicago *Democrat*, the Chicago *Journal*, the Bloomington (Ill.) *Pantagraph*, the New York *Tribune*, the New York *Herald*, the Washington *Union*, and the Richmond *Enquirer*.

All biographies of Lincoln give some attention to his career in the 1850's, but nothing compares in scope, detail, and literary quality with the second volume of Albert J. Beveridge's *Abraham Lincoln, 1809–1858* (2 vols.; Boston, 1928). Next in importance is William Baringer, *Lincoln's Rise to Power* (Boston, 1937), which takes up where the Beveridge work leaves off. James G. Randall, generally regarded as the greatest Lincoln scholar, offers a thoughtful discussion of the pre-presidential years in the early chapters of *Lincoln the President; Springfield to Gettysburg* (2 vols.; New York, 1945). Donald W. Riddle carries his competent monograph, *Congressman Abraham Lincoln* (Urbana, Ill., 1957), as far as the senatorial election of 1855. For the election of 1860, Reinhard H. Luthin, *The First Lincoln Campaign* (Cambridge, Mass., 1944), is indispensable. Harry V. Jaffa, *Crisis of the House Divided: An Interpretation of the Issues in the Lincoln–Douglas Debates* (New York, 1959), is a superior study of Lincoln's political thought. No interpretation has had greater influence than the brilliant but somewhat cynical essay in Richard Hofstadter, *The American Political Tradition and the Men Who Made It* (New York, 1948). There are also excellent chapters on Lincoln the politician in David Donald, *Lincoln Reconsidered* (2d ed.; New York, 1961); and in Richard N. Current, *The Lincoln Nobody Knows* (New York, 1958). Another perceptive essay is T. Harry Williams, "Lincoln and the Causes of the Civil War," in O. Fritiof Ander, ed., *Lincoln Images* (Rock Island, Ill., 1960). Less well known, but important because of their influence on other historians, are William O. Lynch, "The Convergence of Lincoln and Douglas," Illinois State Historical Society *Transactions*, 1925; and Arthur C. Cole, *Lincoln's*

"House Divided" Speech: Did It Reflect a Doctrine of Class Struggle? (Chicago, 1923).

A notable development of recent years is the publication of biographies of Lincoln's contemporaries. David Donald, *Lincoln's Herndon* (New York, 1948), is the most important for the period of the 1850's, but Willard L. King, *Lincoln's Manager, David Davis* (Cambridge, Mass., 1960), is also of great value. Others are Maurice G. Baxter, *Orville H. Browning, Lincoln's Friend and Critic* (Bloomington, Ind., 1957); Don E. Fehrenbacher, *Chicago Giant: A Biography of "Long John" Wentworth* (Madison, Wis., 1957); and Jay Monaghan's overenthusiastic biography of Charles H. Ray, *The Man Who Elected Lincoln* (Indianapolis, Ind., 1956). Horace White's *The Life of Lyman Trumbull* (Boston, 1913), is still the only one available, but it can be supplemented with Ralph J. Roske, "Lincoln and Lyman Trumbull," in Ander, ed., *Lincoln Images*. George Fort Milton, *The Eve of Conflict: Stephen A. Douglas and the Needless War* (Boston, 1934), is strongly biased, but it remains the most thorough study of the Little Giant. There are several good biographies of Greeley, but most useful for the 1850's is Jeter A. Isely, *Horace Greeley and the Republican Party, 1853–1861* (Princeton, N.J., 1947).

Of the many general and special histories consulted in the preparation of this work, the following are particularly important: Allan Nevins, *Ordeal of the Union* (2 vols.; New York, 1947); Nevins, *The Emergence of Lincoln* (2 vols.; New York, 1950); Roy Franklin Nichols, *The Disruption of American Democracy* (New York, 1948); Avery Craven, *The Coming of the Civil War* (New York, 1942); Craven, *The Growth of Southern Nationalism, 1848–1861* (Baton Rouge, La., 1953); Arthur Charles Cole, *The Era of the Civil War, 1848–1870* (Springfield, Ill., 1919); Andrew Wallace Crandall, *The Early History of the Republican Party, 1854–1856* (Boston, 1930); and Milo M. Quaife, *The Doctrine of Non-Intervention with Slavery in the Territories* (Chicago, 1910).

The biographers of Lincoln are themselves the objects of scrutiny in Benjamin P. Thomas, *Portrait for Posterity* (New Brunswick, N.J., 1947). Other scholars have contributed briefer critiques of Lincoln historiography, notably: David M. Potter, *The Lincoln Theme and American National Historiography* (Oxford, 1948); David Donald, "The Folklore Lincoln," in his *Lincoln Reconsidered*; J. G. Randall, "Has the Lincoln Theme Been Exhausted?" *American Historical Review*, XLI (1936); and Clyde C. Walton, "An Agonizing Reappraisal," in Ander, ed., *Lincoln Images*. Thomas saw Lincoln biography of the nineteenth and early twentieth centuries as a struggle between "realists" like Herndon and "romanticists" like Nicolay and Hay. Yet, as Potter and Donald have pointed out, both groups created legendary Lincolns—one, the incarnation of frontier America; the other, the great national hero, Christlike in his character and fate. Neither legend has lost its popular appeal, for the very good reason that neither is essentially false. Both are imaginative extensions of the truth. But the folklore tradition of a simple rail splitter who became the Great Emancipator makes it all the more difficult to delineate the transitional Lincoln of the 1850's.

Although the first two generations of biographers produced some meritorious works and at least two classics—Herndon's *Life* (1889) and Lord Charnwood's *Abraham Lincoln* (1916)—Lincoln historiography entered its most brilliant phase in the 1920's. Within a span of four years, Randall's first Lincoln book was published, Carl Sandburg charmed the public with *Abraham Lincoln: The Prairie Years* (2 vols.; New York, 1926), Beveridge's unfinished but magnificent work appeared, and the Lincoln Centennial Association (later renamed the Abraham Lincoln Association) was converted by Logan Hay into a research organization. The position of executive secretary was filled by a succession of trained scholars, and the Association launched a program of study and publication that culminated in the issuance of the *Collected Works*. Meanwhile, other academic historians were following Randall into the Lincoln field, and the opening of the Robert Todd Lincoln Collection in 1947 served as an added stimulus to scholarship. The result was a steady output of new Lincoln studies which corrected many errors, contributed much new information, and conformed to high standards of professional competence.

But now a curious coincidence must be noted. At the very time that Lincoln scholarship was rising to a new level of distinction, historical interpretation of the causes of the Civil War took a turn that was decidedly anti-Republican and thus, to a certain extent, anti-Lincoln. Furthermore, the "revisionist" group of historians, who regarded the Civil War as a tragic mistake produced by the unnecessary agitation of an artificial issue, included or strongly influenced some of the most prominent Lincoln scholars. Randall was one of the leading revisionists, and his sympathies, in his treatment of the prewar years, were primarily with the advocates of compromise. Beveridge's correspondence, as he worked away on Lincoln in the 1920's, was punctuated with exclamations of admiration for Douglas. Both Luthin and Riddle followed the revisionist line of interpretation, and Nevins was not unaffected by it. There were, however, many Lincoln specialists who stood aloof from the trend, among them Benjamin P. Thomas, whose *Abraham Lincoln; a Biography* (New York, 1952) is the best synthesis of modern scholarship. After the Second World War revisionism began to fall out of favor; one of the most vigorous attacks upon it within Lincoln literature has been Jaffa's *Crisis of the House Divided*. But it is still a potent influence in Lincoln historiography, and it was recently given emphatic restatement by Luthin in his *The Real Abraham Lincoln* (Englewood Cliffs, N.J., 1960).

Revisionism, when applied to Lincoln's pre-presidential career, has tended to question the ultimate wisdom of his anti-slavery stand, to minimize his sympathy for the Negro, to underscore his social and political conservatism, to stress his political opportunism at the expense of his idealism, and, above all, to reduce his stature in the 1850's and confine his greatness to the presidential years. Such an interpretation is not necessarily rendered invalid by the preconceptions of its authors, but it should be accepted only if it stands up under the most rigorous scrutiny.

NOTES

Notes

CHAPTER ONE

1. For Lincoln's criticism of the Mexican War, see Donald W. Riddle, *Congressman Abraham Lincoln* (Urbana, Ill., 1957), pp. 32–69. His famous "Spot" resolutions are in Roy P. Basler, Marion Dolores Pratt, and Lloyd A. Dunlap, eds., *The Collected Works of Abraham Lincoln* (8 vols. plus Index; New Brunswick, N.J., 1953–55), I, 420–22. Hereafter cited as *Collected Works*.

2. Giddings to George W. Julian, May 25, 1860, Giddings-Julian Collection, Manuscript Division, Library of Congress.

3. *The Seventh Census of the United States: 1850; Embracing a Statistical View of Each of the States . . .* (Washington, 1853), p. 702; *Population of the United States in 1860; Compiled from the Original Returns of the Eighth Census* (Washington, 1864), pp. v–vi, 103.

4. *Seventh Census*, pp. xxxvi–xxxvii; *Eighth Census, Population*, pp. 102–4.

5. Chicago *Tribune*, February 14, 1857.

6. *Preliminary Report on the Eighth Census, House Executive Document* No. 116 (Serial 1137), 37 Congress, 2 session, p. 235.

7. Harry E. Pratt, *The Personal Finances of Abraham Lincoln* (Springfield, Ill., 1943), p. 53; see also Robert M. Sutton, "Lincoln and the Railroads of Illinois," in O. Fritiof Ander, ed., *Lincoln Images* (Rock Island, Ill., 1960), pp. 49–54.

8. *Seventh Census*, p. lxv; *Eighth Census, Preliminary Report*, p. 211; Don E. Fehrenbacher, "Illinois Political Attitudes, 1854–1861," unpublished Ph.D. dissertation, University of Chicago, 1951, pp. 68–69, 74.

9. Jay Monaghan's *The Man Who Elected Lincoln* (Indianapolis, 1956) is a biography of Charles H. Ray.

10. Fehrenbacher, "Illinois Political Attitudes," pp. 118–20; Charles Baumer Swaney, *Episcopal Methodism and Slavery* (Boston, 1926), pp. 226–31.

11. Reverend C. H. Palmer of Middleport, Ill., September 10, 1856, American Home Missionary Society Collection, University of Chicago.

12. Arthur Charles Cole, *The Era of the Civil War, 1848–1870* (Springfield, Ill., 1919), pp. 205–10.

13. Chicago *Tribune*, February 5, 1856.

14. Weekly Chicago *Democrat,* June 5, December 4, 1858.

15. Bureau County *Republican* (Princeton, Ill.), August 16, 1860; see also Chicago *Press and Tribune,* August 10, 1860.

16. Roy Franklin Nichols, *The Disruption of American Democracy* (New York, 1948), p. 515.

17. Weekly Chicago *Democrat,* August 23, 1856.

CHAPTER TWO

1. In a letter to Lyman Trumbull written June 7, 1856 (*Collected Works,* II, 342–43), Lincoln declared: "Nine tenths of the Anti-Nebraska votes have to come from old whigs." This was an overstatement, but William O. Lynch, after a careful study, estimated that Whigs furnished nearly two-thirds of the Republican votes in 1856. See his "The Convergence of Lincoln and Douglas," in Illinois State Historical Society *Transactions,* 1925, p. 157n.

2. The quotations are from Allan Nevins, *Ordeal of the Union* (2 vols.; New York, 1947), II, 490; and Gerald M. Capers, *Stephen A. Douglas; Defender of the Union* (Boston, 1959), p. 88. See also Albert J. Beveridge, *Abraham Lincoln, 1809–1858* (2 vols.; Boston, 1928), II, 353–61; Reinhard H. Luthin, *The Real Abraham Lincoln* (Englewood Cliffs, N.J., 1960), pp. 180–82.

3. *Collected Works,* III, 512; IV, 67.

4. John J. Duff, *A. Lincoln; Prairie Lawyer* (New York, 1960), pp. 162–63, echoes the belief of various earlier writers that Lincoln "renounced politics" between 1850 and 1854. Benjamin P. Thomas, *Abraham Lincoln; a Biography* (New York, 1952), titles his chapter on the year 1854: "Lincoln Re-enters Politics."

5. Riddle, *Congressman Abraham Lincoln,* pp. 198–235; *Collected Works,* II, 41, 43–44, 49–51, 54, 57–61.

6. J. G. Holland, *The Life of Abraham Lincoln* (Springfield, Mass., 1866), pp. 134–43; Isaac N. Arnold, *The Life of Abraham Lincoln* (Chicago, 1885), pp. 114–20.

7. Riddle, *Congressman Abraham Lincoln,* p. 249.

8. Paul M. Angle, ed., *Herndon's Life of Lincoln* (New York, 1961), p. 304.

9. J. G. Randall, *Lincoln the President; Springfield to Gettysburg* (2 vols.; New York, 1945), I, 125–27, 240–41; *Lincoln the Liberal Statesman* (New York, 1947), pp. 16, 19.

10. It was in the aftermath of the Kansas-Nebraska controversy that Lincoln began to think along the lines of his "House Divided" speech. For further discussion, see Chapter Four.

11. *Collected Works,* II, 255, 274.

12. See especially the debate with Douglas at Alton in 1858, *ibid.,* III, 312–16.

13. Lynch, "Convergence of Lincoln and Douglas," p. 160n.

14. Riddle, *Congressman Abraham Lincoln,* p. 245.

15. Weekly Chicago *Democrat,* July 23, 1853.

16. Andrew Wallace Crandall, *The Early History of the Republican Party, 1854–1856* (Boston, 1930), pp. 20–26, 31–34; Malcolm Moos, *The Republicans; a History of Their Party* (New York, 1956), pp. 16–18.

17. *Illinois [State] Journal* (Springfield), July 27, 1854.

18. *Collected Works,* IV, 67.

19. *Illinois State Register* (Springfield), September 28, 1854.

20. Angle, ed., *Herndon's Lincoln,* pp. 299–300.

21. The quotation is from Beveridge, *Abraham Lincoln,* II, 265. Lincoln left Springfield for Pekin on October 5, 1854, and handled several cases in court immediately after his arrival. In both 1855 and 1856 he made the same trip during the first week of October. See Paul M. Angle, *Lincoln, 1854–1861* (Springfield, Ill., 1933), pp. 40, 92, 145.

22. David Donald, *Lincoln's Herndon* (New York, 1948), pp. 77–78. The story is still generally accepted, however. See Thomas, *Abraham Lincoln,* p. 152; and Luthin, *The Real Abraham Lincoln,* p. 178.

23. *Collected Works,* II, 273.

24. *Ibid.,* p. 288.

25. Riddle, *Congressman Abraham Lincoln,* p. 249; David C. Mearns, *The Lincoln Papers* (2 vols.; Garden City, N.Y., 1948), I, 189–90. Historians tend to agree with Mearns. See Donald, *Lincoln's Herndon,* p. 78; Thomas, *Abraham Lincoln,* p. 146; Angle, *Lincoln, 1854–1861,* p. xii.

26. That the men who invited Lincoln to speak in Chicago had the senatorship in mind is plainly indicated in the letter of Horace White to Lincoln, October 25, 1854, Robert Todd Lincoln Collection, Manuscript Division, Library of Congress.

27. *Collected Works,* II, 286–90.

28. *Ibid.,* pp. 287–88; E. N. Powell to Lincoln, November 16, 1854; H. Grove to Lincoln, November 18, 1858, Robert Todd Lincoln Collection, Library of Congress; Riddle, *Congressman Abraham Lincoln,* p. 250 n.

29. *Collected Works,* II, 296–98.

30. Beveridge, *Abraham Lincoln,* II, 279–87; *Collected Works,* II, 304–7. The following table summarizes the votes given the four leading candidates on each of the ten ballots, as recorded in the *Journal of the House of Representatives,* 19 Illinois General Assembly, pp. 348–61 :

BALLOTS:	1st	2d	3d	4th	5th	6th	7th	8th	9th	10th
Lincoln	45	43	41	38	34	36	38	27	15	0
Shields	41	41	41	41	42	41	1	0	0	0
Trumbull	5	6	6	11	10	8	9	18	35	51
Matteson	1	1	0	2	1	0	44	46	47	47

31. *Collected Works,* II, 306.

32. See especially Reinhard H. Luthin, "Abraham Lincoln Becomes a Republican," *Political Science Quarterly,* LIX (1944), 425–27.

33. *Collected Works,* II, 316–17.

34. *Ibid.,* pp. 320–23.

35. Luthin, "Abraham Lincoln Becomes a Republican," p. 427.

36. Trumbull to Owen Lovejoy, August 20, 1855, Lyman Trumbull Papers, Illinois State Historical Library; Palmer to Trumbull, January 11, February 28, 1856; Bissell to Trumbull, May 5, 1856; Browning to Trumbull, May 19, 1856, Lyman Trumbull Papers, Manuscript Division, Library of Congress; Trumbull to Palmer, January 24, 1856, in George Thomas Palmer, ed., "Letters from Lyman Trumbull to John M. Palmer, 1854–1858," *Journal of the Illinois State Historical Society,* XVI (1923), 28–29; Thomas J. McCormack, ed., *Memoirs of Gustave Koerner, 1809–1896* (2 vols.; Cedar Rapids, Iowa, 1909), I, 617–18; Don E. Fehrenbacher, *Chicago Giant; a Biography of "Long John" Wentworth* (Madison, Wis., 1957), pp. 135–41; Beveridge, *Abraham Lincoln,* II, 566.

37. *Collected Works,* II, 333; Paul Selby, "The Editorial Convention, February 22, 1856," McLean County Historical Society *Transactions,* III (1900), 30–43.

38. Luthin, "Abraham Lincoln Becomes a Republican," pp. 431–34; Angle, ed., *Herndon's Lincoln,* pp. 310–11.

39. Donald, *Lincoln's Herndon,* p. 87.

40. *Collected Works,* IV, 67.

CHAPTER THREE

1. *Collected Works,* II, 522, 528–32.

2. George H. Haynes, *The Senate of the United States; Its History and Practice* (2 vols.; Boston, 1938), I, 99.

3. *Collected Works,* III, 174.

4. Philadelphia *Pennsylvanian,* quoted in *Illinois State Register,* November 13, 1858; Springfield (Mass.) *Republican,* September 7, 1858; Boston *Daily Advertiser,* November 6, 1858.

5. Herndon to Trumbull, June 24, 1858, Trumbull Papers, Library of Congress.

6. *Collected Works,* II, 472.

7. Beveridge, *Abraham Lincoln,* II, 564–72. Allan Nevins, *The Emergence of Lincoln* (2 vols.; New York, 1950), I, 357–58, follows the Beveridge interpretation, as do George Fort Milton, *The Eve of Conflict; Stephen A. Douglas and the Needless War* (Boston, 1934), pp. 304–5; and Monaghan, *The Man Who Elected Lincoln,* pp. 103–4. For the opposite view, see Thomas, *Abraham Lincoln,* pp. 177–80; Angle, *Lincoln, 1854–1861,* p. xx; and Don E. Fehrenbacher, "The

Nomination of Lincoln in 1858," *Abraham Lincoln Quarterly,* VI (1950), 24–36.

8. Douglas's speech is in the New York *Times,* June 23, 1857. Lincoln's is in *Collected Works,* II, 398–410.

9. Beveridge, *Abraham Lincoln,* II, 529. James Ford Rhodes, no admirer of Douglas, calls it a "noble act" in his *History of the United States from the Compromise of 1850,* II (New York, 1899), 285. Nevins, *Emergence of Lincoln,* I, 257, says that Douglas's opening attack upon the Lecompton constitution was "one of the most honest, impassioned, and therefore greatest speeches of his life."

10. *Collected Works,* II, 446–47, 463, 488, 508–10.

11. *Congressional Globe,* 35 Congress, 1 session, pp. 14–18.

12. *Ibid.,* p. 16.

13. Milton, *Eve of Conflict,* pp. 228–29, 240, 243, 271–73; Nichols, *Disruption of American Democracy,* p. 129; Charles H. Ray to Lyman Trumbull, November 24, 1857, Trumbull Papers, Library of Congress. It is significant that David C. Broderick, one of the two Democratic senators who joined Douglas in vigorous opposition to the Lecompton constitution, was also feuding with Buchanan over the patronage in California.

14. G. C. Lanphere to Douglas, December 24, 1857; James Williams to Douglas, January 26, 1858; and see also Joseph Thomas to Douglas, December 20, 1857; H. Buck to Douglas, January 1, 1858; E. Wilcox to Douglas, January 12, 1858; E. Currier to Douglas, January 29, 1858, all in the Stephen A. Douglas Papers, University of Chicago.

15. Norman B. Judd to Lyman Trumbull, December 1, 1857, Trumbull Papers, Library of Congress.

16. Lyman Trumbull to Lincoln, January 3, 1858, Robert Todd Lincoln Collection, Library of Congress; O. J. Hollister, *Life of Schuyler Colfax* (New York, 1886), p. 119; George S. Merriam, *The Life and Times of Samuel Bowles* (2 vols.; New York, 1885), I, 232; Henry Wilson, *History of the Rise and Fall of the Slave Power in America* (3 vols.; Boston, 1875–77), II, 567. For the alleged Douglas-Seward agreement, see the New York *Herald,* April 6, 13, November 20, 1858; William H. Herndon to Theodore Parker, September 20, 1858, printed in Joseph Fort Newton, *Lincoln and Herndon* (Cedar Rapids, Iowa, 1910), pp. 215–16; George W. Jones to Sidney Breese, September 17, 1858, Sidney Breese Papers, Illinois State Historical Library. A meeting between Douglas and Seward at Chicago on October 22, 1857 (reported in the *Illinois State Register,* October 26, 1857) was pointed to as the beginning of the alliance.

17. Hayes to Douglas, January 1, 1858, Douglas Papers, University of Chicago. There are similar letters from many other Republicans in the collection.

18. Chicago *Tribune,* March 19, 1858.

19. Wilson to Theodore Parker, February 28, 1858, quoted in Newton, *Lincoln and Herndon,* p. 148.

20. Hollister, *Schuyler Colfax,* p. 121.

21. Ray to Trumbull, March 9, 1858, Trumbull Papers, Library of Congress.

22. Donald, *Lincoln's Herndon,* pp. 114–17; Newton, *Lincoln and Herndon,* pp. 153, 203, 209, 215–16, 219, 241–42, 245–47.

23. See, for example, Lincoln's letter to Samuel Galloway, July 28, 1859, *Collected Works,* III, 394–95. There is further discussion of this point in Chapter Four.

24. Horace Greeley, *Recollections of a Busy Life* (New York, 1868), pp. 357–58; New York *Tribune,* December 17, 21, 23, 1857; March 3, May 4, 11, 27, 1858; Greeley to Colfax, March 15, May 6, 12, June 2, 14, 1858, Horace Greeley–Schuyler Colfax Correspondence, New York Public Library.

25. New York *Times,* April 15, May 10, 1858; Albany *Evening Journal,* May 15, 1858; Springfield (Mass.) *Republican,* April 30, 1858; "Mr. Buchanan's Administration," *Atlantic Monthly,* I (April 1858), 756–57.

26. Dixon *Republican and Telegraph,* May 20, 27, 1858.

27. Trumbull to Lincoln, January 3, 1858, Robert Todd Lincoln Collection, Library of Congress; Palmer to Trumbull, May 25, 1858, Trumbull Papers, Library of Congress.

28. *Collected Works,* II, 430.

29. Chicago *Tribune,* April 21, 1858.

30. Herndon to Washburne, April 10, 1858, and Jason Marsh to Washburne, April 28, 1858, Elihu B. Washburne Papers, Manuscript Division, Library of Congress; Jesse K. Dubois to Trumbull, April 8, 1858, Trumbull Papers, Library of Congress. Herndon used similar language in a letter to Charles Sumner. See Donald, *Lincoln and Herndon,* p. 117. Marsh, although violently opposed to supporting Douglas, was one of the few Illinois Republicans to express doubt about the propriety of electing Lincoln. He preferred someone from the northern part of the state like Washburne or William B. Ogden.

31. *Illinois State Journal,* April 19, May 17, 1858; Bureau County *Republican* (Princeton), April 22, May 6, 1858; Ottawa *Republican,* April 24, 1858; Alton *Weekly Courier,* May 27, 1858; Chicago *Journal,* April 15, 24, May 4, 19, 1858. The Chicago *Journal* of May 20 printed quotations from numerous Illinois newspapers on the subject.

32. Greeley to Schuyler Colfax, May 12, June 2, 1858, Greeley-Colfax Correspondence, New York Public Library.

33. Koerner to Hatch, April 20, 1858, and Lincoln to Hatch, March 24, 1858 (photostat), Ozias M. Hatch Papers, Illinois State Historical Library.

34. Herndon to Trumbull, April 12, 1858, Trumbull Papers, Library of Congress.

35. George T. Brown to Lyman Trumbull, April 25, 1858, *ibid.*; Charles H. Ray to Elihu B. Washburne, May 2, [1858], Washburne Papers, Library of Congress. Washburne, especially, was suspected for a time of having adopted the Greeley viewpoint. See *Collected Works,* II, 443–46; Fehrenbacher, *Chicago Giant,* pp. 155–56.

36. *Collected Works,* II, 456.

37. David L. Phillips to Lincoln, June 9, 1858, Robert Todd Lincoln Collection, Library of Congress; Bloomington *Pantagraph,* June 7, 15, 1858; Chicago *Tribune,* June 9, 14, 15, 1858; *Illinois State Journal,* June 10, 14, 15, 1858; Greenville *Advocate,* June 10, 1858; Ottawa *Republican,* June 12, 1858.

38. *Collected Works,* II, 429.

39. Chicago *Tribune,* November 23, 25, 1857.

40. Beveridge, *Abraham Lincoln,* II, 564–72. The other writers cited in note 7 for this chapter all relied on Beveridge's judgment.

41. *Illinois State Register,* April 30, May 21, June 4, 1858; Chicago *Times,* May 19, 25, June 2, 1858.

42. Chicago *Tribune,* May 25, 1858; Chicago *Journal,* May 27, 28, 1858; Chicago *Democratic Press,* May 20, 1858. By this time, some Republican leaders believed that Wentworth had shifted his sights to the governorship race in 1860. One of them, significantly, was Charles L. Wilson, who secured the explicit endorsement of Lincoln by the state convention. See his letter to Elihu B. Washburne, May 3, 1858, Washburne Papers, Library of Congress. Lincoln was eventually forced to deny rumors that he had agreed to support Wentworth for the governorship. See E. T. Bridges to Lincoln, May 18, 1858, and Wilson to Lincoln, May 31, 1858, Robert Todd Lincoln Collection, Library of Congress, together with Lincoln's reply to Wilson on June 1, 1858, in the *Collected Works,* II, 456–57. Wilson's letter is published in Mearns, *Lincoln Papers,* I, 207–8.

43. Chicago *Tribune,* June 9, 1858.

44. *Illinois State Register,* June 17, 1858; *Illinois State Journal,* June 17, 18, 1858; Bloomington *Pantagraph,* June 18, 19, 1858. Wentworth, by the way, probably did not even attend the state convention. Historians, myself included, have been misled by the published list of delegates, which bore his name. But on June 6, he had informed Lincoln that he expected to leave for the East before the appointed day, and the *State Register* of June 17 specifically noted his absence.

CHAPTER FOUR

1. Chicago *Tribune,* June 19, 1858.

2. This and all other quotations from the speech are taken from *Collected Works,* II, 461–69.

3. Angle, ed., *Herndon's Lincoln,* p. 323. Herndon's recollection that he was the only man to respond favorably is supported by the

testimony of others who were present, but one may be permitted to doubt that he actually predicted: "Lincoln, deliver that speech as read and it will make you President." See Donald, *Lincoln's Herndon,* pp. 118–19.

4. Scripps to Lincoln, June 22, 1858, Robert Todd Lincoln Collection, Library of Congress.

5. Swett to William H. Herndon, July 17, 1866, in Emanuel Hertz, ed., *The Hidden Lincoln* (New York, 1938), pp. 295–302.

6. Angle, ed., *Herndon's Lincoln,* pp. 321–24. In reconstructing Lincoln's words, Herndon drew upon his own memory and upon that of John Armstrong, a local Republican leader in Springfield who was apparently present at the pre-convention reading of the speech. Herndon's interview with Armstrong in 1870 is in the Ward Hill Lamon Papers, Henry E. Huntington Library. In another account of the meeting written many years later by William Jayne (brother-in-law of Lyman Trumbull), Lincoln is made to appear even more dedicated and pompous. He responds to the protests against the speech by reciting six stanzas from a poem by Bryant, quoting the Apostle Paul, and pointing to the example of Martin Luther. William Jayne, *Personal Reminiscences of the Martyred President Abraham Lincoln* (Chicago, 1908), pp. 38–42.

7. Nevins, *Emergence of Lincoln,* I, 360.

8. Beveridge, *Abraham Lincoln,* II, 585.

9. Richard Hofstadter, *The American Political Tradition and the Men Who Made It* (New York, 1948), p. 114n. Hofstadter reinforces this particular statement with a yarn from the pen of Joseph Medill. In 1862, Medill allegedly asked Lincoln why he had delivered "that radical speech" back in 1858, and Lincoln allegedly replied: "Well, after you fellows had got me into that mess and begun tempting me with offers of the Presidency, I began to think and I made up my mind that the next President of the United States would need to have a stronger anti-slavery platform than mine. So I concluded to say something." Unless Lincoln uttered these words in jest, the whole story is absurd.

10. *Collected Works,* II, 476–81.

11. "If we could first know *where* we are, and *whither* we are tending," Lincoln began, "we could then better judge *what* to do, and *how* to do it." This was a terse paraphrase of the opening sentence in Webster's reply to Hayne. Near the end of his speech, Lincoln also borrowed from Webster's peroration when he described the Democrats as "wavering, dissevered and belligerent."

12. *Collected Works,* III, 8, 111; Newton, *Lincoln and Herndon,* p. 173.

13. Several times during the debates with Douglas, Lincoln made it plain that he expected the slavery controversy to be settled peace-

ably. "There will be no war, no violence," he assured his audience at Alton. *Collected Works,* III, 316.

14. *Ibid.,* II, 491.

15. Nevins, *Emergence of Lincoln,* I, 359, 361.

16. *Collected Works,* II, 471.

17. *Ibid.,* III, 18. See also his statements at Jonesboro, Charleston, Quincy, and Alton, *ibid.,* pp. 117, 180–81, 276, 306–8.

18. *Ibid.,* pp. 18, 92–93, 181.

19. *Ibid.,* p. 78. These words are from the newspaper report of a speech that Lincoln delivered at Carlinville, Illinois, on August 31, 1858, but he identified his own views with those of the "fathers of the republic" in his speech at Peoria in 1854, and many times thereafter. See *ibid.,* II, 274, 276, 501, 513, 520–21; III, 18, 87, 92–93, 117–18, 181, 276, 306–8, 333, 484, 488, 489, 496, 498, 535, 537–38, 550, 551, 553; IV, 17–18, 21–22.

20. *Ibid.,* II, 498; III, 92–93, 254–55, 312–13.

21. Seward's remark, made on the floor of the Senate, is in *Congressional Globe,* 35 Cong., 1 sess., p. 521 (February 2, 1858). The New York *Times* of March 1, 1858, said that the statement "substantially dissolved" the loose alliance constituting the Republican party. The Chicago *Democratic Press,* March 9, 1858, carried an angry reply to the *Times.*

22. Nevins, *Emergence of Lincoln,* I, 361–63; Randall, *Lincoln the President,* I, 107–8. A notable exception is Harry V. Jaffa, *Crisis of the House Divided: An Interpretation of the Issues in the Lincoln-Douglas Debates* (New York, 1959), pp. 275–301, which contains an elaborate and persuasive defense of Lincoln's argument.

23. Nevins, *Emergence of Lincoln,* I, 362.

24. *Collected Works,* II, 521; III, 20–22, 27–30, 232–33.

25. *Congressional Globe,* 35 Cong., 1 sess., p. 18 (December 9, 1857). This remark, which Republicans lifted from context and quoted repeatedly, was directed specifically at the slavery clause of the Lecompton constitution, due to be submitted to the voters of Kansas on December 21. Douglas was merely announcing his opposition to the constitution no matter which way the vote went on the clause. Nevertheless, Lincoln believed that the phrase was an accurate summary of popular sovereignty, which, he said, "acknowledges that slavery has equal rights with liberty." *Collected Works,* IV, 155.

26. *Collected Works,* III, 29–30, 233, 316, 369, 404–5, 442, 469; IV, 5, 20–21.

27. These words, which so crisply sum up Lincoln's view of the Douglas doctrine, are from the Cooper Institute address of February 27, 1860. Such "sophistical contrivances," Lincoln said, were as "vain as the search for a man who should be neither a living man nor a dead man." *Ibid.,* III, 550.

28. Herndon to Jesse W. Weik, October 29, 1885, Herndon-Weik Collection, Manuscript Division, Library of Congress.

29. Arthur C. Cole, *Lincoln's "House Divided" Speech: Did It Reflect a Doctrine of Class Struggle?* (Chicago, 1923), an address delivered before the Chicago Historical Society, March 15, 1923, and published as a pamphlet.

30. *Ibid.,* pp. 11–30.

31. Notably, in his eulogy of Henry Clay on July 6, 1852, in his Peoria speech of October 16, 1854, and in his speech at a Republican banquet in Chicago on December 10, 1856. Also, the brief newspaper report of his famous "lost speech" at the Bloomington convention on May 29, 1856, reports him as saying: "The sentiment in favor of white slavery now prevailed in all the slave state papers, except those of Kentucky, Tennessee and Missouri and Maryland." *Collected Works,* II, 130, 255, 275–76, 341, 385.

32. Cole, *Lincoln's "House Divided" Speech,* pp. 14, 15, 34.

33. *Collected Works,* II, 514.

34. *Ibid.,* p. 255.

35. Beveridge, *Abraham Lincoln,* II, 273.

36. *Collected Works,* II, 318.

37. *Ibid.,* III, 431, 451; IV, 6–7, 23. Lincoln repeatedly cited the Richmond *Enquirer's* use of the concept in 1856, but he also asserted that "almost every good man" since the formation of the government had uttered the same sentiment, including Washington, Jefferson, Jay, and Monroe. Prudently, he neglected to add that the idea of the incompatibility of slavery and freedom, together with the theory of a great slave power conspiracy, had long been a stock-in-trade of the abolitionists. See Russel B. Nye, *Fettered Freedom: Civil Liberties and the Slave Controversy, 1830–1860* (East Lansing, Mich., 1949), pp. 217–49.

38. See especially his form letter to Fillmore men in *Collected Works,* II, 374.

39. Dickey to William H. Herndon, December 8, 1866, Herndon-Weik Collection, Library of Congress. Dickey told substantially the same story in a letter to Isaac N. Arnold, February 7, 1883, Arnold Papers, Chicago Historical Society. Herndon included the incident in his biography (Angle, ed., *Herndon's Lincoln,* pp. 322–23), but said only that it took place "at Bloomington in 1856." This may have led some of his readers to connect the incident with the Republican convention at Bloomington on May 29, 1856, thus contributing to the development of a tradition that Lincoln used the house-divided doctrine in his famous "lost speech." The error may have begun with Ward H. Lamon, *The Life of Abraham Lincoln* (Boston, 1872), p. 398. The manuscript of Dickey's letter to Herndon removes all doubt. It states that the speech was given at "a political meeting"

held in the evening of "some day in September or October of 1856."

40. *Collected Works,* II, 375.

41. Henry B. Rankin, in his *Personal Recollections of Abraham Lincoln* (New York, 1916), pp. 235–36, asserted that Lincoln used the house-divided doctrine in a speech at Petersburg on August 30, 1856. He, too, misinterpreted Dickey's story as a reference to the Bloomington convention of May 29 (see note 39 above), and thus concluded, mistakenly, that in uttering the doctrine at Petersburg, Lincoln broke his promise to Dickey. Rankin's statement, published sixty years after the event, is of dubious value but perhaps adds something to the credibility of Dickey's recollection. Petersburg, it may be noted, was also in the heart of old Whig territory, and the newspaper account of Lincoln's speech shows him making an appeal to the Fillmore supporters. *Collected Works,* II, 366–68.

42. John G. Nicolay and John Hay, eds., *Abraham Lincoln: Complete Works* (2 vols.; New York, 1894), I, 422–27. It seems likely that Nicolay and Hay were influenced in their selection of this date by the location of the manuscript in Lincoln's files. Since they used it, the manuscript itself has disappeared, except for the final page, which is in the Pierpont Morgan Library, New York City. The Morgan Library associates two other pages of manuscript with this page, but there is apparently no convincing reason for doing so. See *Collected Works,* II, 552n.

43. The fragment appears in *Collected Works,* II, 448–54. All quotations from the fragment are taken from this source. The editors followed Nicolay and Hay and the page of manuscript in the Pierpont Morgan Library. The date which they assign obviously takes into account Herndon's statement that Lincoln spent about one month writing the House Divided speech (see note 28 above). They suggest May 18 specifically because on that day Lincoln delivered a speech at Edwardsville, but there is apparently no evidence of any kind linking the fragment with that speech. On the other hand, the contents of the fragment indicate beyond any doubt that it was written much earlier. For instance, Lincoln discusses the question of "whether the Lecompton constitution should be accepted or rejected" by Congress. But the Lecompton bill was, in effect, defeated on April 1 in the House, and the chief topic of public discussion in the latter part of April was the substitute English bill. This measure, which is not mentioned in the fragment, became law several weeks before May 18.

44. *Ibid.,* p. 430.

45. This is Lincoln's first recorded use of the biblical quotation in connection with the sectional controversy. In 1843, he and two other Whig leaders had quoted it in a circular pleading for party unity. (*Ibid.,* I, 315.) By 1858, the sentence had been used so often in one context or another that it was almost a cliché. Beveridge, *Abraham*

Lincoln, II, 575n, gives several examples. In the John J. Crittenden Papers, Manuscript Division, Library of Congress, there is a letter from G. D. Jaquess, dated March 1, 1858, which reads in part: "The good book says where a house is divided against its self it cannot stand. It appears this republic is fast drifting to that position." See also the *Northwestern Christian Advocate* (Chicago), March 29, 1854; Chicago *Tribune,* March 22, 1858; New York *Herald,* June 8, 1858.

46. Cole, *Lincoln's "House Divided" Speech,* p. 33.

47. Sacramento *Union,* February 12, 1858.

48. *Congressional Globe,* 35 Cong., 1 sess., p. 617.

49. *Collected Works,* III, 24–27, 48–49, 73–76.

50. *Ibid.,* p. 367.

51. *Ibid.,* p. 379.

52. *Ibid.,* pp. 265–66, 323.

53. This question, implicit in Lincoln's approach to the sectional controversy by 1858, was forcefully posed in his First Inaugural address. *Ibid.,* IV, 267–68.

54. *Ibid.,* VIII, 405.

CHAPTER FIVE

1. Beveridge, *Abraham Lincoln,* II, 585n.

2. Jackson *Mississippian* (semiweekly), September 14, 1858. The summary of Southern editorial opinion in this paragraph is based upon a survey of approximately twenty newspapers.

3. Ray to Lincoln, July 27, 1858, Robert Todd Lincoln Collection, Library of Congress.

4. The Chicago and Springfield speeches of both Douglas and Lincoln are in Paul M. Angle, ed., *Created Equal?: The Complete Lincoln-Douglas Debates of 1858* (Chicago, 1958), pp. 12–82. Douglas's speech at Bloomington is in Alonzo T. Jones, ed., *Political Speeches and Debates of Abraham Lincoln and Stephen A. Douglas, 1854–1861* (Battle Creek, Mich., 1895), pp. 92–119.

5. *Collected Works,* III, 84.

6. The correspondence between Lincoln and Douglas concerning the debates is in *ibid.,* II, 522, 528–30, 531–32.

7. Chicago *Press and Tribune,* July 28, 1858; *Illinois State Journal,* August 3, 1858.

8. Harry E. Pratt, *The Great Debates* (Springfield, Ill., 1956), p. 9, reprinted from *Illinois Blue Book, 1953–1954* (Springfield, 1955).

9. *Ibid.,* p. 5.

10. Angle, ed., *Created Equal,* p. xxiv.

11. New York *Evening Post,* quoted in Cincinnati *Enquirer,* September 30, 1858.

12. Chicago *Press and Tribune,* August 23, 1858.

13. New York *Evening Post,* September 2, 1858.

14. *Collected Works,* III, 63.

15. Chicago *Times,* September 2, 1858; Joliet *Signal,* September 7, 1858.

16. *Schuyler Citizen* (Rushville), October 27, 1858.

17. Alexander Sympson to John Bagby, October 25, 1858, Bagby Papers, Illinois State Historical Library.

18. *Illinois State Register,* September 23, 1858; *Illinois State Journal,* October 4, 1858.

19. *Missouri Republican* (St. Louis), September 27, 1858; *Illinois State Register,* September 23, 1858.

20. Chicago *Times,* August 20, 1858.

21. Chicago *Press and Tribune,* August 23, 1858.

22. Portland *Transcript,* October 23, 1858.

23. "Solely on their merits," wrote Beveridge in *Abraham Lincoln,* II, 635, "the debates themselves deserve little notice." He then proceeded to a ten-page summary of the Ottawa debate.

24. *Collected Works,* III, 3–4, 6, 43–45, 56, 119, 146–58, 159–66, 168, 183–86, 227–29, 239, 251, 319–20.

25. *Ibid.,* pp. 8–9, 67–68, 110–12, 178, 218–19, 274, 285–86, 297, 325.

26. *Ibid.,* p. 45.

27. *Ibid.,* p. 10.

28. *Ibid.,* pp. 213–15, 262–64.

29. *Ibid.,* pp. 13–16, 19, 40–41, 122, 145–46, 246–49, 308–9.

30. Harry V. Jaffa and Robert W. Johannsen, eds., *In the Name of the People; Speeches and Writings of Lincoln and Douglas in the Ohio Campaign of 1859* (Columbus, Ohio, 1959), p. 44.

31. *Collected Works,* III, 312–16.

32. *Ibid.,* p. 43.

33. Randall, *Lincoln the President,* I, 123–26; *Lincoln the Liberal Statesman,* pp. 21–22.

34. Lincoln, while conceding the "right of the States to do as they please," insisted that the federal government too must have "a policy in relation to domestic slavery." *Collected Works,* III, 311, 498.

35. Randall, *Lincoln the President,* I, 123.

36. *Collected Works,* III, 249.

37. *Ibid.*

38. *Ibid.,* pp. 211, 226–27; Chicago *Tribune,* May 25, 1858. See also Lincoln to Trumbull, June 23, 1858, *Collected Works,* II, 471–72.

39. Harry E. Pratt, *Concerning Mr. Lincoln* (Springfield, Ill., 1944), p. 12; Herndon to Trumbull, July 8, 1858, Trumbull Papers, Library of Congress.

40. Medill to Trumbull, April 22, 1858; E. L. Baker to Trumbull, May 1, 1858, Trumbull Papers, Library of Congress.

41. Fehrenbacher, *Chicago Giant,* pp. 151–52.

42. Herndon to Trumbull, July 8, 1858, Trumbull Papers, Library of Congress; A. Sherman to Ozias M. Hatch, September 27, 1858, Hatch Papers, Illinois State Historical Library. When Sherman, who was employed by the Chicago *Journal,* failed to receive his money from the editor of the *State Democrat,* he asked the Republican organization to pay it.

43. Chicago *Press and Tribune,* August 18, September 8, 10, October 7, November 8, 1858.

44. Randall, *Lincoln the Liberal Statesman,* p. 211.

45. A study of the election abstract for 1858 (MS, Illinois State Archives, Springfield) reveals that a shift of less than 150 votes from the Democratic to the Republican columns in each of three counties (Fulton, Madison, and Tazewell) would have given Lincoln a 51 to 49 majority in the legislature. Some of the Republican victories were equally close, however.

46. Chicago *Press and Tribune,* October 2, 12, 23, 1858; Ottawa *Republican,* October 16, 1858; *Missouri Democrat* (St. Louis), October 22, 1858; Ray to Hatch, no date, Hatch Papers, Illinois State Historical Library; Newton, *Lincoln and Herndon,* p. 233. A copy of the central committee's form letter, dated October 22, 1858, is in the Washburne Papers, Library of Congress.

47. *Collected Works,* III, 329–30. See also an earlier letter to Judd on the same subject in *ibid.,* p. 202.

48. G. W. Rives to Hatch, November 10, 1858; Grimshaw to Hatch, November 11, 1858, Hatch Papers, Illinois State Historical Library.

49. Davis to Lincoln, November 7, 1858, Robert Todd Lincoln Collection, Library of Congress; John M. Palmer to Trumbull, December 9, 1858; Peck to Trumbull, November 22, 1858; Judd to Trumbull, December 26, 1858, Trumbull Papers, Library of Congress; Benjamin L. Wiley to Hatch, December 7, 1858, Hatch Papers, Illinois State Historical Library; *Central Transcript* (Clinton), December 17, 1858; *Weekly Chicago Democrat,* December 4, 1858; Chicago *Press and Tribune,* November 17, 29, 1858.

50. Peck to Trumbull, November 22, 1858, Trumbull Papers, Library of Congress.

51. A poll taken on one of the trains carrying Republican delegates to their state convention in June revealed that Seward was still the most popular presidential candidate. He received 139 out of 225 votes. (Chicago *Journal,* June 21, 1858.) Through intermediaries, Seward assured Lincoln that he had no intention of interfering in Illinois politics. See James Watson Webb to George Bates, June 9, 1858, Robert Todd Lincoln Collection, Library of Congress.

52. Scammon to Lincoln, May 28, 1860, Robert Todd Lincoln Collection, Library of Congress.

53. Ottawa *Republican,* August 14, 1858; Bloomington *Pantagraph,* August 16, 17, 30, 1858; Dickey to Crittenden, July 19, 1858, John J. Crittenden Papers, Manuscript Division, Library of Congress; Crittenden to Lincoln, July 29, 1858, Robert Todd Lincoln Collection, Library of Congress; Mrs. Chapman Coleman, *The Life of John J. Crittenden, with Selections from His Correspondence and Speeches* (2 vols.; Philadelphia, 1871), II, 164–66; *Collected Works,* III, 335–36.

54. *Illinois State Journal,* November 8, 9, December 7, 1858; Chicago *Press and Tribune,* November 5, 1858.

55. Nevins, *Emergence of Lincoln,* I, 398; Luthin, *The Real Abraham Lincoln,* p. 202; Cole, *Era of the Civil War,* pp. 179, 181; Nichols, *Disruption of American Democracy,* p. 220.

56. The votes for the General Assembly by counties, taken from the election abstract in the State Archives, were rearranged according to the provisions of the defeated Republican apportionment bill as given in *Illinois State Journal,* February 11, 1857.

CHAPTER SIX

1. *Collected Works,* III, 43, 51–52.

2. Nathaniel W. Stephenson, "Abraham Lincoln," *Encyclopaedia Britannica* (23 vols.; Chicago, 1959), XIV, 141. Similar statements can be found by the score in writings about Lincoln over the past hundred years. Examples in recent publications are Monaghan, *The Man Who Elected Lincoln,* p. 117; Harry V. Jaffa, " 'Value Consensus' in Democracy: The Issue in the Lincoln-Douglas Debates," *American Political Science Review,* LII (September 1958), 746, 753; Angle, ed., *Created Equal,* pp. v, xxx. The growth of the Freeport legend is well illustrated in Winston Churchill's popular historical novel, *The Crisis* (New York, 1901), pp. 144–45. In a chapter entitled "The Question," the author writes: "the fate of the United States of America was concealed in that Question,—was to be decided on a rough wooden platform that day in the town of Freeport."

3. Two writers who express doubt about Lincoln's "bigger game" remark, but otherwise accept the story that he asked the Freeport question over the protests of various advisers, are Beveridge, *Abraham Lincoln,* II, 656; and William Baringer, *Lincoln's Rise to Power* (Boston, 1937), p. 24.

4. John L. Scripps, *Life of Abraham Lincoln* (Chicago, 1860), p. 28; Henry J. Raymond, *The Life and Public Services of Abraham Lincoln* (New York, 1865), p. 66; J. G. Holland, *The Life of Abraham Lincoln* (Springfield, Mass., 1866), pp. 188–89; Isaac N. Arnold, *The History of Abraham Lincoln and the Overthrow of American Slavery* (Chicago, 1866), p. 133; Ward H. Lamon, *The Life of*

Abraham Lincoln (Boston, 1872), pp. 415–16; John G. Nicolay and John Hay, *Abraham Lincoln, A History* (10 vols.; New York, 1890), II, 160; Lord Charnwood, *Abraham Lincoln* (New York, 1917), pp. 148–49; Carl Sandburg, *Abraham Lincoln: The Prairie Years* (2 vols.; New York, 1926), II, 154–55.

5. White's account is in a chapter on the debates that he wrote for the second edition of William H. Herndon and Jesse W. Weik, *Abraham Lincoln: The True Story of a Great Life* (2 vols.; New York, 1892), II, 109.

6. Ray to Elihu B. Washburne [August 23, 1858], Washburne Papers, Library of Congress. See also Monaghan, *The Man Who Elected Lincoln,* pp. 115–20. Monaghan's effort to make Ray the real author of the Freeport question is unpersuasive, however.

7. Herndon to Weik, October 2, 1890, Herndon-Weik Collection, Library of Congress. The letter is published in Hertz, ed., *The Hidden Lincoln,* pp. 255–56.

8. Edwin Erle Sparks, ed., *The Lincoln-Douglas Debates of 1858* (Springfield, Ill., 1908), pp. 203–6; Beveridge, *Abraham Lincoln,* II, 656; Nevins, *Emergence of Lincoln,* I, 381–82.

9. The letter to Peck is not in the *Collected Works.* The Illinois State Historical Library has a photostatic copy of it.

10. Medill's letter was dated only "Friday morning," but beyond question it was written on August 27. Peck and Judd apparently hoped to confer with Lincoln at Dixon or Amboy on their way to Springfield, but if they did, the views that they expressed presumably coincided with those in the Medill letter.

11. Before answering the seven questions put to him, Lincoln tried to extract from Douglas a promise that he would answer as many in return. *Collected Works,* III, 15, 39.

12. J. Jordan to Lincoln, August 24, 1858; Henry C. Whitney to Lincoln, August 26, 1858, Robert Todd Lincoln Collection, Library of Congress. For the opinion of Theodore Parker that Douglas "had the best of it" at Ottawa, see his letter to Herndon of September 9, 1858, in Newton, *Lincoln and Herndon,* p. 208.

13. The phrase is from John D. Hicks, *The Federal Union* (Boston, 1937), p. 594.

14. *Collected Works,* II, 487. See pp. 136–37.

15. Wilson to Lincoln, undated, but obviously written between August 21 and August 27, 1858, Robert Todd Lincoln Collection, Library of Congress. See also *Illinois State Journal,* July 30, 1858; Chicago *Press and Tribune,* August 4, 1858.

16. Henry Asbury to Lincoln, July 28, 1858, Robert Todd Lincoln Collection, Library of Congress.

17. *Collected Works,* II, 530–31.

18. For example, Nathaniel W. Stephenson, *Lincoln* (Indianapo-

lis, 1922), p. 89; Samuel E. Morison and Henry S. Commager, *The Growth of the American Republic* (4th ed., 2 vols.; New York, 1950), I, 629; Hicks, *Federal Union,* p. 594. The common belief that the Freeport doctrine actually cost Lincoln the election in 1858 has no doubt been partly induced by the tradition that his advisers predicted such a result.

19. Only if we had public-opinion polls taken before and after the Freeport debate would it be possible to estimate its influence upon the election. For an interesting, but, in my opinion, less than satisfactory effort to measure the effect of the campaign as a whole upon the voters, see Forest L. Whan, "Stephen A. Douglas," in William Norwood Brigance *et al.,* eds., *A History and Criticism of American Public Address* (3 vols.; New York, 1943–55), II, 821–24.

20. W. Dean Burnham, *Presidential Ballots, 1836–1892* (Baltimore, 1955), p. 86; D. E. Fehrenbacher, "The Historical Significance of the Lincoln-Douglas Debates," *Wisconsin Magazine of History,* XLII (Spring 1959), 196–97.

21. Nichols, *Disruption of American Democracy,* p. 513.

22. Cass based his doctrine upon a strict construction of the Constitution which limited Congress to merely establishing territories and ordering their forms of government. See his statement in *Congressional Globe,* 34 Cong., 1 sess., Appendix, pp. 519–20, but his fullest exposition of popular sovereignty is in *ibid.,* 31 Cong., 1 sess., Appendix, pp. 58–74. Douglas's views were similar in many respects to those of Cass, but were less clear and consistent.

23. Milo M. Quaife, *The Doctrine of Non-Intervention with Slavery in the Territories* (Chicago, 1910), pp. 67–69.

24. Nichols, *Disruption of American Democracy,* pp. 49–50.

25. *Senate Reports,* 34 Cong., 1 sess., No. 34 (Serial 836), pp. 1–5, 39.

26. *Congressional Globe,* 34 Cong., 1 sess., pp. 1369–75.

27. *Ibid.,* 3 sess., pp. 67, 103–4.

28. Horace Montgomery, "A Georgia Precedent for the Freeport Question," *Journal of Southern History,* X (May 1944), 205–6.

29. *Congressional Globe,* 34 Cong., 1 sess., pp. 1371, 1374; Appendix, p. 797.

30. The words "consistent with the Constitution" in the 1850 acts and "subject only to the Constitution" in the Kansas-Nebraska Act, together with special provisions for carrying slavery cases to the Supreme Court, furnished the statutory basis for the subsequent assertion that the matter had been left to the judiciary. See especially the remarks of Judah P. Benjamin in 1856, 1858, and 1860 in *ibid.,* p. 1093; 35 Cong., 1 sess., p. 615; 36 Cong., 1 sess., p. 1969.

31. James D. Richardson, ed., *A Compilation of the Messages and Papers of the Presidents* (11 vols.; [New York], 1913), IV, 2962.

32. *Congressional Globe,* 34 Cong., 3 sess., p. 67. Smith's statement is unusually interesting because he made the same distinction between power and right that was to become so important after 1858 in discussions of the Freeport doctrine. See p. 139.

33. *Ibid.,* pp. 103–4. Orr was especially close to the position of Douglas at Freeport in that he asserted the finality of territorial non-protection. His statement that there was no remedy for the latter amounted to a repudiation of congressional intervention in the form of a territorial slave code.

34. For example, the New Orleans *Courier,* April 2, 1854 (quoted in Washington *National Intelligencer,* April 11, 1854), declared that a Southerner had the right to carry his slaves anywhere, "provided the local authority of State or Territory permitted him to locate his habitation within their limits."

35. The pertinent passage in Chief Justice Taney's opinion is as follows: "And if Congress itself cannot do this—if it is beyond the powers conferred on the Federal Government—it will be admitted, we presume, that it could not authorize a Territorial Government to exercise them. It could confer no power on any local Government established by its authority, to violate the provisions of the Constitution." (19 Howard 451.) However, this dictum was not a part of the Court's decision because the constitutionality of a territorial law was not under consideration. Furthermore, it is by no means certain that the concurring Justices agreed with Taney on this particular point. None of them said they did, and one, Justice John A. Campbell, indicated that popular sovereignty was a political rather than a judicial question: "How much municipal power may be exercised by the people of the Territory, before their admission to the Union, the courts of justice cannot decide." (*Ibid.,* p. 514.) Douglas also insisted that Taney's statement referred only to powers specifically forbidden in the Constitution, and not to the slavery question, but his argument was based upon an outrageous misreading of Taney's words and betrayed Douglas's weakness as a constitutional theorist. See his *Harper's* essay, "Popular Sovereignty in the Territories," p. 530.

36. New York *Times,* June 23, 1857. This was not Douglas's first use of the argument that the will of the people in a given locality would always triumph over an unpopular restraint imposed by outside authority. Previously, however, he had used it to demonstrate the ineffectiveness of federal laws *prohibiting* slavery in the territories. The Ordinance of 1787, he declared during the Compromise debates of 1850, had not prevented slavery from flourishing for a time in Indiana and Illinois. "A law passed by the national legislature to operate locally upon a people not represented, will always remain practically a dead letter upon the statute book, if it be in opposition to the wishes and supposed interests of those who are to be affected

by it, and at the same time charged with its execution." *Congressional Globe,* 31 Cong., 1 sess., Appendix, pp. 369–70.

37. Washington *Union,* June 23, 1857.

38. *Congressional Globe,* 35 Cong., 1 sess., p. 524.

39. *Ibid.,* p. 616.

40. Nichols, *Disruption of American Democracy,* pp. 212–15.

41. Angle, ed., *Created Equal,* pp. 12–17.

42. *Collected Works,* II, 487.

43. Jones, ed., *Speeches and Debates of Lincoln and Douglas,* p. 110; Angle, ed., *Created Equal,* pp. 58–60.

44. *Collected Works,* III, 316–18. This was Lincoln's final point in the final debate at Alton. His closing words were: "Why there is not such an Abolitionist in the nation as Douglas, after all."

45. Lincoln expected him to do just that. See *ibid.,* II, 530.

46. Portland *Eastern Argus,* September 13, 1858.

47. Dunbar Rowland, ed., *Jefferson Davis, Constitutionalist: His Letters, Papers, and Speeches* (10 vols.; Jackson, Miss., 1923), III, 344–48. For a good discussion, see Nevins, *Emergence of Lincoln,* I, 416–18.

48. Richmond *Enquirer,* September 10, 17, 30, October 15, November 12 (semiweekly), 1858. The *Enquirer* angrily denied the suggestion of the Washington *Union* (September 14) that its defense of Douglas had been written "ironically." Yet the editors must have known that if Douglas took their lifeline he would hang himself on it, and one cannot but suspect calculation in their fantastic misreading of the Freeport doctrine. The suspicion deepens when it is noted that the *Enquirer* conveniently ignored Douglas's subsequent repudiation of a territorial slave code. The presidential ambitions of Governor Henry A. Wise, whose son was one of the editors of the newspaper, are visible in its curious policy.

49. *Collected Works,* III, 132. See O. M. Dickerson, "Stephen A. Douglas and the Split in the Democratic Party," in *Proceedings of the Mississippi Valley Historical Association,* VII (1913–14), 204.

50. *Collected Works,* III, 141–42, 270.

51. *Congressional Globe,* 35 Cong., 2 sess., pp. 1241–59; 36 Cong., 1 sess., p. 658; Nichols, *Disruption of American Democracy,* pp. 296–305; Robert W. Johannsen, "Stephen A. Douglas, 'Harper's Magazine,' and Popular Sovereignty," *Mississippi Valley Historical Review,* XLV (March 1959), 606–31. The decision of the Charleston Convention to write a platform before choosing a candidate has inflated the part played by doctrinal controversy in the break-up of the party. The Southern demand for a slave-code plank was an attack not so much upon the mild and reasonable platform of the Douglas delegates as upon their distasteful candidate.

52. *Congressional Globe,* 36 Cong., 1 sess., p. 1970.

53. Nichols, *Disruption of American Democracy*, p. 321. Two prominent historians who differ widely in their interpretations of the Civil War, but substantially agree in asserting the superficial nature of the slave-code controversy that grew out of the Freeport question, are Nevins, *Emergence of Lincoln*, I, 418, and Avery O. Craven, *Civil War in the Making, 1815–1860* (Baton Rouge, La., 1959), p. 86.

CHAPTER SEVEN

1. Henry P. H. Bromwell to Lincoln, November 5, 1858; Horace White to Lincoln, November 5, 1858; Benjamin C. Lundy to Lincoln, November 22, 1858, Robert Todd Lincoln Collection, Library of Congress; George W. Rives to Ozias M. Hatch, November 5, 1858; Josiah M. Lucas to Hatch, November 20, 1858, Hatch Papers, Illinois State Historical Library. The Weekly Chicago *Democrat* of October 2, 1858, mentioned Lincoln's name in connection with the presidency, and on November 20 the same newspaper proposed to make him a candidate for president, vice-president, or governor. Baringer, *Lincoln's Rise to Power*, pp. 51–64, gives a full account of the early announcements for Lincoln in the press.
2. *Collected Works*, III, 337, 395.
3. *Ibid.*, pp. 378–79, 380, 384, 394–95; IV, 34.
4. *Ibid.*, III, 396.
5. See *ibid.*, p. 397, for Lincoln's letter declining an invitation to campaign in Minnesota. He was also invited to speak in Pennsylvania and New York. Russell Errett to Lincoln, September 13, 1859; Joshua R. Giddings to Lincoln, September 12, 1859, Robert Todd Lincoln Collection, Library of Congress.
6. Jaffa and Johannsen, eds., *In the Name of the People*, gives a summary of the Ohio campaign, together with the principal speeches.
7. *Collected Works*, III, 510–12. The invitation which resulted in his Cooper Institute address was received by Lincoln in October of 1859. See *ibid.*, p. 494; Angle, ed., *Herndon's Lincoln*, p. 359.
8. Chicago *Press and Tribune*, February 16, 1860.
9. *Collected Works*, III, 522–54; IV, 1–30. Lincoln spoke at Providence and Woonsocket, R.I.; Concord, Manchester, Dover, and Exeter, N.H.; Hartford, New Haven, Meriden, New London, Norwich, and Bridgeport, Conn. The Manuscript Division of the Library of Congress now has the letter from Lincoln to his wife, written from Exeter on March 4, 1860, which is only partly reproduced in *ibid.*, III, 555. "I have been unable to escape this toil," he wrote. "If I had foreseen it I think I would not have come East at all."
10. *Collected Works*, IV, 34.
11. Luthin, *The Real Abraham Lincoln*, pp. 194, 196, 204, 206, 210,

336, 400. See also his *The First Lincoln Campaign* (Cambridge, Mass., 1944), pp. 73, 80–81.

12. *Collected Works,* III, 379, 380, 388, 396, 461–62.

13. *Ibid.,* p. 384.

14. *Ibid.,* pp. 379, 380, 390–91. Lincoln, for example, thought that the tariff question "ought not to be agitated in the Chicago convention." *Ibid.,* IV, 49.

15. *Ibid.,* III, 401–4, 439, 453, 460, 484, 501, 504, 535, 538–39, 546, 550, 552; IV, 17. The quotation is from Lincoln's speech at New Haven on March 6, 1860. *Ibid.,* IV, 21.

16. *Ibid.,* III, 369, 404–5, 407–8, 421, 424, 438–39, 441–42, 460, 469, 547–50, 551, 553–54; IV, 3, 5, 6–7, 8, 17, 20–21, 28–29.

17. Fehrenbacher, *Chicago Giant,* pp. 161, 163–64; "The Judd-Wentworth Feud," *Journal of the Illinois State Historical Society,* XLV (Autumn 1952), 199–200; "Lincoln and the Mayor of Chicago," *Wisconsin Magazine of History,* XL (Summer 1957), 242.

18. Weekly Chicago *Democrat,* March 26, October 8, November 12, 26, December 10, 1859; Davis to Lincoln, January 1, 1859 (misdated 1858); February 25, 1860; Judd to Lincoln, December 1, 1859; January 31, 1860; Wentworth to Lincoln, December 21, 1859; N. Niles to Lincoln, December 16, 1859, Robert Todd Lincoln Collection, Library of Congress; Fehrenbacher, *Chicago Giant,* pp. 170–71; Willard L. King, *Lincoln's Manager, David Davis* (Cambridge, Mass., 1960), pp. 129–30; *Collected Works,* III, 516.

19. *Ibid.,* pp. 507–9; Fehrenbacher, *Chicago Giant,* pp. 171–72; King, *Lincoln's Manager,* pp. 130–33. The terms of the truce proposed by Lincoln are quoted in Davis to Lincoln, February 21, 1860, Robert Todd Lincoln Collection, Library of Congress.

20. *Collected Works,* III, 517.

21. Chicago *Press and Tribune,* February 16, 1860; Judd to Lincoln, February 21, 1860, Robert Todd Lincoln Collection, Library of Congress.

22. Judd, in the letter cited above, had explained his painful dilemma to Lincoln and added, "What shall I do[,] write me." Lincoln's reply, if he made one, has not been found, but Herndon spoke in support of Wentworth at a mass meeting shortly before the election. See Fehrenbacher, *Chicago Giant,* pp. 173–74.

23. S. York to Trumbull, November 30, 1859; January 9, 1860; G. O. Pond to Trumbull, December 28, 1859; Benjamin L. Wiley to Trumbull, January 10, 1860; F. R. Payne to Trumbull, January 14, 1860; Jubal C. Brock to Trumbull, January 15, 1860; Alexander B. Morean to Trumbull, January 23, 1860, Trumbull Papers, Library of Congress; Greenville *Advocate,* March 31, 1859; March 22, 1860; Lincoln *Herald,* cited in *Illinois State Journal,* February 17, 1859.

24. *Collected Works,* IV, 46; Ralph J. Roske, "Lincoln and Lyman Trumbull," in Ander, ed., *Lincoln Images,* p. 72.

25. In April, Joseph Medill wrote a long letter to Trumbull suggesting that a McLean-Trumbull ticket would be a very strong one. Trumbull wrote immediately thereafter to McLean, telling him that he was the only man who could beat Seward at Chicago. He also wrote to Lincoln proposing McLean as the best candidate. Medill to Trumbull, April 16, 1860, Trumbull Papers, Library of Congress; Trumbull to McLean, April 21, 1860, John McLean Papers, Library of Congress; Trumbull to Lincoln, April 24, 1860, Robert Todd Lincoln Collection, Library of Congress.

26. The Chicago *Journal* favored Seward, with Lincoln as its second choice, right up to the time of the national convention. So did the *Illinois Staats-Zeitung,* leading German newspaper in Chicago. A Seward supporter raised the only objection to the instruction of delegates for Lincoln by the Decatur convention. See Baringer, *Lincoln's Rise to Power,* pp. 186–87.

27. Bissell to Chase, February 4, 1860, quoted in Baringer, *Lincoln's Rise to Power,* pp. 144–45.

28. *Ibid.,* p. 183.

29. Lincoln is supposed to have told his supporters early in 1860 that he would not allow his name to be used in connection with the vice-presidency. See Angle, ed., *Herndon's Lincoln,* pp. 358–59. But such statements are standard practice in American politics and seldom irrevocable. It is almost inconceivable that Lincoln would have refused a vice-presidential nomination. "As to the Presidential nomination," he wrote a month before the national convention, "claiming no greater exemption from selfishness than is common, I still feel that my whole aspiration should be, and therefore must be, to be placed anywhere, or nowhere, as may appear most likely to advance our cause." (*Collected Works,* IV, 43.) Baringer, *Lincoln's Rise to Power,* pp. 143–44, maintains that Lincoln entered the presidential race in order to make capital for a return engagement with Douglas in the senatorial contest of 1864. This theory can be neither proved nor disproved, but it assumes that Lincoln had no interest in the vice-presidency, a cabinet post, or any of the other honors that might have been offered to a prominent but defeated candidate for the presidential nomination if the Republicans won in 1860.

30. The fullest and best study of the various candidates is in Luthin, *The First Lincoln Campaign,* pp. 23–119.

31. In the 36th Congress, three of the free-state delegations in the House of Representatives were controlled by the Democrats (Illinois, Oregon, California), and the Rhode Island delegation consisted of one Republican and one American. This left the Republicans with

only 14 sure votes out of 33 in the election of a president. The admission of Kansas on January 29, 1861, gave the Republicans another state, but the admission might have been delayed if the presidency had been at stake. In any case, it increased the number of votes necessary for election to 18.

32. M[urat] Halstead, *Caucuses of 1860: A History of the National Political Conventions of the Current Presidential Campaign* . . . (Columbus, Ohio, 1860), pp. 145–49.

33. Compare Baringer, *Lincoln's Rise to Power*, pp. 214, 266–67, 277, 334, with King, *Lincoln's Manager*, pp. 137–38, 141, 162–64.

34. Claude G. Bowers, *Beveridge and the Progressive Era* (New York, 1932), p. 565.

35. Luthin, *The Real Abraham Lincoln*, p. 242.

INDEX

Index

Albany *Evening Journal,* 61
Alton, Ill.: debate at, 100, 108
American Almanac, 97
American party, *see* Know-Nothings
Angle, Paul M., 101
Anti-Nebraska movement, 7, 22, 31, 41; carries Illinois, 37, 38–39. *See also* Republican party
Antislavery movement, *see* Anti-Nebraska movement; Free-Soil party; Republican party; Slavery
Archy slave case, 93
Arnold, Isaac N., 21
Atlantic Monthly, 61
Augusta *Constitutionalist,* 135
Aurora, Ill., 36

Baringer, William E., 154
Bates, Edward, 43; as presidential candidate, 150, 153, 154, 155
Bell, John, 142, 156, 159, 160
Benjamin, Judah P., 93, 140, 189
Beveridge, Albert J.: on Lincoln's conversion to Republicanism, 42, 43; explains senatorial nomination of Lincoln, 50; on Wentworth as senatorial candidate, 66; on House Divided speech, 73, 85, 97; disappointed with Lincoln, 160–61
Bissell, William H., 8, 9, 16, 62; as candidate for governor, 43, 44, 46; elected, 47; death of, 151; on Lincoln's presidential candidacy, 153–54
Bloomington, Ill.: Republican state convention at, 43, 44, 45, 46; Lincoln speaks at, 86–87, 91, 99, 182–83; Douglas speaks at, 99, 137
Bloomington *Pantagraph,* 80, 126
Breckinridge, John C., 142, 159, 160

Brown, John, 145, 156
Browning, Orville H., 43, 46
Buchanan, James, 51, 79, 87; as presidential candidate, 17, 46–47, 51, 86, 147; quarrels with Douglas, 49, 56, 136, 177; supports Lecompton constitution, 53, 54–55, 58, 89; supporters of, in Illinois, oppose Douglas, 112–14; and popular sovereignty, 130–31, 133
Burlingame, Anson, 59
Butler, Andrew P., 26

Calhoun, John C., 129, 133
California: Know-Nothings carry, 43; Archy slave case in, 93
Cameron, Simon, 43, 148–49, 153, 155
Campaigns, *see* Elections
Cass, Lewis, 129, 130, 189
Catholic Church, 7, 13–14, 115
Charleston, Ill.: debate at, 100, 105
Charleston, S. C.: Democratic convention at, 129, 156, 191
Charleston *Mercury,* 135
Chase, Salmon P., 26, 43, 147; as presidential candidate, 148, 153, 155
Chicago, Ill., 10, 32; Republican convention at, 2, 144, 145, 154–59; Lincoln speaks at, 37, 78, 94, 99, 100, 136; feud among Republicans in, 149–51
Chicago and Rock Island Railroad, 8
Chicago *Democrat,* 13, 31, 65, 66
Chicago *Press and Tribune, see* Chicago *Tribune*
Chicago *Times,* 11, 98, 103
Chicago *Tribune,* 13, 59, 103; supports Lincoln for president, 11, 146, 150; on senatorial contest, 62, 64–65, 68; becomes *Press and*

Tribune, 98; and Lincoln-Douglas debates, 98, 99, 100; on Buchanan Democrats, 113, 114; and Judd-Wentworth feud, 149, 151

Churches and politics, 11–14

Cincinnati, Ohio, 144

Clay, Henry, 26, 27

Clayton compromise, 131

Codding, Ichabod, 36

Cole, Arthur C., 83–85, 92–93, 182

Colfax, Schuyler, 59, 60

Collected Works of Abraham Lincoln, The, 88, 89, 183

Columbus, Ohio, 144

Compromise of 1850, 28–29, 30; and popular sovereignty, 130, 132, 189

Constitutional Union party, 156

Cook County, Ill., 67, 119

Cooper Institute: Lincoln's speech at, 18, 145–47, 148, 154, 181

Crittenden, John J., 117, 128

Cuba, 110

Cutts, James Madison, 56

Dallas City, Ill., 103

Danville, Ill., 103

Davis, David, 43, 117, 149, 159

Davis, Jefferson, 26, 82, 140; enunciates Freeport doctrine, 137–38

Dayton, Ohio, 144

Dayton, William C., 46

Decatur, Ill.: convention of Republican editors at, 44, 45; state Republican convention at, 148–49, 151, 152, 154

Declaration of Independence, 106, 111–12

Democratic party, 3, 6, 25, 38, 51, 88; divided by slavery question, 25–26, 29; in elections, 27, 30, 43, 46–47, 159–60; and Dred Scott decision, 51–52; divided by Lecompton issue, 53, 57, 58–59; disruption of, 120, 129, 141, 142, 156, 160; effect of Freeport doctrine on, 122, 128–42

—of Illinois, 4, 16, 33, 38, 57; defeated in 1854, 36–37; and 1855 senatorial election, 38–39; divided into Douglas and Buchanan fac-

tions, 63–64, 112–14; and election of 1858, 115–20, 186

Dickey, T. Lyle, 86–87, 91, 118, 182–83

District of Columbia: slavery in, 34, 106

Donald, David, 35, 45

Dougherty, John, 113

Douglas, Stephen A., 6, 11, 34, 36, 62, 86; anti-Catholic clamor against, 13–14; plays dominant role in politics, 17–18; admired by revisionist historians, 21, 109, 161; and Kansas-Nebraska Act, 25, 33, 57; in senatorial contest with Lincoln, 48–49, 96–120; quarrels with Buchanan, 49, 56, 136, 177; receives Republican support, 49–50, 61, 62, 63, 64, 78, 92, 117–18; on Dred Scott decision, 52, 88, 93, 190; and Freeport doctrine, 52, 108, 112–14, 127, 131, 133–34, 136–37, 190–91; opposes Lecompton constitution, 53–60, 136, 181; speaks at Springfield in 1857, 55–56; cooperates with Republicans, 59–61; Illinois Republicans refuse to support, 68, 94; Lincoln warns Republicans against, 70–71, 84, 90–91, 148; denounces House Divided speech, 74, 95, 99, 105, 107; and Lincoln's conspiracy charge, 79–82, 93, 181; House Divided speech directed against, 83, 85, 89, 92; sponsors enabling act for Kansas, 89–90; opposition of South to, 98, 127, 134–35; compared with Lincoln as orator, 104; strategy of, in debates, 105–6; on Negro, 106, 111–12; on slavery, 110–11; wins re-election, 115, 119, 186; effect of Freeport doctrine on, 121–22, 123, 127–28, 134, 135, 137, 139–40, 142; deprived of committee chairmanship, 139–40; campaigns in Ohio, 144–45; as presidential candidate, 156, 159, 160

Dred Scott decision, 3, 23, 51–52, 93, 141; Lincoln and, 79–80, 87–89, 91, 92, 140, 148; and popular sovereignty, 108, 125, 126, 133, 136–37, 190

Elections: interest in, 14–16; *1848*, 26, 27; *1850*, 21; *1852*, 21, 27–28, 31; *1853*, 29; *1854*, 4, 30, 32, 36–37, 85; *1855*, 43; *1856*, 4, 17, 46–47; *1858*, 4, 114–20, 127–28, 142, 143, 186, 189; *1860*, 2, 4, 128–29, 142, 156, 159–60, 194–95
English compromise, 58–59, 61, 108, 125, 135

Fessenden, William P., 93
Fillmore, Millard, 25, 47, 86, 87, 155
Fitzhugh, George, 84
Foreign-born, *see* Germans; Irish
Freeport, Ill.: debate at, 93, 100, 102, 108, 110
Freeport question and doctrine, 52, 108–9, 121–42, 187–92; Lincoln and, 122–27, 136–37, 139–40; effect of, on Lincoln-Douglas contest, 127–28, 189; effect of, on Democratic party and election of 1860, 128–42; early manifestations of, 132–33, 134, 136–37; Jefferson Davis and, 137–38; and slave-code question, 139–41, 191; overemphasized, 141–42
Free-Soil party, 19, 23, 26, 27–28, 30
Frémont, John C., 46, 47, 51, 86
Fugitive Slave Law, 28, 30, 106; Lincoln on, 34, 36, 147

Galena, Ill., 75
Galesburg, Ill.: debate at, 100, 113
Germans: in Illinois population, 6; in politics, 6–7, 13, 40, 153, 155
Giddings, Joshua, 5
Greeley, Horace, 32, 70, 98, 114; supports Douglas, 49–50, 60–61, 62–63, 64, 68, 135; blamed for Lincoln's defeat, 117, 128
Grimshaw, Jackson, 117
Grow, Galusha, 131, 132

Hale, John P., 27
Harper's Magazine: Douglas's article in, 93, 140, 145
Hay, John, 89, 91, 183

Hayes, Rutherford B., 59
Haynes, George H., 49
Herndon, William H., 22, 113–14, 116, 149, 160; on Lincoln and early Republican party, 19–20, 35, 45; on Eastern Republicans, 50, 60, 62; on House Divided speech, 72, 83, 89, 179–80, 182–83; on Freeport question, 123–24
Hillyer, Junius, 131, 132
Hofstadter, Richard, 73, 180
Holland, Josiah G., 21
House Divided speech, 14, 48, 68, 114, 146; Douglas attacks, 74, 95, 99, 105, 107; origins and purpose of, 70–95, 179–80, 182–84; as step toward presidency, 73, 97, 180

Illinois: as pivotal state, 5, 17, 154; population of, 5–7; political sectionalism in, 6, 71; economic growth of, 7; election pattern in, 9, 21, 40; newspapers in, 10–11; politics in, 14–16 and *passim*
Illinois Central Railroad, 7, 8–9
Illinois General Assembly: Lincoln elected to, 1, 37; senatorial elections in, 38–39, 49, 175; apportionment of seats in, 115; 118–20, 152
Illinois State Democrat, 114
Illinois State Journal, 11, 14–15, 42, 85, 100, 113
Illinois State Register, 34, 36, 66, 67
Indiana: as pivotal state, 17, 154; Republicans of, support Lincoln, 157
Indianapolis, Ind., 144
Iowa: election of 1854 in, 32; Lincoln speaks in, 143
Irish: in Illinois politics, 6–7; as railroad workers, 8; and election of 1858, 115–17, 128

Jackson, Mich., 31
Jackson *Mississippian,* 98, 135
Jaffa, Harry V., 107
Joliet, Ill., 102
Jonesboro, Ill.: debate at, 100, 139
Journalism, *see* Newspapers
Judd, Norman B., 8, 39, 116; and Freeport debate, 124, 125, 126,

188; as candidate for governor, 149, 150, 151; quarrels with Wentworth, 149–51, 193

Kansas, 22, 54, 90, 108, 110, 140; turmoil in, 23, 41, 44, 51, 52; Lincoln speaks in, 144, 145. *See also* Lecompton constitution
Kansas-Nebraska Act, 3, 41, 43, 51, 57, 80; effects of, 6, 23, 24, 25, 30, 37, 51; Lincoln's opposition to, 19, 21, 23–24, 25, 29–30, 34, 74, 83, 107, 161; interpretation of, 22; and Lincoln's conspiracy charge, 79; and beginnings of house-divided doctrine, 85–86; and popular sovereignty, 130, 132, 189; Douglas interprets, 131
Koerner, Gustave, 38, 43, 63
Know-Nothings, 3, 19, 28, 46, 47, 86–87; in Illinois, 7, 33; Lincoln and, 14, 41, 155; in 1854 elections, 32; in 1855 elections, 43; division of, 41, 44; in 1858 election, 73; in 1860 election, 147, 154–55, 156

Lawrence, Kans., 46, 52
Lawyers and politics, 9
Lecompton constitution, 49, 78–79, 82, 107, 113, 127, 134–35, 142; struggle over, in Congress, 53–59; and Lincoln's house-divided doctrine, 88–89
Liberty party, 30
Lincoln, Abraham: retires from Congress, 1; path to presidency of, 1–2; profits from death of Whig party, 4; fortunate in residence, 5, 16, 17; as railroad lawyer, 8–9; law practice of, and politics, 9; cultivates newspaper editors, 11; and religious influences in politics, 14; wins prominence as opponent of Douglas, 17–18; factors in emergence of, 18; and founding of Republican party, 19–20, 34–35, 42–43, 44–46, 47; refuses governorship of Oregon territory, 20; alleged retirement from politics of, 20–21; supports Scott, 21; motives of, in opposing Kansas-Nebraska Act, 21–22, 24–25; arguments of, against Kansas-Nebraska Act, 23–24; remains a Whig, 25, 27, 28, 29–30, 33; as candidate for legislature, 33; in 1854 campaign, 34–35; refuses to join "Republicans" of 1854, 35–36, 175; elected to legislature and resigns, 37; candidate for Senate, 37–39, 175; political position of, in 1855, 40–42; letters of, to Lovejoy and Speed, 41–42; at Decatur convention of editors, 44; at Bloomington convention, 46; campaigns for Frémont, 46–47; nominated for Senate, 48–50, 64, 67–68; criticizes Dred Scott decision, 52, 79–80, 88, 92; warns Republicans on popular sovereignty, 60; claims of, to senatorship, 61–62; worried by Republican support of Douglas, 62; proposes state convention, 63; supported by county conventions, 64; alleged plot of Wentworth against, 66–68, 179; resolution of state convention supporting, 67; explains nomination, 67–68; consequences of nomination of, 68–69

Delivers House Divided speech, 70–83, 180–81; on ultimate extinction of slavery, 76–79; charges conspiracy to nationalize slavery, 79–82; rejects Greeley view, 82; directs House Divided speech against Douglas, 82–83, 88–89; and doctrine of class struggle, 83–85, 182; early use of house-divided doctrine by, 85–87, 182–83; House Divided fragment by, 89–94, 183–84; faith of, in Republican program, 94–95; in senatorial contest with Douglas, 96–120; debates with Douglas increase fame of, 98; challenges Douglas, 99–100; debates of, with Douglas described, 100–103; compared with Douglas as debater, 104; expects progression in debates, 105; pursued by cry of Negro equality, 106; argument of, in debates, 106–8; queries Douglas at Freeport, 108–9; arguments of, compared

with Douglas's, 109–12, 185; lacks full support of party, 112; consults with Buchanan leader, 113; loses election, 115, 118–20, 186, 187; on illegal voters, 116; blames Crittenden for defeat, 118; emerges as national figure, 120 Asks second Freeport question, 121; urged by advisers to ask Freeport question, 122–27, 142, 188; Freeport question as factor in defeat of, 127–28, 189; influence of Freeport doctrine on presidential election of, 128–29, 189; earlier use of Freeport question by, 136–37; queries Douglas on slave code for territories, 139; attacks Freeport doctrine, 139–40; early support of, for presidency, 143; makes speeches in Ohio, 144–45; speaks in Wisconsin and Kansas, 145; Cooper Institute speech of, 145–46, 181; speaks in New England, 146, 192; alleged conservatism of, 146–48; supported for presidency by state convention, 148–49, 154; and Judd-Wentworth feud, 149–50, 193; passes Trumbull as state leader, 151–52, 194; warns Trumbull, 152–53; reservations concerning candidacy of, among Illinois Republicans, 153–54, 194; nominated for presidency, 155–56, 157–59; elected president, 159–60, 194–95; interpretations of pre-presidential career of, 160–61
Lincoln-Douglas debates, *see* Lincoln-Douglas campaign of 1858; Freeport question and doctrine
Lincoln-Douglas campaign of 1858, 8, 16, 69, 77, 96–120; anti-Catholicism in, 13; uniqueness of, 48–49; effect of, on Lincoln's career, 120, 143, 152, 155; and Freeport question, 121–28, 136–37, 141–42
Louisville *Democrat*, 135
Lovejoy, Owen, 36, 41, 42, 102
Luthin, Reinhard H., 44–45, 146–47, 161

McLean, John, 46, 152, 153, 154, 194

McLean County tax case, 8–9
Maine: in election of 1854, 32
Marshall, Humphrey, 131, 132
Mason, James M., 26
Massachusetts: politics in, 28, 32
Matteson, Joel A., 8, 38–39, 175
Mattoon *National Gazette*, 93
Mearns, David C., 37
Memphis *Appeal*, 135
Medill, Joseph, 113, 194; on Freeport question, 124–26, 127, 188; on House Divided speech, 180
Methodist Church, 12
Mexican War, 1, 21, 26, 104
Michigan: Republican party in, 31–32
Milwaukee, Wis., 145
Missouri Compromise, 3, 24, 36, 51, 130. *See also* Kansas-Nebraska Act
Mobile *Register*, 135
Montgomery Confederation, 135

Nativism, *see* Know-Nothings
Negroes, 31; Lincoln and Douglas on rights of, 34, 106, 111. *See also* Slavery
Nevins, Allan, 72, 76
New England: 1855 elections in, 43; Lincoln speaks in, 81–82, 146–47, 154, 192; delegates from, and nomination of Lincoln, 158
New Jersey: as pivotal state, 17, 154; slow to accept Republican name, 47
Newspapers: and politics, 9–11; reporting of Lincoln-Douglas campaign in, 97–98
New York: politics in, 28, 29, 32, 43
New York *Post*, 112
New York *Times*, 61
New York *Tribune*, 11, 61, 62, 90
Nichols, Roy F., 15, 129, 136, 141
Nicholson letter, 129, 130
Nicolay, John G., 89, 91, 183
North Carolina Standard, 135
Northwest Ordinance, 24, 190

Ohio: politics in, 32, 43; Lincoln speaks in, 81–82, 91, 144, 145; delegates from, and nomination of Lincoln, 159

Oregon, Ill., 15–16
Oregon Territory, 20
Orr, James L., 132, 133, 134, 137, 138, 190
Ottawa, Ill.: "forgery" at, 36, 104; debate at, 77, 93, 100, 102, 103, 110; Douglas's questions at, 106, 122, 124–25; criticism of Lincoln's performance at, 126, 188

Palmer, John M., 39, 43, 62, 117
Parker, Theodore, 116, 188
Peck, Ebenezer, 117, 125, 126, 188
Peeples, Cincinnatus, 131
Pekin, Ill., 35, 175
Pennsylvania: as pivotal state, 17, 154; politics in, 32, 43; slow to accept Republican name, 47; delegates from, swing to Lincoln, 157, 158
Peoria, Ill.: Lincoln's speech at, 22, 24, 34, 36, 85
Pierce, Franklin, 25, 27, 28, 29, 79
Political Debates between Lincoln and Douglas, 145, 146
Politics: importance of, in American life, 14–17
Popular sovereignty, 54, 110; Lincoln attacks, 24, 85; and Dred Scott decision, 51–52, 108, 125, 126; Republicans lean toward, 60, 78; and nationalization of slavery, 81–82; and Freeport doctrine, 129–40, 189–91
Portland, Me., 138
Presidency: Lincoln as candidate for, 2, 4, 5, 143–61
Prohibition, 12–13

Quincy, Ill.: debate at, 100

Railroads of Illinois, 7–8; Lincoln and, 8–9
Randall, James G.: on Kansas-Nebraska Act, 22, 110, 114, 161; minimizes differences between Lincoln and Douglas, 109; on racial views of Lincoln and Douglas, 111
Ray, Charles H., 60, 98, 116; on Freeport debate, 123, 126, 188
Religion and politics, 11–14

Republican party, 2, 17, 75, 127, 143, 147; national conventions of, 2, 5, 39, 46, 154–59; rise of, 3, 19, 25, 30–33, 35–36, 40–47; objectives of, 3, 76, 77; courts nativists and foreign-born, 7, 13–14, 147, 154–55; pro-Douglas sentiment in, 49–50, 57, 59–64, 78–79, 84, 90, 92, 112, 117; and Dred Scott decision, 51–52, 88; opposes Lecompton constitution, 53, 54; nominates Lincoln for presidency, 144, 154–59; opposition to Seward within, 145, 152–57 *passim*; 1860 platform of, 156–57; wins presidential election, 159–60
—of Illinois, 4, 16, 69, 71–72, 105; Lincoln as a founder of, 18–20, 33–36, 40, 42–47, 161; composition of, 19; beginnings of, 32–33, 34, 35–36; formal organization of, 44–46; state conventions of, 46, 48–50, 63, 67–68, 70, 148–49, 151, 154; elects state officers, 47; refuses to support Douglas, 61–63, 94; nominates Lincoln for Senate, 64, 67–68; encourages Buchanan Democrats, 112–14, 186; and election of 1858, 115–20, 186; supports Lincoln for presidency, 144, 148–49, 151, 152, 154; dissension in, 149–51
Richmond *Enquirer,* 96, 135, 182; on Freeport doctrine, 139, 191
Riddle, Donald W., 21–22, 27, 37
Ripon, Wis., 31
Robertson, George, 85–86
Rushville, Ill., 102, 103

Sangamon County, Illinois, 38
Scott, Winfield, 27–28
Scripps, John L., 71, 76
Senate, U.S.: Lincoln as candidate for, 1, 4, 36, 37–39, 48–49, 72, 94, 96–120, 127
Seward, William H., 11, 32, 42, 78, 146; as presidential candidate, 2, 96, 145, 152, 154, 155, 156; allegedly friendly to Douglas, 59, 135, 186; Rochester speech by, 74, 148; blamed for Lincoln's defeat, 117–

18; compared with Lincoln on slavery issue, 147, 155; supported in Illinois, 150, 153, 186, 194; defeated by Lincoln, 157–59

Shields, James, 38–39, 175

Slavery: and political revolution, 3, 7, 15, 25–26, 30; churches and, 11–14; Lincoln's attitude toward, 14, 36, 106, 107–8, 147–48; in Kansas, 22; in District of Columbia, 34, 106; provisions for, in Lecompton constitution, 53, 55; Lincoln's discussion of, in House Divided speech, 74–82, 83–85, 86, 94–95, 182; views of Lincoln and Douglas on, compared, 110–11, 185; planks on, in Republican platform, 156–57

—in territories, 3–4, 22–23, 121–22, 129–42, 157, 189–91; views of Lincoln and Douglas on, compared, 110; Lincoln opposes, 23, 42, 78, 87

Smith, Samuel A., 132, 133, 134, 137, 138, 190

South and Southerners: and slavery in territories, 3, 4; in Illinois population, 6; economic opposition to, 30; Lincoln's attitude toward, 34; and Dred Scott decision, 51–52, 133; Lincoln misunderstands, 95; and Douglas, 96, 98, 108, 120, 127, 134–35, 137, 140, 141, 191; on popular sovereignty, 130–33, 190; demand of, for slave code, 139–41; reaction of, to John Brown raid, 156

Speed, Joshua F., 41–42

Springfield, Ill., 16; Lincoln speaks at, 34, 35, 52, 88, 99; Douglas speaks at, 34, 52, 55–56, 99, 137; antislavery convention of 1854 at, 35, 36; state Republican convention of 1858 at, 48, 63–64, 67

Springfield *Republican,* 61

Sullivan, Ill., 103

Sumner, Charles, 25–26, 31, 46

Swett, Leonard, 71, 150

Taney, Roger B., 13, 51, 79, 134, 190

Taylor, Zachary, 1, 20, 27

Territories, *see* Slavery in territories

Thomas, Benjamin P., 50

Toombs bill, 105

Trumbull, Lyman, 16, 17, 43, 50, 60, 62, 90, 105, 113; elected to Senate, 38–39, 120, 175; acknowledges debt to Lincoln, 62; asks equivalent of Freeport question, 131, 136; and 1860 presidential contest, 151–53, 194

Van Buren, Martin, 26

Vermont: election of 1854 in, 32

Vice-presidency: Lincoln and, 4, 5, 39, 46, 194

Virginia: election of 1855 in, 43

Wade, Benjamin F., 31, 135

Washburne, Elihu B., 123

Washington *Union,* 93, 112, 134, 135

Webster, Daniel, 26, 28, 180

Weed, Thurlow, 11, 32, 61, 117

Weik, Jesse W., 123

Wentworth, John, 8, 15–16, 43, 113; alleged senatorial ambitions of, 50, 65–68, 179; elected mayor of Chicago, 65, 150–51; quarrels with Judd, 149–51, 193

Whig party: decline of, 3, 4, 19, 25–29, 44; of Illinois, 4, 21, 27–28, 33, 38; Lincoln and, 25, 42; remnant of, nominates Fillmore, 47

Whigs, former: at Bloomington convention, 46; in 1858 election, 71, 73; in 1860 election, 147, 154–55, 156

White, Horace, 123, 124

Whitney, Henry C., 97

Wilmot Proviso, 3, 22–23, 25, 30, 42, 129

Wilson, Charles L., 67, 68, 126, 179

Wilson, Henry, 59, 60, 135

Wisconsin: Republican party in, 31–32; Lincoln speaks in, 144, 145

Yates, Richard, 16, 43; as candidate for Congress, 21, 33, 37; as candidate for governor, 150, 151